THE LIFE
in your
GARDEN

THE LIFE
in your
GARDEN

Gardening for Biodiversity

Reeser Manley and Marjorie Peronto

TILBURY HOUSE
PUBLISHERS

Tilbury House Publishers
12 Starr Street, Thomaston, Maine 04861
800-582-1899
www.tilburyhouse.com

First hardcover edition October 2016
ISBN 978-0-88448-472-1
eBook ISBN 978-0-88448-475-2

Library of Congress Cataloging-in-Publication Data

Names: Manley, Reeser, author. | Peronto, Marjorie, author.
Title: The life in your garden : gardening for biodiversity / Reeser Manley
  and Marjorie Peronto.
Description: First hardcover edition October 2016. | Thomaston, Maine :
  Tilbury House Publishers, 2016.
Identifiers: LCCN 2016036052 (print) | LCCN 2016037206 (ebook) | ISBN
  9780884484721 (hardcover) | ISBN 9780884484752 (ebook)
Subjects: LCSH: Gardening—Environmental aspects. | Biodiversity
  conservation. | Garden ecology.
Classification: LCC SB454.3.E53 M36 2016 (print) | LCC SB454.3.E53 (ebook) |
  DDC 577.5/54—dc23
LC record available at https://lccn.loc.gov/2016036052

Printed in the USA by Versa Press, East Peoria, IL

15 16 17 18 19 20 VER 5 4 3 2 1

Designed and produced by Frame25 Productions.
Chapter-closing illustrations by Lynne Hundhammer.
Range maps in Chapter 8 and Appendix 3 adapted
courtesy of the United States Department of Agriculture.

This book is dedicated to Joan Peronto (1929–2016), Marjorie's mother, a lifelong inspiration and role model, wife, mother of seven, grandmother to seven, gardener, reference librarian, poet.

Margie's Garden, Ellsworth, Maine, 2005

by Joan Peronto

Her garden started in the Peace Corps
1983, in heat so thick
you had to douse your head
with water just to sleep.

A vision, on the road to Ouagadougou
by the dry fields of millet
beneath the baobab trees
planted upside down by God.

Now the garden glows
in the late August sun
humming birds, wings blurring
attend delphinium and larkspur.

Butterflies, like ashes in the wind
float over bleeding heart, lavender
night-scented nicotiana
love-in-the-mist.

Nearby, white delicata squash
red heritage tomatoes
purple eggplant and one forgotten
football-sized zucchini.

Wind chimes shiver a single tone
pause, sound another.

All dreamed in Africa
when the Harmattan
turned air red with dust
and women fought for water at the well.

Table of Contents

Chapter 1

Getting Back to the Garden

"A recent tally of threatened species by the World Conservation Union lists more than a thousand mammals, nearly a quarter of all those we know, and more than a thousand birds. Each year's list is longer. We can reverse those trends . . . by living more lightly and by making way for wildness in our yards and parks and forests and farms. Nothing keeps us from doing so, except habit and haste and lack of faith. Faith in what? In our capacity for decent and loving work, in the healing energy of wildness, in the holiness of creation."
—Scott Russell Sanders, *Earth Works*

"We are stardust / billion year old carbon. / We are golden, / caught in the devil's bargain. / And we've got to get ourselves / back to the garden." These lyrics from "Woodstock," the song Joni Mitchell wrote to commemorate the 1969 music festival on Max Yasgur's farm in upstate New York, are even more relevant today than they were a half century ago.

We live in the sixth mass extinction period of Earth's history, a period of unprecedented plant and animal species loss. The fifth mass extinction period, called the Cretaceous-Tertiary extinction, occurred about 65 million years ago, likely caused by the impact of a several-mile-wide asteroid with Earth. Resulting extinctions included 16 percent of marine families, 46 percent of marine genera, and 18 percent of land vertebrate families, including the dinosaurs.

Conservation biologists tell us that overall extinction rates are now 1,000 times higher than the historical background rate of one to five species per year, with future extinction rates likely to be 10,000 times higher. Some 31 percent of U.S. bird species and 12 percent of the nearly 10,000 bird species worldwide are on the brink of extinction. Amphibians, the hardest hit class of animal life on Earth, are experiencing extinction rates at least 25,000 times background, with more than a third of the 6,300 known species at risk of extinc-

Of the 46 bumble bee species in North America, five are currently threatened with extinction. Major threats include diseases introduced through commercial bumble bee rearing, habitat destruction, invasive species, and climate change.

tion. Thirty percent of all invertebrates, including insects, are threatened, and half of Earth's mammal populations are declining, with a third of mammal species at risk of extinction. Of the 12,914 plant species studied to date, 22 percent are threatened with extinction.

These alarming figures refer only to the 1.7 million known species. Scientists estimate the total number of species on Earth at between 3 and 30 million, with new ones being discovered every day. We have identified only a fraction of our planet's total biodiversity. Sadly, many plants and animals will disappear from our planet before they are discovered, their immense contributions to our lives gone before being understood.

The current period of mass extinction is unique in two ways: It is the first such event in the short history of the human species, and we are the cause of it. In his recent book *Half-Earth: Our Planet's Fight for Life,* biologist E. O. Wilson frames one of the great moral ques-

tions of our time: "Will we continue to degrade the planet to satisfy our own immediate needs, or will we find a way to halt this mass extinction for the sake of future generations?"

Wilson summarizes the causes of this unprecedented species loss in the acronym HIPPO: **H**abitat loss due to human activities; **I**nvasive species introduced around the world by human activity; **P**ollution of all types; human **P**opulation growth; and **O**verharvesting of Earth's resources, particularly in our oceans. These five causes of our planet's biodiversity crisis appear in the acronym in the order of their impact on species loss. Habitat loss

The Xerces Society's Red List of endangered North American solitary bees includes 53 species.

caused by human activity is the number one cause of Earth's biodiversity crisis.

Why should gardeners be concerned about a loss of biodiversity?

Most importantly, biodiversity allows the garden ecosystem to adjust to disturbances. For example, if one species of bumble bee disappears from a garden that hosts several species, the others will likely adapt to fill the vacated pollinator role. But if the garden has only one kind of bumble bee, there can be no adaptation to its loss, and plants that depend on bumble bees for pollination will bear no fruit.

Without a diversity of microbial life in garden soil, the variety and quality of garden

Fifty-nine North American butterfly and moth species are listed on the Xerces Society's Red List of endangered species.

plants would be severely limited. Without a diversity of predatory insects, garden plants would be overwhelmed by herbivores (the plant munchers).

Outside the garden's borders, biodiversity provides us with a wide array of essential products, including foods, fibers, and other materials. Medical discoveries to cure diseases

Seven species of beetles are listed as endangered by the Xerces Society.

depend on research into plant and animal biology and genetics. Every time a species goes extinct, we lose a potential opportunity to discover a new vaccine or drug.

Finally, biodiversity enriches our lives. There is nothing as beautiful, wonderful, and inspiring as the diversity of life that can exist in your garden.

What role can our gardens play in reversing the current trend in biodiversity loss?

Studies show that public and private gardens represent a growing percentage of suitable habitat for many threatened species, particularly if these gardens can be linked by vegetation corridors for wildlife, a concept already being applied in some urban areas of our country. Certainly our gardens can play a significant role in sustaining native plant diversity and, as a consequence, provide refuge for threatened species of insects, the creatures described by Wilson as "the little things that run the world," as well as providing sanctuary for birds, amphibians, reptiles, and small mammals.

This book is about making way for wildness in your garden. We will share our experiences in gardening for biodiversity, placing a strong emphasis on insect diversity as a bellwether of success, and we will introduce plants that can be grown for their ability to nurture insects, birds, and other creatures. Properly managed gardens provide essential habitat, protecting many of Earth's creatures, known and still unknown, from the HIPPO juggernaut.

A path through Marjorie's garden in mid-June with summersweet clethra on the left, fringetree (*Chionanthus virginicus*) in flower on the right, and pagoda dogwood flowering in the background.

Biodiversity in Marjorie's Garden

Marjorie laid out the lines of our garden and did the initial digging, raising the garden beds from a shelf of granite rock, four years before Reeser arrived on the scene. The garden has been our joint enterprise for 16 years now, but Reeser still calls it Marjorie's garden.

It is surrounded by woods, conifers and hardwoods that feed and shelter countless animal species. Many deer and a few black bears are denizens of these woods and occasionally make their presence known in the garden. On early autumn mornings, a red fox makes her final round along the border between the garden and the woods; one summer we spotted her sunning on an old oak log at the back of the garden, and in spring we hear her calling to her kits. Chipmunks and red squirrels are a year-round presence in the garden, on the firewood pile, and on the porch under the bird feeders. Raccoons make occasional visits to those feeders, and skunks dig in the compost piles at the back of the vegetable garden. Every so often, a rotund porcupine lumbers out of the woods for a dinner of dandelion greens.

Virginia creeper in autumn.

Turkeys, traveling in a gang of twenty or so, leave prehistoric tracks in the snow as they strut out of the woods and through the garden, scratching for insects, acorns, and spruce seeds. Pileated woodpeckers drill for insects in an old birch snag left standing in the garden. A solitary spruce grouse appears every so often, sunning on an old log or pecking at seed catkins in the top of a yellow birch. We are frequently awakened by the early morning tremelo of a loon flying down to the Union River. Songbirds in the garden include a pair of cardinals, catbirds, robins, white-throated sparrows, juncos, black-capped chickadees, red- and white-breasted nuthatches, winter wrens, downy and hairy woodpeckers, hermit thrushes with their haunting songs, phoebes, and numerous warblers in the treetops. One particularly cold and snowy winter, a flock of redpolls flew down from Canada to overwinter in the garden.

Over the years we have planted native understory trees, including mountain maples (*Acer spicatum*), a pagoda dogwood (*Cornus alternifolia*), and a gray birch (*Betula populifolia* 'Whitespire'), and several native shrub species including summersweet clethras (*Clethra alnifolia*), mapleleaf viburnums (*Viburnum acerifolium*), common elderberries (*Sambucus canadensis*), winterberry hollies (*Ilex verticillata*), a gray dogwood (*Cornus racemosa*), a round-leaved dogwood (*C. rugosa*), and a common snowberry (*Symphoricarpos albus*). In a shady corner of the garden, a Virginia creeper vine (*Parthenocissus quinquefolia*) wraps its sinuous stems around a tall black cherry stump. These plants, as well as many others, including numerous herbaceous species, produce flowers and fruits for insects, birds, and other wildlife.

The garden's pagoda dogwood in late September, at the peak of its fall foliage color.

The blue-black fruits of mapleleaf viburnum are quickly eaten by the garden's white-throated sparrows in early October.

The portion of our garden devoted to vegetables and small fruits nourishes wildlife as well as us. Catbirds, red squirrels, and chipmunks eat most of the grapes, while a variety of bird species help themselves to the elderberries, raspberries, and highbush blueberries. We do manage to harvest plenty of the berry crops for our own use.

As we began a lifetime of gardening together, we found common ground in our concern about the biodiversity crisis facing planet Earth and in our shared belief that gardens, large and small, can serve as refuges for many forms of life, including soil organisms (both micro- and macroscopic), plants, insects, amphibians, reptiles, birds, rodents, and small mammals. We are convinced that this approach to gardening provides full enjoyment of the ornamental beauty of garden plants, both native and non-native, while adding another dimension, that of *functionality*, to the selection of plants we choose to grow.

Elderberries do double duty in the garden, providing food for gardeners and birds.

Our most significant epiphanies have occurred during our observations of the garden's insect life. This is not surprising, since insects comprise 60 percent of Earth's biodiversity. While often overlooked because of their small size, insects deserve to be recognized as the creatures that run our gardens. They are unsurpassed in variety and beauty, and many are the gardener's best friends for controlling herbivores, the insect species that eat garden plants.

While not native to North America, the Sargent crabapple, *Malus sargentii*, is a multi-season functional small tree. Its flowers are swarmed by pollinators in spring, and the small red apples (shown here) are a favorite of songbirds.

A gardener may not recognize the importance of insects in her garden without taking the time to seek them out, identify each discovery, and learn as much as possible about the newly identified insect's links to the garden food web. In recent years, work in our garden has evolved to include time spent looking under leaves and investigating sudden movements on nearby plants. We keep a camera handy, and the images of each day guide many an eve-ning hour with books and the Internet as we give a name to each new discovery and learn all we can about its life cycle and its place in the garden ecosystem. Each new discovery strengthens our view of the gar-den as a refuge for biodiversity.

Summersweet clethra, shown here in full flower, provides nectar and pollen for a wide variety of insects in late summer.

It is an unfortunate reality that there are still books being published with titles that are variations on the theme "Good Bugs and Bad Bugs: Everything You Need to Know about Attracting the Good Guys and Controlling the Bad Guys." It is equally disturbing that organizations that otherwise do good work in promoting gardening continue to use the word "pest" in reference to any gar-den creature that eats plants. If we want to get serious about gardening for biodiversity, we must drop these concepts and words from our book jackets, our websites, our thinking, and

This beautiful metallic-blue-green cuckoo wasp (*Hedychrum sp.*) resting beneath a sunflower head would be easily missed by anyone not taking the time to look. (For more about cuckoo wasps, see Chapter 7.)

our vocabularies. If gardeners can eliminate the word "pest" from their gardening lexicon, they can dispense with the word "pesticide" as well, thus eliminating these toxins from store and shed shelves, from waterways, and from landfills.

You will not find the word "pest" in the remaining pages of this book. An insect species that munches on garden plants is an herbivore, while a predator is any insect species that feeds on other insects. A pollinator is any creature that moves pollen from anther to stigma. Some insect species fill two or all three of these roles in their various life stages.

It is not the gardener's job to eliminate insect herbivores that munch on leaves, suck the sap from stems, bore holes in fruits, or graze on roots. This is the work of predatory insects such as ladybird beetles, hoverfly larvae, praying mantises, and certain wasps, which feed on herbivores as adults, larvae, or both. And it is the work of predatory arachnids such as spiders and harvestmen. The gardener's task is to cultivate populations of these predatory arthropods.

Certainly there are times when a gardener must take on the role of predator, hand-picking a horde of Japanese beetles from the grape leaves or rising at dawn to harvest sluggish cucumber beetles from the undersides of leaves. Such interventions minimize damage to the plants without the use of insecticides, and are required when herbivore populations reach a "standing room only" level. More often, the wisest course of action is to do nothing, at least for a while, and give the garden's insect predators a chance to bring things under control.

In order for your garden to support a healthy population of predators, there must be a constant population of herbivores. Kill off the herbivores with poisons and the predators disappear, leaving you with chemicals as your only defense against the next wave of herbivores. As time goes by, you will notice that the pesticides have lost their punch as the herbivores build up resistance, but not before the chemicals have eliminated pollinators and other beneficial insects from your garden.

A reader of Reeser's newspaper column once sent him an email with a photo attachment showing a squash leaf covered with cucumber beetles. She wanted to know what kind of insect this was and what she could do about it. He identified the beetle for her and suggested hand-picking and, perhaps, yellow sticky traps placed close to the squash leaves, provided she left the traps up for only a day or two to help reduce the beetle population. (Yellow sticky traps will also attract many other insects, including beneficial predators.) Two days later she sent another email, thanking him for identifying the beetle and inform-

ing him that "my husband went right out and bought a sack of Sevin dust to kill those pesky bugs." Reeser wrote back to tell her that her husband had not only eliminated the beetles, but also any chance of her squash flowers being pollinated, as bees are extremely sensitive to Sevin.

Tree leaves riddled in late September by the chewing of caterpillars and other herbivores are sure signs of a functional garden.

In our garden we live with a small population of cucumber beetles every year. If they start to get out of hand, we may pick a few, tossing them into a can of soapy water just as we do with invading Japanese beetles, but mostly we just live with them, and we still harvest plenty of cucurbits for our own use and for the food pantry in our community.

Turning your garden into a refuge for all forms of wildlife may demand a new way of thinking about insects and spiders. When, at the end of summer, you notice that most of the leaves on your oak tree are riddled with holes, rejoice! The caterpillars that create those holes are what bird food looks like! When you spot a colony of aphids on the stem of a favorite plant, leave them for the ladybird beetles and woodpeckers. In late summer, as you notice the population of harvestmen (relatives of daddy-long-legs) has boomed, give thanks, for they are working on your behalf. And rather than be frightened by that two-inch-long black wasp crawling across a cluster of milkweed blossoms, greet her as the friendly predator she is.

The Plan of This Book

Chapter 2 of this book offers an account of several garden epiphanies. The insights we gained from these events have reinforced our view that gardens can serve as refuges for much of Earth's biodiversity.

Chapter 3 describes the mostly invisible world of the garden's soil life, and Chapter 4 offers advice on how you can sustain soil life using organic mulches and compost, cover cropping with oats, and starting a new bed with minimal disturbance of the soil. Our advice stems from decades of combined experience gardening in tune with nature.

Insects and other arthropods are vital members of the garden food web. In Chapters 5 through 7 we discuss the three major groups of arthropods—pollinators, herbivores, and predators—using as examples the diversity of creatures that we have discovered in our garden. (Neither of us is an entomologist, and thus in some cases we have been unable to identify an arthropod to the level of species, or even to genus in a few cases.)

The lives of garden arthropods are intertwined with the phenology of garden plants. In Chapters 8 through 11, we describe the functional plants in our garden and their relationships with garden life. The introduction to these chapters describes the concept of a "garden insectary," the collection of plants that provide food and nesting habitat for garden insects.

Appendices discuss the importance of using scientific names for plants and animals (Appendix 1), species of milkweed (*Asclepias*) for gardens in each state (Appendix 2), regional recommendations for functional understory trees and shrubs (Appendix 3), and selected references for further reading.

Enjoy the life in your garden.

Paddled Dagger Moth Caterpillar
(*Acronicta funeralis*)

Chapter 2

Garden Epiphanies

"This curious world which we inhabit is more wonderful than it is convenient; more beautiful than it is useful; it is more to be admired and enjoyed than used."

—Henry David Thoreau, "The Commercial Spirit of Modern Times,"
Harvard University commencement address, 1837

Remember the food chains we studied in elementary school? Every creature was some other creature's lunch, as indicated by the arrows connecting one species group to another. The owl eats the rabbit that eats the plant that is fed by the sun's energy. The owl's fate is decomposition by fungi. These food chains existed in forests and oceans, deserts and swamps, each chain proceeding from plant (primary producer) to herbivore (primary consumer) to predator (secondary consumer) to decomposer, with each creature in its assigned place. In higher grades, of course, we learned that these straight-arrow drawings were oversimplifications and should be replaced by more complex drawings of food webs. We learned that the owl, one of many carnivores, eats several types of herbivores, and that all predators except the apex predator in a particular habitat are themselves preyed upon, with tertiary consumers preying upon secondary consumers and sometimes, in turn, being preyed upon by quaternary consumers in a dog-eat-dog world.

Food webs, viewed as several interconnected food chains, more accurately encompass the complexity of a garden ecosystem. When you attempt to fit a newly discovered creature into the food web of your garden, picture connecting arrows flowing to and from the new species. Who does this creature eat, and who might depend on it for energy? The story of Lucy the garter snake, the first snake of any kind found in our garden, serves as a good example.

We found Lucy sleeping in tight loops atop a pile of wood chips used to mulch garden walkways. She was not disturbed when we pulled back her blanket, a tarp to keep the wood chips dry, and we watched her closely for several minutes before resuming the morning's work. When we returned several hours later to recover the pile, she was gone. Late in the afternoon we found her sunning atop one of the firewood logs used to hold down the tarp.

Lucy, the garden garter snake. "Watch me," she whispered.

At dusk we went out to the garden with the camera, looking for Lucy. She was still coiled on the log, but as we crept closer she slowly unwound and slithered across the ground until the distance between us seemed safe. She stretched out in front of us, three feet long with a dark gray back, red-brown stripes along her sides, and a light gray belly. Her eyes were cloudy blue.

Lucy let us take her picture, several frames with long exposures, then several more with a flash, before she slid away. "Watch me," she whispered, and we did, until she was out of sight.

Two days later, when the sun came out, we slowly pulled back the tarp, hoping to find Lucy sleeping among the wood chips. Instead we found her just-shed skin stuck to the bottom of the tarp. We've since learned that cloudy blue eyes mean a garter snake is about to shed.

To fit Lucy, an Eastern garter snake, *Thamnophis sirtalis,* into our mental picture of the garden food web, we had to do some research, learning that she eats insects, primarily grasshoppers, as well as earthworms, small rodents, salamanders, frogs, and tadpoles. Imagine all the connecting arrows!

And what eats the garter snake? Birds of prey, like the sharp-shinned hawks and kestrels that lord over the garden from the top of an old spruce snag, are probably the major predators. Perhaps a skunk or raccoon, creatures that prowl the garden at night, would make a meal of her, but Lucy is likely safe, sleeping under her tarp blanket.

We haven't seen Lucy since that first encounter, but we suspect she is around, watching us, seeing us even though we don't see her.

With every new species that you find in the garden ecosystem, known biodiversity increases by one and the food web becomes more complex. New arrows are drawn, connections that seem to make sense based on your knowledge of the creatures involved. If connections are carried far enough, plants enter the picture as the primary producers that capture the energy of sunlight, converting it to chemical energy that moves through the food web from herbivores to carnivores and omnivores.

Adding Snakes to the Life in Your Garden

Gardeners should be glad to see snakes gliding through the garden. Depending on where you live, your garden might harbor slug-eating garter snakes or perhaps sharp-tailed snakes, which prey on grubs, including those of Japanese beetles. Garter snakes like Lucy are the most abundant snake in urban and suburban gardens.

A few simple guidelines will ensure that your garden is snake-friendly:

* Walk through your lawn before mowing to scare snakes into hiding. Lawn mowers are deadly to snakes. They do not hear the engine like we do and often do not sense the mower's vibrations until it is too late.

* Provide habitat for snakes in your garden. Old stumps, large rocks, brush piles, and dense patches of shrubs provide suitable habitat, as will a piece of old plywood left on the ground.

* Do not use chemicals, including pesticides and synthetic fertilizers.

Pets reportedly limit the possibility of harboring snakes in the garden, although Lucy shared our garden with two dogs and a cat. It is likely, however, that garden snakes will be far less visible when pets are around.

Insects predominate in any garden food web, yet many gardeners have little awareness of the diversity or importance of insects in their gardens with the possible exception of the role of pollinators in a vegetable garden. Some insects are herbivores, much to the gardener's vexation; some are predators, consuming other insects (including herbivores). Some species, such as butterflies, are pollinators in one stage of their life cycle and herbivores in another. And some species, like the syrphid flies (hoverflies), are predators as larvae and pollinators as adults.

What follows is an overview of a few insect species that we have discovered in our garden. Each discovery, along with insights into its role in the garden, has helped inform our view of the garden as an ecosystem, one that can be a bastion of biodiversity.

No doubt many of these insects, or similar species in the same genera, are residents of your garden too, yet you will never discover them if you do not spend time standing quietly among the flowers to watch pollinators at work, or turning over a leaf to discover aphids, the ants that farm them for their honeydew, and the syrphid fly larvae that devour aphids. A whole new world of garden life awaits discovery! These small creatures are the little things that run your garden.

Great Black Wasp: A Gardener's Best Friend (*Reeser*)

On a warm August afternoon, I was visiting a coastal Maine landscape filled with native plants, a garden close enough to home to provide visual ownership of plants that we do not grow in our own garden. On one edge was a rain garden planted with native herbaceous species that love wet feet, including swamp milkweed, *Asclepias incarnata*.

I stood in the midst of the blooming milkweeds, astonished by the diversity of insects swarming and crawling among the flowers and along the stems. On some plants, the earliest flower clusters had produced bunches of immature green seed pods, the stems of which were crowded with orange aphids that I later determined to be oleander aphids, *Aphis nerii*, a common herbivore associated with milkweeds worldwide.

I looked up from photographing the aphids and there, inches from my nose, was a giant black wasp crawling purposefully across a cluster of milkweed blossoms. About two inches long, she was both beautiful and threatening, black except for wings that reflected a shining metallic blue in sunlight. (I determined the wasp's sex later in the day, when a field guide showed the male to be much smaller.)

She ignored me and the myriad other insects swarming around her, completely focused on foraging for nectar while moving pollen from flower to flower. After a few moments of

A great black wasp sipping nectar from swamp milkweed flowers.

feeling intimidated by the size of her stinger, I followed her from one flower cluster to another with the camera.

Later that day I sat down with field guides to learn as much as I could about the wasp named *Sphex pensylvanicus*. Also known as "katydid hunter" and the "steel-blue cricket hunter," she belongs to a group of solitary hunting wasps collectively called digger wasps, a reference to the construction of their nesting tunnels in soft soil.

It is the male wasp's responsibility to pick the nest site and keep competitors away while choosing a mate. The female is the digger, using her heavy-duty mandibles to loosen the soil. Using her legs as a rake, she compacts a lump of subterranean soil, holds it in place under her chin with her front pair of legs, and transports it to the surface where she deposits it in a pile. Her nesting tunnel is long, with multiple egg chambers. While not social insects, several females may excavate nesting tunnels in the same area.

After constructing the nesting tunnels, the wasp provisions each egg chamber with food for the developing larva. Katydids and grasshoppers, often much larger than she, are her primary prey. She first supplies each chamber with one captured insect paralyzed with three stings, laying one egg to its underside. Although immobile, the prey will live until the egg hatches and the larva begins to feed.

During its development, a larva will consume between two and six katydids or grasshoppers, so the adult female spends a good portion of her time provisioning each chamber of her nest. (Forget the male at this point; he's just the sperm donor.) When a chamber is fully provisioned, she fills it, pushing in soil and tamping it down with her head, often with the aid of a small leaf or pebble, placing the "tool" on the loose earth and pressing her head against it while vibrating her abdomen. After the egg hatches, the larva spends about 10 days feeding and then pupates through the winter.

Provisioning each nest chamber with sufficient food takes up much of the female's time, and the task is made even more arduous when a captured and paralyzed insect never makes it to the nest. The female wasp can become a victim of kleptoparasitism (parasitism by theft) by house sparrows and gray catbirds as she drags her prey back to the nest. Researchers at University of Rhode Island determined that as many as one third of a wasp's provisioning attempts are thwarted by avian theft.

As often happens, a few days after my first encounter with a great black wasp, I met another female foraging on Queen Anne's lace in our garden insectary. Paying me no heed, she moved deliberately across the cluster of tiny flowers, filling up on nectar. I smiled at the thought that somewhere in the garden, perhaps along the back edge of a bed where the soil had been softened by digging, there was a nesting tunnel where well-fed pupae would spend the winter.

Paddled Dagger Moth Caterpillar: An Experience of a Lifetime (*Reeser*)

We share our highbush blueberry harvest with white-throated sparrows, blue jays, robins, black-capped chickadees, mourning doves, and other birds, as well as the garden's chipmunks. In addition to birds and small mammals, blueberry plants also serve as a larval host for several lepidopteran species, including brown elfin, striped hairstreak, and spring azure butterflies and hummingbird clearwing, major datana, and saddleback moths. While we have yet to encounter all of these caterpillars in our garden, the adults are common nectar feeders there.

One late mid-August afternoon, Marjorie came in from the garden with a bowl of berries and announced that there was an unusual caterpillar on one of the blueberry shrubs. I rushed to the garden with camera in hand and took several shots of the creature as it munched the tip of a blueberry leaf.

A paddled dagger moth caterpillar munching on a highbush blueberry leaf.
The caterpillar can rotate the paddles on its back as a means of deterring would-be predators.

Typically when you find one caterpillar there are others of the same species nearby, but a thorough search of the garden's blueberry shrubs turned up no other like it. The back of its coal-black body was lined with orange and white football-shaped pads, each sporting a slender black filament with a paddle-shaped tip. That evening I keyed it out as the larva of a paddled dagger moth, *Acronicta funeralis*.

Whenever we find a new species in our garden, we try to understand how it fits into the garden food web. We learned that the highbush blueberry was but one of several larval host plants for *A. funeralis*. We might also find it feeding on alder, apple, birch, dogwood, hazel, maple, oak, or willow, all of which occur in or around our garden. And we learned that our sighting of this creature was a rare event, that some lepidopterists go their entire lives without seeing the larva of the paddled dagger moth.

From my research on this species we learned that the adult moth is mostly gray with distinctive black markings that account for its common name, the funerary moth. But other questions remain unanswered. What eats the paddled dagger moth caterpillar? Do the paddle-tipped hairs deter birds, or is this rare creature another example of what bird food looks like? We have yet to find answers, but we did add *Acronicta funeralis* to the list of creatures with whom we share our garden.

Monarch Butterflies: Plant It and They Will Come

We knew that populations of the monarch butterfly *(Danaus plexippus)* in their Mexican overwintering forests had decreased in recent years, but we didn't know how dire the situation had become until we read Gabriel Popkin's article "Plight of the Butterfly" in *The American Gardener* (March/April 2014). The monarch overwintering area in 2013 was the lowest ever recorded, 1.65 forest acres compared with a peak of 45 acres in the mid-1990s.

The number of monarch butterflies summering in Maine has also declined in recent years. Ann Judd, leader of the monarch project at Charlotte Rhoades Butterfly Garden in Southwest Harbor, Maine, reported all-time lows of monarchs spotted in a nearby field of common milkweed in the summer of 2013: only two monarchs were seen.

A male monarch butterfly nectaring on tropical milkweed.

Causes of this drastic decline include winter habitat loss to timber cutting in Mexico and several consecutive spring droughts that desiccated monarch eggs, reducing the number that hatched. But most scientists agree that the number one cause is reduction in milkweed populations along the monarch's migration routes due to the use of herbicides on fields of herbicide-resistant genetically engineered corn and soybean varieties. All other plants are killed, including nearby milkweed. This short-sighted and ecologically destructive farming strategy is lethal to monarchs, as milkweeds are the only plants that monarch caterpillars will eat; without them, the species cannot complete its life cycle.

After reading Popkin's article, we asked Ann which species of milkweed she would recommend to gardeners who want to help restore summer monarch populations in New England. She suggested planting the native *Asclepias syriaca*, common milkweed, in open fields or other areas where its rhizomatous habit can be tolerated. It is the best native perennial species from the monarch's point of view, simply because of its abundance, but too aggressive for the home garden. Another native perennial species, swamp milkweed (*A. incarnata*), the same plant that the great black wasp found so inviting, works well in the perennial border, where it is a magnet for butterflies and other pollinators.

"Even a tub of the South American annual species *A. curassavica*, tropical milkweed, a continuous bloomer, can get a family interested in the monarch cycle if they don't have a back yard for a garden," said Ann. "My goal is to have schools and senior centers, libraries, golf courses—everyone, really—get something started. It would make a difference in any community if everyone tried."

In early March there were only a handful of young swamp milkweed plants in our garden, too small to attract passing monarchs, so we purchased several packets of tropical milkweed seeds, germinated them indoors, and in early June transplanted about three dozen seedlings into the garden. Most went into two small beds in the vegetable garden, and a dozen were planted in a large "whiskey barrel" tub at the porch steps. We waited to see if any monarchs would find us.

Our milkweeds, both the perennial and the tropical annual, grew slowly through the spring, but as the days lengthened and temperatures rose, the annuals burst into bloom. By the end of June, each plant bore several clusters of orange-red flower buds that soon opened to reveal deep-yellow petals.

On a warm early-July morning, while working in the garden, we caught a glimpse of a monarch soaring over the deer fence and into the vegetable garden—the first monarch butterfly ever to visit our garden, as far as we knew. It flitted about for a few minutes and then disappeared. That afternoon there were two monarchs flying about the garden. We kept watch as we worked, hoping to see them come to rest on the tropical milkweeds, but saw no monarchs touch down.

Yet monarchs did touch down, for on July 20 there were small monarch caterpillars munching on all the tropi-

Monarch caterpillars devouring the foliage of annual tropical milkweed.

cal milkweeds. Slender and hard to find at first, they grew rapidly as the leaf area on the milkweed plants grew smaller. By the first of August we counted 24 fat caterpillars nearing the end of their two-week larval stage, almost ready to pupate.

When monarch caterpillars are ready to pupate, they leave the milkweed plants and disperse. Before this could happen, we transferred nine caterpillars to hatching cages for tagging. Of the remaining 15, we easily discovered six chrysalises attached to plastic strands of the deer fence, but the rest of the pupating larvae were hidden in the garden.

One of the monarch caterpillars attached its chrysalis to the stem of a sweet pea plant.

In the hatching cages, each caterpillar continued to feed on cuttings of milkweed for a while before crawling up the mesh side of its cage to the top, where it attached itself upside-down to the plastic roof, assuming the shape of a "J." What followed was merely chemistry, but it had the aura of lepidopteran magic. The caterpillar at dusk transformed into a translucent lime green chrysalis by dawn, the contents of the chrysalis little more than a bag of fluid.

Daily checks over the next two weeks showed little change in the chrysalises. They were buffeted by winds, pounded by rain, and baked by the sun, but otherwise remained the same color and size. As the time approached for the emergence of adult butterflies from these tiny capsules, we could see the orange and black markings of wings through the thin shells of the chrysalises.

And then, about 24 hours before emergence, the color of each chrysalis changed to a dark gray-green, almost black in poor light. Often this color change occurred late in the day, and by dawn the adult had emerged. We would find it clinging to the transparent shell of its chrysalis, to a nearby stem, or to the mesh walls of the hatching cage, pumping its wings to fill them with fluid.

A monarch adult ready to emerge from the chrysalis, as evidenced by the outline of the markings on its wings.

Making our rounds of known chrysalis locations in the garden, we came across a chrysalis from which the adult was just emerging, its wings crinkled like tissue paper around its swollen abdomen. Over a thirty-minute period, the wings slowly expanded until they appeared nearly full size but still very fragile, easily creased as the butterfly slowly crawled about the empty chrysalis shell. It would be several hours before the monarch could fly.

Monarch Watch, a nonprofit education, conservation, and research program based at the University of Kansas, runs a monarch tagging program to keep track of monarch numbers and to track any shifts in the origins of monarchs that reach Mexico. Ann Judd manages the Monarch Watch tagging project at Charlotte Rhoades Butterfly Garden in Maine, transferring mature caterpillars from the garden to hatching cages for pupation. At the end of the two-week pupation period, on the day after the adult butterfly emerges from its chrysalis, it is carefully removed from the cage, and the center of one wing is tagged with a small sticky-backed paper disk. A number on the tag identifies the butterfly's tagging location and sex. If recovered, the tag provides information on mortality during migration. Since the total number of butterflies tagged each year roughly parallels the numbers overwintering in Mexico, tagging also provides a benchmark of shifts in the number of migrating monarchs.

An adult monarch just after emergence from its chrysalis, not yet able to fly.

Of the nine caterpillars that we placed in hatching cages, eight adults were successfully tagged over a three-day span (one never emerged from its chrysalis). As one of us gently

A just-tagged monarch nectaring on tropical milkweed flowers.

grasped the folded wings of a butterfly, the other applied the tiny paper disc to the outer wing. We then released the monarch on a cluster of tropical milkweed to begin nectaring.

Each mid-August day brought more monarch butterflies in the air above our garden. They sipped nectar from summersweet clethra, purple coneflowers, Mexican sunflowers, zinnias, and, of course, milkweed. They soared over the deer fence into the vegetable garden. They floated gently into the high canopy of a birch tree, their orange-and-black markings distinctive among the dark green leaves.

The two monarch butterflies that had flown into our garden in early July were third-generation descendants of butterflies that spent the previous winter in Mexico. In some mysterious way they found the small patches of milkweed plants growing in our little garden, deposited eggs on the leaves of those plants, and moved on. In late August, the adult monarchs raised in our garden were winging south to the oyamel fir forests of Mexico to begin the cycle anew.

There is a vital truth in this modest story: two gardeners tending a small garden can make a difference. Imagine a world in which every garden included a patch of milkweed. (See Appendix 2: "*Asclepias* Species for the Garden and Insectary.")

Milkweed Tussock Moth Caterpillars and Milkweed Aphids: Unexpected Guests at the Table

While the 25 monarch caterpillars in our garden munched on the annual tropical milkweed, the young swamp milkweed plants grew unmolested to three feet in height. Preoccupied with the monarch larvae, we were surprised one August morning to find the leaves of one of the perennial milkweed plants, both upper and lower surfaces, covered with a horde of small caterpillars, later identified as milkweed tussock moth larvae (*Euchaetes egle*). Grazing like a herd of tiny cows, these caterpillars skeletonized each plant's leaves in a matter of days, so that by summer's end all of the swamp milkweed plants had been reduced to slender leafless stalks while the caterpillars grew fat.

Milkweed tussock moth caterpillars devouring a leaf of swamp milkweed.

E. egle larvae go through four molting stages as they mature, and the first stage looks nothing like the fourth. The first stage is a small, thin, gray caterpillar that is only slightly hairy, while the fourth stage looks like Cousin Itt of Addams Family fame, much larger and covered with long black and orange hairs.

Making frequent stops at our little milkweed patch to watch the tussock moth caterpillars (we were hoping to see a predator at work), we noticed that the color of one of the stems had changed from green to orange. Close inspection revealed a growing colony of oleander aphids (*Aphis nerii*), so named for their primary host plants in more southern regions of the country, but also called milkweed aphids in New England.

Oleander aphids on swamp milkweed stems—standing room only!

It took only a few days for every swamp milkweed stem to become completely covered with orange aphids, each tapped into the phloem sap of the stem. This is not surprising, since every aphid is a female capable of giving birth to 80 live young, called nymphs, every week, and each nymph, also a female, becomes sexually mature in about a week. It's an interesting math exercise to start with a single aphid and calculate the number of aphids after just five weeks. Of course, aphid population explosions are usually tempered by ladybird beetles, thrip larvae, syrphid fly larvae, woodpeckers, and other predators.

We were so captivated by the presence of both herbivores—the tussock moth larvae and the aphids—that we overlooked the likelihood that no predators would show up to control their population growth. Both the tussock moth larvae and the aphids were ingesting the same glycosides that are toxic to potential predators of monarch butterflies. The orange color of the aphids and the vivid orange and black coloration of the tussock moth larvae— the same color combination of adult monarchs—serve as warnings to would-be predators: Don't Eat Me!

Thus, over the course of the last few weeks before first frost, our young swamp milkweed plants took a beating. Based on experience with this species at Marjorie's office garden, we knew that mature plants could take the abuse and come back the next spring with vigor, but we were asking a lot of one-year-old plants. As it turned out, their underground crowns were up to the task.

The Garden as Habitat

What a difference those milkweed plants, both annual and perennial, made in our garden! Three insect species, each dependent on milkweeds to complete their life cycle, suddenly appeared in the garden in the first year milkweeds had ever been grown there. How did the female monarch butterfly or the female tussock moth find a little patch of milkweed where before there had been none? Where did that first milkweed aphid come from? What we do know is that planting milkweeds increased our garden's insect biodiversity by at least three species.

The garden experiences described above were seminal. They strengthened our view of the garden as ecosystem and define our work as caretakers of a community of life, a haven for biodiversity.

Nursery Web Spider
(*Pisaurina mira*)

Chapter 3

The Living Soil

"Once you are aware of and appreciate the beautiful synergisms between soil organisms, you will not only become a better gardener but a better steward of the earth."
—Jeff Lowenfels and Wayne Lewis, *Teaming with Microbes: The Organic Gardener's Guide to the Soil Food Web*

Soil is an ecosystem, one that teems with life. Plant roots exploring the soil's matrix of minerals and organic matter probe a domain of bacteria, fungi, nematodes, earthworms, arthropods, and other life forms. Gardeners should nurture that ecosystem. The more we read and think about soil biodiversity, the less inclined we are to take a spade to a garden bed or to disturb the complex food web that healthy soil contains.

Plants control the soil food web, including the numbers and kinds of bacteria and fungi, a dynamic mix of which compete for the carbohydrates and proteins in root exudates. These well-fed beneficial organisms in turn attract bigger microbes, including nematodes and protozoa, who eat the bacteria and fungi. Anything they don't need is excreted as waste, which plant roots absorb as nutrients.

From the gardener's point of view, the primary role of the soil food web is to pass nutrients through the web until they become temporarily immobilized in the bodies of bacteria and fungi. When these organisms die, the nutrients are released in a form that plants can utilize. The most important of these nutrients is nitrogen, and the biomass of bacteria and fungi in the soil determines, for the most part, the amount of nitrogen readily available for plant use.

Life in the Rhizosphere

The soil food web is a complex interweaving of food chains, and it starts with plants. Photosynthesis in leaves provides energy that roots use to produce chemicals and to secrete those

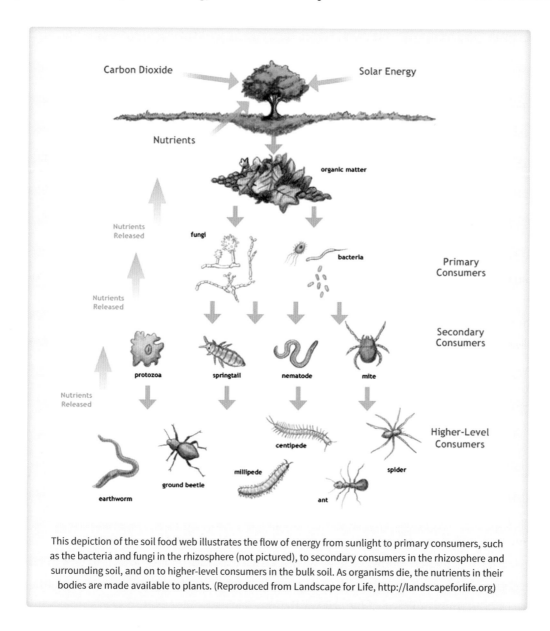

This depiction of the soil food web illustrates the flow of energy from sunlight to primary consumers, such as the bacteria and fungi in the rhizosphere (not pictured), to secondary consumers in the rhizosphere and surrounding soil, and on to higher-level consumers in the bulk soil. As organisms die, the nutrients in their bodies are made available to plants. (Reproduced from Landscape for Life, http://landscapeforlife.org)

chemicals into the soil to form the rhizosphere, a thin layer of intense microbial activity surrounding plant roots. Sugars, amino acids, proteins, and material sloughed from dead root cells are leaked into the rhizosphere, which electron micrographs tell us is a mucigel, or gelatinous material, covering plant roots. To soil-dwelling microorganisms, the rhizosphere resembles a donut shop, a great source of carbohydrates. As a result, this zone of plant exudates, located within a tenth of an inch of the plant roots, is filled with microbes, including bacteria, fungi, nematodes, protozoa, and other organisms that feed on the exudates. Bacteria levels in the rhizosphere can be ten to one thousand times higher than in surrounding soil.

These microbes sequester nutrients in their bodies, and when they die, some of the released nutrients, such as nitrogen, are reabsorbed by the plant roots, while other released nutrients become food for rhizosphere life.

Here is the take-home message for gardeners: Soil life provides the nutrients needed for plant life, and plants initiate and fuel the cycle by secreting root exudates into the rhizosphere. Without the rhizosphere system, most nutrients would be leached from the soil. Instead, they are retained in the bodies of living organisms, a reservoir to be tapped by growing plants.

In a Teaspoon of Soil

One billion bacteria live in a single teaspoon of productive soil, the equivalent of a ton of bacteria per acre. These microbes live in the water-filled pores of the soil, on the moist surfaces of mineral particles and decaying organic debris, and, most importantly from the plant's point of view, in the rhizosphere.

Many soil bacteria are decomposers, converting the energy held within the carbon-to-carbon bonds of organic matter into forms of energy useful to all organisms in the soil food web. Nitrogen and other elements essential to plants are stored in decomposer cells, preventing their loss from the root zone. When the bacteria die, the stored nutrients can be absorbed by plant roots.

Nitrogen-fixing bacteria form mutualistic relationships with the roots of legumes such as peas and beans and trees such as alder. The plant supplies carbon-based energy sources to the bacteria, and the bacteria convert nitrogen from the air into a form the plant can use.

Other soil bacteria species, the nitrifying bacteria, convert ammonium produced by the decomposition of organic matter into nitrate, a preferred form of nitrogen for most garden crops. And the actinomycetes, a large group of bacteria that are responsible for the earthy smell of healthy soil, decompose a wide variety of organic materials, including chitin and cellulose, the tough stuff of plant cell walls.

The billion bacteria in a teaspoon of healthy garden soil represent thousands of species. This diversity keeps pathogens in check, perhaps outcompeted, until they disappear. In the rhizosphere, beneficial bacteria can coat root surfaces so thoroughly that pathogens have no room to take hold.

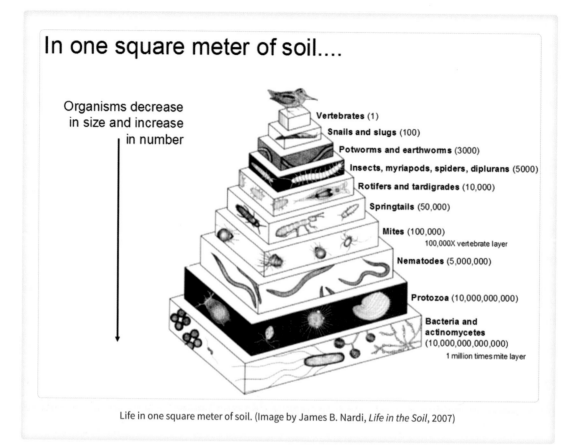

In one square meter of soil....

Organisms decrease in size and increase in number

Vertebrates (1)
Snails and slugs (100)
Potworms and earthworms (3000)
Insects, myriapods, spiders, diplurans (5000)
Rotifers and tardigrades (10,000)
Springtails (50,000)
Mites (100,000)
  100,000X vertebrate layer
Nematodes (5,000,000)
Protozoa (10,000,000,000)
Bacteria and actinomycetes (10,000,000,000,000)
  1 million times mite layer

Life in one square meter of soil. (Image by James B. Nardi, *Life in the Soil*, 2007)

Joining the bacteria as important decomposers of dead organic matter are saprophytic fungi, species that feed on decomposing organic material, breaking it down into humus, minerals, and nutrients that plant roots can absorb. That teaspoon of healthy garden soil will contain several yards of fungal hyphae, thread-like strands of fungal bodies that bind soil particles together to form stable soil aggregates. These aggregates increase the soil's water-holding capacity and water infiltration. The fungal hyphae form nets or webs around roots, creating physical barriers to invasion by pathogens. And like bacteria, saprophytic fungi retain nutrients that would otherwise leach away.

Other fungi, called mycorrhizal fungi, colonize plant roots in mutualistic relationships. Capable of increasing the root surface absorbing area by one hundred or more times, these fungi provide physical protection, water, and nutrients to plant roots in return for the carbon-containing exudates secreted by the roots into the rhizosphere. You scratch my back, I'll scratch yours.

In addition to bacteria and fungi, a teaspoon of healthy garden soil contains several thousand nutrient-mobilizing protozoa—microscopic, single-celled microbes that eat bacteria. Since the bacteria contain more nitrogen than the protozoa can use, some nitrogen in the form of ammonium is released to plants.

A teaspoon of garden soil will also contain a few dozen nematodes (microscopic unsegmented worms), most of them beneficial. They spend their lives in water-filled spaces between soil particles, eating bacteria and fungi. There are also predatory nematodes that eat the few nematode species that feed on plant roots.

Each square foot of healthy garden soil contains up to 100 beneficial arthropods (insects, spiders, mites, and others) and between 5 and 30 earthworms. Earthworms are particularly important to maintaining healthy soil structure. Their tunnels provide aeration and drainage, and their excretions (worm castings) bind soil crumbs together.

It is an eat-and-be-eaten world in the soil. And since most organisms eat more than one kind of prey, food chains are not straight lines but rather complex webs of food chains linked and cross-linked to each other.

The Good Earth

Many gardeners live their entire lives without appreciating the complex ecosystem beneath their feet or acknowledging the importance of this ecosystem to their gardening success. This is why garden center shelves are stacked with insecticides, herbicides, fungicides, and synthetic fertilizers.

This is a gardener's truth: Putting toxic chemicals into the soil destroys the soil ecosystem. Pesticides kill off important members of the soil food web, destroying ecosystem function. Once the soil is dead, the gardener becomes totally dependent on the toxic chemicals and must forever add more and more synthetic fertilizer, more and more chemicals to deal with plant pathogens and herbivores. And some of those chemicals end up in the gardener.

The healthy alternative is to nurture the soil ecosystem.

Black Ground Beetle
(*Pterostichus melanarius*)

Chapter 4

Sustaining Soil Biodiversity

"The soil is the great connector of lives, the source and destination of all. It is the healer and restorer and resurrector, by which disease passes into health, age into youth, death into life. Without proper care for it we can have no community, because without proper care for it we can have no life."
—Wendell Berry, *The Unsettling of America*

It is a clear, blue-sky day in early spring, and the garden is waking from a long winter's sleep. The vegetable beds are bare, and their dark soil—having soaked up yesterday's rain—is now being warmed by the sun. At the soil surface or just below, signs of the garden's awakening abound. Scarab beetles, tossed up in the digging of postholes for the garden's new gate, lumber sleepily over clods of damp, loamy soil. Earthworms tunnel just below the soil surface, while a stubby banded woolly caterpillar crawls lazily above them. All around, birds argue about nesting territory.

A bumble bee queen stirs in her underground winter nest at the edge of the garden, where she spent the long winter alone, the sole survivor of a teeming summer colony. In a day or so she will be flying over the garden in search of early nectar. She will be joined by adult solitary bees, awakened from their winter's sleep in cramped cells stacked end-to-end in an old fence post, searching first for mates, then for dandelions in bloom.

A native solitary bee forages for pollen and nectar on a dandelion head.

And the life the gardener cannot see, but knows must be there, is also waking. Single-celled and multicellular, these invisible soil-builders—bacteria, fungi, and nematodes—begin their work of breaking down organic matter into nutrients that the garden's plants must have to grow. As the soil warms, microbe populations expand.

Into this community of life, this ecosystem called the garden, comes the gardener. She treads lightly on paths made for walking, circling beds raised by years of topdressing with compost. She brings with her only tools she can carry in her hand. No plow, no tiller, has ever been in this garden.

She sows seeds and transplants seedlings with the least possible disturbance of the life around them, for it is this living soil that will feed the growing plants and enable them to mature, put forth leaves, and bear fruit. Weeds, if they are troublesome, are pulled by hand. She has a helper, a partner, and between them the garden thrives.

What follows are a few tips on managing garden soil to sustain soil biodiversity. Over the years, we have abandoned many conventional methods of soil management, opting for less disruptive methods including minimal tillage; the use of organic mulches such as shredded leaves, compost, and composted manures; and cover cropping with oats. We also offer advice on using wood ashes in the garden and starting a new bed.

The Minimum-till Garden

When both of us started gardening several decades ago, double-digging of garden beds was the prevailing paradigm. Now we know better, having arrived at a view of the gardener as caretaker of the life in the garden. In this view, disrupting the community of soil life with a rototiller is anathema to us.

We can find no good in rototilling or deep-digging established garden beds. These actions disturb the natural growing environment for plant roots, breaking up fungal hyphae, killing worms and arthropods, destroying soil structure, and eventually reducing soil aeration. Tillage disrupts the complex cycling of nutrients through the soil food web. It brings dormant weed seeds to the surface, where they will sprout.

Minimal-till gardens harbor fewer insect herbivores and plant diseases, likely due to the more balanced community of life in an undisturbed soil environment.

We have had some interesting discussions on the question of when, if ever, soil should be invaded by a spade, considering the disruption of life that this act creates. For example, is cover-cropping with winter rye worth the disruption of soil life caused by digging in the cover crop?

Perhaps not. There are other annual cover crops, such as winter-killed oats, that do not need to be turned into the soil in order to plant vegetables in the spring. And perhaps the same goal, increasing the organic matter content of the soil, can be accomplished by top-dressing with composted manure. Think about how many earthworms are killed when you turn over a cover crop of winter rye. (No, they don't grow back the missing half. They die.) Not to mention the disruption of microbial life in the soil caused by digging.

When we plant peas in early spring, we do it as non-invasively as possible, using our hands to make shallow furrows in the soil and cover the seeds. We may relocate a worm or two, but we won't bisect any. Microbial life below the furrows will go on undisturbed. When we transplant tomato seedlings in early June, we dig the planting holes by hand, throwing a handful of compost in the bottom of each hole as penance for the disturbance.

Nourishing life in the garden, treading lightly, providing habitat for pollinators and other wildlife, this is the gardener's work. Leave the deep tilling to earthworms.

Organic Mulches Sustain Healthy Garden Soil

Every spring, as soon as the soil has thawed and drained, we pick a sunny afternoon to plant peas and onions. Typically, these first activities in the vegetable garden capture the attention of several crows who watch from a nearby birch.

We feel the sun's warmth on our backs and the soil's warmth in our fingers as we form two shallow furrows down the length of a garden bed. Into each furrow we scatter pea seeds, plump from soaking in water, then cover them with the warm soil, gently patting it down by hand. The crows watch.

A thin layer of shredded leaves makes an excellent moisture-retaining mulch for newly planted onions.

We push twiggy birch branches into the soil between the rows, forming a four-foot scaffold for future pea tendrils and an immediate barrier to the scheming seed scavengers. Defeated, the crows fly off as we soak the bed with a gentle shower.

Finally, we spread over the bed a thin blanket of shredded leaves, a handful at a time, pulled from a bag stored in the basement since fall when we spread them in an open space on the drainfield and shredded them with a lawn mower. Dry leaf dust drifts downwind as we settle the leaf mulch into place with a final watering.

We also use shredded leaves to mulch the onion transplants, just enough to cover the soil, hold in the moisture, keep the root run cool, and perhaps make it a little harder for weed seeds to get started. Later, after the plants are established and growing, we lay down a deeper mulch.

We also do a lot of mulching with "nannyberries," a composted mixture of goat manure, urine, and bedding (wood shavings)—hereafter referred to as composted goat manure—applying it liberally around garden shrubs and small trees as well as the highbush blueberries, raspberries, and grape vines when these small fruit crops begin their new growth in early spring. Nannyberries have replaced straw as our mulch of choice for these crops since we learned that mulching with straw can increase the chances of mice girdling the bases of the plants.

Nannyberries are too coarse for use where vegetable seeds will be sown, and they often contain too much nitrogen to place in direct contact with tender transplants. We spread

All of the garden's shrubs and small trees are mulched with nannyberries, including this Sargent crabapple.

nannyberries over the soil of most vegetable beds in the fall, relying on shredded leaves as mulch for these beds after planting.

We mulch the next year's potato bed with nannyberries in autumn. When it's time to plant, we rake this mulch aside to make furrows for the seed potatoes, then spread it back over the bed once the cut tubers are covered with soil. In two or three weeks, when the first potato leaves appear, the composted manure mulch will be well seasoned, its nutrients seeping into the soil with every rain.

Finished garden compost is another excellent mulch. A mixture of vegetable scraps from the kitchen, spent plants from the garden, shredded leaves, seaweed, and nannyberries, our compost pile decomposes through the summer and, by October, yields a modest amount of rich, crumbly mulch. We screen it first, eliminating tough stems and other coarse materials that need more time to break down, then spread it where it is needed most, often on the strawberry beds.

And we mulch with worm castings. Over the course of a year, the worm bin occupants transform pounds of coffee grounds, banana peels, and other kitchen vegetable scraps into buckets of nutrient-rich castings. Blueberries and raspberries are the usual beneficiaries.

Organic mulches are the only fertilizer for our trees, shrubs, and perennials. In the vegetable garden, organic mulches and an occasional watering with a fish emulsion solution supply sufficient quantities of nitrogen and other essential nutrients for sustained vegetable and fruit production, year after year.

Screened compost, ready for spreading on the strawberry beds.

Organic mulches should be in the final stages of decomposition. Wood chips, shredded wood, and sawdust are excellent mulches for garden walkways but should never be used where plants are grown. The wood in these products consists of large molecules, mostly lignin and cellulose, which must be decomposed by legions of soil bacteria into smaller molecules. These hard-working microbes utilize the bulk of the soil's nitrogen as they work, leaving the garden plants nitrogen-starved.

Good Reasons to Rake Leaves (*Reeser*)

I can think of a couple of good reasons to rake autumn leaves into huge piles. Neither involves stuffing them into plastic bags left at curbside until trash day.

Most important when I was younger was the need to jump feet first from a running start into the pile, to hide perfectly still below the surface, breathing in the pungent organic odor, until routed out by an old dog's cold nose. I am too old to fly into the pile as I once did, but not too old to retain the memory of being ten years old on a crisp October afternoon, my father heaping up the leaves after every flying leap.

Now I gather leaves to recycle their nutrients into leaf mold and compost for the garden. True, much of a leaf's nutrient content is transferred to roots and stems before the leaf dies. But those dry, brown remnants of summer retain a surprisingly high nutrient element analysis. Fallen leaves of deciduous trees such as maple, beech, ash, and oak contain about 0.5 percent nitrogen, 0.1 percent phosphorus, and 0.5 percent potassium, along with equally substantial amounts of calcium and magnesium, all of which are essential for plant growth.

Because leaf decomposition is a slow process, these nutrients are released gradually—nature's version of a slow-release fertilizer. Indeed, annual top-dressing with a mixture of decomposing leaves and composted manure is all the fertilizer that trees, shrubs, and many perennials need for healthy growth. Even lawns are healthier for the nutrients released from fallen leaves by a mulching lawn mower.

Shredded leaves make an excellent mulch for vegetable crops like these leeks.

Nutrients, however, are only one of the benefits of autumn leaves; leaf mold (leaves in the final stages of decomposition) also improves both the structure and water-holding capacity of the soil. While rich topsoil can hold 60 percent of its weight in water (compared with 20 percent for subsoil), leaf mold can retain 300 percent or more of its weight.

To make leaf mulch, start by shredding dry leaves into small pieces that will break down quickly. This can be done with special grinders designed for the task—or with a lawn mower. I know one gardener who puts dry leaves in a trash can and then shreds them with a weed whacker.

Some of the shredded leaves can be added to the compost pile, but only sparingly unless they are mixed with high-nitrogen materials such as fresh grass clippings or stable manure. Too many leaves will stall the composting process, but a mixture of two parts shredded leaves to one part green grass clippings (by volume) will decompose quickly.

Reluctant to rob nutrients from our woodland garden, we rely on a willing neighbor for an endless supply of autumn leaves. We wait for a sun-washed Saturday afternoon to walk down the road, rakes in hand, to make the piles. We build them tall and broad for Sophie, our black lab puppy, to run through, and only when she has had enough do we haul the leaves home and spread them out for the mower.

Composting (*Reeser*)

I once joined a group of adult students under Marjorie's tutelage to construct a compost pile in 30 minutes. It was impressive and made me think of community members gathering together to raise a barn in a day.

A compost thermometer is an essential tool for successful composting.

Everyone arrived with a key ingredient in the recipe for compost: dry straw, stable manure, seaweed, vegetable and fruit peelings, coffee grounds, egg shells, grass clippings, dried leaves (whole and shredded). The bin, a closed wire fence measuring three feet in each direction, was the minimum size for a successful compost pile. I worked in amazement as something that takes most gardeners months to build was accomplished in half an hour.

We began by turning over the soil beneath the bin to provide easy access to the pile for earthworms, ground beetles, and microbial agents of decomposition. Because a compost bin in full sun will dry out easily, slowing down decomposition, we located our bin in a well-drained spot with partial shade.

We started with a 12-inch layer of fluffed straw—not hay, which contains weed seeds that will survive the composting process and germinate in garden beds. Dry straw, the hollow stems of harvested grain, is used as the initial layer because it is stiff enough to resist compaction and will allow air to enter the pile from the bottom. Like dry leaves, straw is also an excellent source of carbon, the primary energy source for the bacteria and fungi that decompose organic matter.

Six inches of fresh grass clippings were added next, providing the compost-manufacturing bacteria with nitrogen, which is essential for reproduction. Grass clippings are not the only source of nitrogen, however, and many gardeners prefer to leave them on the lawn. Livestock manures are excellent nitrogen sources, as are coffee grounds, vegetable and fruit waste, and seaweed collected from above the high tide line.

Layer by layer the pile grew, shredded leaves followed by garden weeds that had been chopped into small pieces with a digging spade, then dry whole leaves. At this point, with the bin about one-third full, we mixed everything together with a garden fork and thoroughly watered the pile.

Next came additional layers of chopped seaweed, straw, composted goat manure, shredded leaves, chopped kitchen wastes, more leaves. Again we thoroughly stirred and watered the pile, then topped it off with final layers of seaweed and leaves.

Chopping bulky ingredients such as garden weeds, vegetable and fruit peelings, and seaweed increases the surface areas of these ingredients. Bacteria and fungi work at the surfaces of decaying materials.

Decomposition occurs quickly when the pile's carbon to nitrogen ratio (C:N) is approximately 30:1. We accomplished this by mixing high-carbon materials (C:N of 50:1), such as straw and dry leaves, in roughly equal amounts with high-nitrogen materials such as manure, seaweed, and grass clippings (C:N of 15:1).

Success in composting is measured with a compost thermometer. A well-constructed compost pile heats up as bacteria do their work, reaching a peak between 90 and 150 degrees F, and then starts to cool. When the pile returns to ambient temperature, it should be turned so that the least decomposed material on the cooler outside of the pile is moved to the middle. While turning, water the pile to the consistency of a wrung-out sponge. Within a day or so, the temperature in the middle should start to rise again.

One week after building our pile, its temperature was a healthy 149 degrees. Four months later, the finished compost was dark brown with a crumbly texture, none of the original ingredients recognizable. Chocolate cake for the garden.

Finished compost, screened and ready for use.

Bringing together everything needed to build a compost pile in half an hour takes either a captive audience of eager students or a lot of space for stockpiling essential ingredients. Most gardeners fill compost bins at a much slower rate, adding materials as they become available but always remembering the need to mix materials high in carbon with those high in nitrogen. A neighbor who would love to have someone rake their autumn leaves for free, a local dairy farmer or horse owner with a growing pile of stable litter (straw and manure), a friend with ready access to seaweed—these are goldmines for the gardener who composts.

Cover Cropping with Oats

Gardening is about feeding soil creatures. Do all you can to nourish them and protect their environment. Do nothing that disturbs their work.

In the vegetable garden, cover cropping—planting a crop to cover the soil—is done in the fall to protect the soil over the winter when otherwise it would be bare, vulnerable to erosion by wind and water. We feel that oats are the least disruptive cover crop when it comes to sustaining soil life.

This early April cover crop of oats can be left on the bed as a mulch around transplants, or parted for direct sowing of seeds or planting transplants. There is no need to work it into the soil, as it will quickly decompose.

Oats, readily available and inexpensive, should be sown between late summer and early fall (not earlier or they could go to seed, leading to a volunteer spring oat crop). They produce good vegetative growth all fall and make an excellent catch crop, trapping soluble nutrients in the soil and keeping them in the top of the soil profile. The oat plants are killed by freezing temperatures, forming a dense mat of dead vegetation that holds the soil in place through the winter. To avoid disturbing the soil and help with weed control, you can transplant seedlings directly through the mulch or part the mulch to make seed furrows.

Using Wood Ashes in the Garden

A lot of gardeners rely on wood-burning stoves and fireplaces to stay warm in winter, resulting in an abundance of wood ashes. Should these ashes be used in the garden?

Wood ashes are valued as a primary source of potassium for both field and garden, as well as a means of raising the pH of acidic soils. Home gardeners can take advantage of a supply of wood ashes to add needed nutrients.

Used in moderation, wood ashes can benefit most garden soils. They contain between five and seven percent potassium and up to two percent phosphorus, both major plant nutrients. Hardwood ashes have higher potassium levels than softwood ashes.

Wood ashes also contain 25 to 50 percent calcium, another essential plant nutrient, along with a number of minor elements. They do not contain a significant amount of nitrogen, so you will need to supply this essential element from compost, green manures, and other sources.

There are two potential problems associated with use of wood ashes: excess soluble salts and alkalinity. Since wood ashes are up to 90 percent water-soluble mineral salts, excessive applications can result in a buildup of these salts in the soil, resulting in root injury and plant death.

Because ashes are alkaline, you should avoid using them in soils above pH 6.5. Also, avoid using them around rhododendrons, blueberries, and other acid-loving plants. Wood ashes act much faster than lime in raising soil pH, so you should have your garden soil tested at least every other year to make sure the use of wood ashes is not raising soil pH above its optimum level.

A safe application rate for most garden soils would be 20 pounds— the equivalent of a five-gallon pail of ashes—per 1,000 square feet. This is the equivalent of six pounds of ground limestone per 1,000 square feet, an amount considered appropriate for yearly applications without disrupting soil pH.

Wood ashes can be raked into soil in the spring, three to four weeks before planting, or they can be side-dressed around growing plants. Apply the ashes evenly, avoiding lumps or piles.

To avoid chemical burns to sensitive plant tissues, do not apply ashes over germinating seeds or young seedlings. Also, rinse applied ashes from foliage.

Store your wood ashes in a metal container to keep them dry. Potassium and other water-soluble nutrients are leached from wood ashes that are left standing in the rain. This leaching not only reduces the nutrient value of the ashes but leaves them more alkaline.

Never put coal or charcoal ashes on the garden! Coal ashes tend to be high in toxic heavy metals, while charcoal ashes contain sodium borate, a chemical toxic to plants.

A final caution: protect yourself when applying wood ash. Use the same precautions you would use when handling household bleach, another strongly alkaline material. Wear eye protection and gloves and, depending on the fineness of the ash and the direction of the wind, you may want to wear a dust mask.

Crevices in the edgings of large stones that frame each of our garden beds are favorite slug bedrooms. Left alone, these slimy creatures spend hot summer days in these cool niches, gliding around the garden at night to munch on succulent stems and leaves. Wood ashes to the rescue! Imagine sliding on your belly over the micro-sharp particles.

In moderation, wood ashes can be an effective part of garden soil management. Gardeners know from experience that the garden demands moderation in all things.

Breaking New Ground

"Perhaps the most radical thing you can do in our time is to start turning over the soil, loosening it up for the crops to settle in, and then stay home and tend them." —Rebecca Solnit

As writer and gardener Rebecca Solnit points out in her article "The Most Radical Thing You Can Do" (*Orion*, November/December 2008), the word "radical" comes from the Latin word for root. Gardeners rooted in the soil of their gardens have always worked diligently to keep it healthy and productive. Now, in times of fluctuating fuel and food prices, the quality of our lives may depend on staying home and breaking new ground.

When we break new ground in our garden, we start with the closest thing we have to lawn, a mixture of grasses (mostly Kentucky bluegrass), wild strawberries, and dandelions. In summer, before beginning the task of turning this diverse patch of vegetation into a garden bed, we sample the soil for testing. The results come back from the university soil lab long before we need them.

In late autumn, we cut the selected patch of weeds as short as possible. We then cover the area with a quarter-inch layer of cardboard or several layers of newspaper, followed by an 8-inch layer of straw (not hay, which contains weed seeds). We throw on a layer of seaweed if we can get it.

Our future garden bed spends the winter under this cover and the snow that accumulates above it. In early spring, as the sun penetrates the cover to warm the soil, most of the perennial plants buried beneath the cover quickly use up food reserves stored through winter in their roots, then die.

In late May we remove what is left of the cover, exposing bare ground to the sun, and set aside the seaweed-straw mix to use as weed-suppressing mulch over the new bed. After the soil dries out, we turn it over with a digging fork, adding amendments recommended by the soil test as well as plenty of composted goat manure. As we turn and rake the soil, we remove any remaining clumps of live grass and roots.

By early June our new bed is ready for its first planting. For many years, the grasses and wild plants that were growing there functioned as a perennial cover crop, recycling nutrients, including those returned to the soil as clippings each time we mowed. Whatever we plant, we expect a good yield.

If early snowfall prevents us from covering the garden-bed-to-be in late autumn, we cover it as early as possible in spring and keep it covered until late spring. This late start delays planting of the first crop until sometime in July, still early enough for a crop of summer squash, cucumbers, or even tomatoes in a good year.

In distressing times, gardeners turn to their gardens. We enlarge our gardens or begin new ones. We stay home, grow our own food, and perhaps discover, as Solnit writes, "a more stately, settled, secure way of living." We find richness rooted in our connection with healthy soil.

Converting Lawns to Insectaries

The conventional lawn, a monoculture of a single species of grass, is a biodiversity wasteland. In the United States there are 40.5 million acres of such lawns, including 24 million acres around homes and the rest surrounding businesses, churches, schoolyards, cemeteries, and golf courses. There are more acres of lawn in the U.S. than of corn, alfalfa, soybeans, and fruit orchards combined.

Those who wish to increase the ability of their gardens to sustain insect biodiversity can use the procedure described above ("Breaking New Ground") to convert some or all of their lawn to an insectary, a place devoted to nurturing pollinators and other insects. No doubt, insectaries also attract herbivores—that is the point. Insectaries are balanced mini-ecosystems designed to ensure the presence of beneficial insects, including herbivore predators, throughout the garden year.

This insectary consists of three plant species, a goldenrod (*Solidago* spp., background), common milkweed (*Asclepias syriaca*, center), and purple coneflower (*Echinacea purpurea*, front). Notice that the early-flowering milkweed (Family Apocynaceae) has finished flowering, while the two composites will continue to bloom into autumn.

Your insectary can be created by converting a section of your lawn to herbaceous perennials and annuals that attract insects. Two plant families, the Asteraceae (composites) and Apiaceae (umbellifers), dominate any list of insectary plants. Composites include cosmos,

Insectary plants form the backbone of this attractive garden. Composites, including mauve pink Joe-pye weed (*Eutrochium purpureum*), white and purple coneflowers (*Echinacea* spp.), and bright yellow sunflowers (*Helianthus* spp.), are well represented.

sunflowers, dandelions, yarrow, artemisia, feverfew, tansy, marigolds, zinnias, thistles, asters, goldenrod, and calendula, as well as artichoke and lettuce (if you let a few of these plants flower). All composites mature their flowers in heads over a long period of time, thus providing a long-term source of nectar and pollen.

Umbellifers include parsley, carrots, parsnips, lovage, angelica, and Queen Anne's lace. They produce large amounts of nectar over a short period of time.

A mixture of plants from these two plant families, as well as the other herbaceous plants discussed in Chapters 8 and 9 of this book, can produce an insectary that has something blooming from early spring until late fall.

A garden insectary should be thought of as a long-term permanent component of your garden. Results are not instant, but the benefits to your garden are cumulative. As resident populations of beneficial insects become established, your garden will become a balanced environment with a complex food web of plants, insects, birds, and, of course, the gardener.

Hoverfly
(*Spilomyia fusca*)

Chapter 5

Garden Pollinators

"The evidence is overwhelming that wild pollinators are declining .... Their ranks are being thinned not just by habitat reduction and other familiar agents of impoverishment, but also by the disruption of the delicate 'biofabric' of interactions that bind ecosystems together. Humanity, for its own sake, must attend to the forgotten pollinators and their countless dependent plant species."

—E. O. Wilson, in the foreword to *The Forgotten Pollinators*,
by Stephen L. Buchman and Gary Paul Nabhan

Pollination, the first process that must occur before a plant can produce fruits that contain seeds, is simply the transfer of pollen from the anther (the topmost portion of the stamen, the male reproductive organ of a flower) to the stigma (the pollen-receptive portion of the pistil, the female reproductive organ). Some plant species have both stamen and pistil in the same flower, while others have unisexual flowers either on the same plant or on separate male and female plants.

One-third of the food we eat depends on pollination, including half of our diet of fats and oils. Of the 1,300 plants grown around the world for human needs—including food, beverages, medicines, spices, and fabrics—75 percent are pollinated by animals. The vast majority of these pollinators are insects, including more than 25,000 species of bees as well as moths, flies, wasps, beetles, and butterflies. (The remaining 25 percent of pollination is performed by wind or water.)

Without these wonderful creatures our world would be impoverished, not only materially but spiritually. Yet all pollinating insect species in this country are in trouble, victims of pesticide use and habitat loss. Gardeners can help mitigate this depletion of pollinator populations by providing pesticide-free habitats for pollinators.

Who are the pollinators? They include the usual suspects and a great many more.

Bumble Bees

Winters are long in our garden. For six months of the year, November through April, the garden lies dormant under snow and ice, and there are few signs of life. As May nears we grow restless, eager for the last of the snow to disappear, desperate for the first dandelion flowers and, with them, the first bumble bees of the year.

The surest sign that spring has finally come to the garden is the sighting of the first queen bumble bee. She is the sole survivor of the former colony, mating in autumn and then spending the long winter hibernating underground, alone. She emerges in early spring, frantic to establish a new colony. Other than sipping a little nectar, she pays scant attention to food until she finds an old mousehole or other suitable nesting site. Once this primary objective is met, she searches earnestly for pollen. You can bet that any queen carrying pollen has already found her nest.

The underground nest secured, the queen mixes wax secreted from her body with pollen to form a mound on which she lays her first brood of eggs. She also collects nectar, which she stores in a waxen "honey pot" located near the brood. Sipping from the pot provides

A bumble bee foraging on a dandelion, one of the earliest sources of nectar and pollen.

her with enough energy to incubate the eggs for several days, waiting for the first batch of larvae to emerge.

For the next two weeks, the queen forages nearby flowers, mostly dandelions in our garden, gathering pollen and nectar to feed the growing larvae. These larvae eventually spin cocoons in which they pupate, emerging as adult workers ready to take on the task of foraging and caring for subsequent broods. From then on, her majesty remains in the nest, laying more eggs and giving orders.

Queen bumble bees are the first bees of spring. Unlike honeybees, they are willing to forage on the cold, damp days of early May. We were in the garden one early spring morning and found a queen bumble bee lying motionless on a dandelion blossom. Taking her for dead, Reeser softly brushed her bristly back with his finger and was surprised to see a leg move. As a shaft of sunlight broke through the trees and washed over her, she began to crawl over the face of the flower, resuming the task she had abandoned at dusk.

There are 46 species of bumble bees native to the U.S. and Canada, their diversity being greatest in mountain regions and other areas of cool temperatures. Each New England state, for example, hosts between 16 and 20 species, the western mountain states each have 23 or 24 species, and the states bordering the Gulf of Mexico each have between 1 and 5 species. Bumble bees occupy a wide variety of habitats, including mountain meadows, prairies, desert uplands, savannas, farms, gardens, and wetlands. Their populations are densest where a continuous supply of pollen and nectar is available throughout the growing season.

Bumble bees are among the largest of garden insects and thus easy to recognize by their hairy bodies and contrasting bright colors, mostly black and yellow, with some species adding orange, red, or white. Most gardeners recognize a bumble bee when they see one, and it is not necessary to identify them at the species level in order to understand their importance to gardening success. Take, for example, the bumble bee's role in growing the perfect tomato.

If there is a universal garden vegetable, it is the perfect tomato, bright red, round, exploding with flavor when bitten or sliced, the favorite subject of summer chats over the garden fence. The veteran gardener assumes the role of teacher, defining her success in terms of choosing the best variety or building the perfect soil or applying a special fertilizer at just the right time. The novice holds his misshapen cat-faced tomato at his side and pretends to listen, but he is distracted by a bumble bee crawling across the face of a sunflower.

Focus your attention on the bumble bee. She is the only character in this story that understands the anatomy of a tomato flower. She alone knows what it really takes to make a perfect tomato.

Tomatoes have perfect flowers, the term "perfect" being used by botanists to describe flowers that have stamens (the pollen-producing organs) and one or more pistils (the ovule-producing organs). The top portion of each stamen is called the anther, and at maturity it contains the pollen grains. The yellow anthers of the tomato flower are collectively fused together to form a ring around a greenish pistil.

In the basal portion of the pistil is the ovary, and it contains the ovules, or egg cells, that will eventually become tomato seeds if two sequential processes, pollination and fertilization, are successful. The botanist will say that when you eat a tomato fruit you are eating a ripened ovary filled with mature seeds, each containing an embryo surrounded by a bit of stored nourishment to see the seedling out of darkness and into the light.

Pollination is no more than the transfer of pollen grains from anthers to the topmost portion of the pistil, the stigma, yet pollination is essential for fertilization, a process that begins with germination of the pollen grains on the surface of the stigma. A slender tube, the pollen tube, grows out of the germinating pollen grain, passing downward through the stigma and the style, a thread of connecting tissue between stigma and ovary. Eventually, if all goes well (a big if), the pollen tube meets one of several multicellular embryo sacs in the tomato ovary. Swimming down the elongating pollen tube are two sperms cells that were formed in the pollen grain. One of these sperms will fuse with an ovule in an embryo sac to form the first cell of an embryo. The other sperm will fuse with another cell in the embryo sac to produce the first cell of a nutrient-rich material, the endosperm, that surrounds the mature embryo. Together, the mature embryo and endosperm constitute a seed, an infant plant surrounded by enough food to see it into the light.

No pollination means no fertilization, no ultimate union of sperm cells with egg cells in the ovary. No fertilization means no seeds. No seeds means no fruit. That fertilization succeeds at all is nothing short of miraculous, a tale worth telling at some later time, but fertilization never gets a chance if pollination, the focus of this story, does not occur.

At this point in the story, it should be emphasized that for every seed found in the mature tomato fruit, a pollen grain must be deposited on the pistil's stigma. Fully successful pollination requires the deposition of many pollen grains. This is analogous to pollination in corn, with every kernel on the cob requiring a separate pollen grain sown by the wind on one of the long, silk-like stigmas that protrude from the end of an ear shoot. Just as inadequate pollination means unfilled ears of corn, it also means misshapen, often lobed, tomato fruits.

If you look closely at the fused ring of pollen-producing anthers in a tomato flower, you notice that the only avenue for pollen escape is through a tiny pore at each anther's tip. The mature pollen grains are smooth-grained and sticky, so they are not likely to simply fall out through this pore. They need to be forced out by agitation of the anthers. This agitation is the job of the bumble bee.

Because they have perfect flowers and because some pollen will be shed with moderate agitation of the anthers by wind, tomatoes are often described as being self-fertile. This is true to the extent that some self-fertilization—some union of sperm and egg produced in the same flower—will occur, depending on the quantity of pollen released. Agitation of the anthers by bumble bees, however, results in a rain of tomato pollen grains.

Imagine the pollination dance of the bumble bee. She grasps a blossom with her legs, pulling the flower down into a vertical position and placing the stigma against her fuzzy abdomen. She then vibrates her wing muscles at just the right frequency to release the flower's pollen, a process called sonication, or "buzz pollination." The released pollen falls onto her abdomen, while pollen obtained from previously visited flowers is transferred to the flower's stigma, resulting in cross pollination.

Coevolution of wild tomatoes with sonicating bees was the choreographer of this beautiful dance. In South America, where wild ancestors of our garden tomatoes still grow, there is a bee that does this dance. North American bumble bees were buzzing wild blueberry flowers, which also benefit from sonication, before there were garden tomatoes.

A bumble bee pollinating a tomato flower.

Our native bumble bees are twice as effective in pollinating many plants, including our food plants, as non-native honeybees. This should come as no surprise, since the honeybee never learned the dance.

Tomato plants pollinated by bumble bees are likely to bear larger fruits and fewer misshapen fruits. Cross pollination between varieties will not affect fruit characteristics in the current year, but seeds from these cross pollinated plants should not be saved as they will likely produce hybrid plants with a wide range of fruit characteristics.

In addition to tomatoes, bumble bees also buzz pollinate eggplant, blueberry, and cranberry blossoms. In the garden at harvest time, when we hear the familiar buzzing nearby, we stop to watch bumble bees at work. Unlike a honeybee, which prefers to forage in a large field of a single plant species, a bumble bee will move from one type of plant to another. It might start with a sunflower head, crawling over each tiny flower until it has filled its hairy hind-leg sacs with bright orange pollen, then dive into the throat of a male squash blossom,

A bumble bee foraging on blueberry flowers.

dusting its bristly body with bright yellow pollen, and then move on to a cluster of tomato flowers, or catmint, or campanulas.

Scientists tell us that many species of North American bumble bees are showing varying degrees of population decline, and that up to half of all species may be at risk of decline. Reasons for this decline include habitat loss, insecticide use, climate change, spill-over of pathogens from populations of bumble bees managed for pollination of greenhouse and field crops, and alteration of natural ecosystems by non-native invasive bees, wasps, and plants. (Can you hear the echo of HIPPO? See Chapter 1 for an explanation of this acronym.)

It is hard to imagine harder working creatures than bumble bees. By midsummer they are everywhere, pollinating a wide variety of plants. We've found them foraging in circles on sunflower and coneflower heads, getting tipsy on the nectar of rhododendron blossoms, and flying frantically from one raspberry flower to another, to name just a few of their favorite haunts in our garden. We've found them foraging on cold mornings and in the rain, conditions under which no honeybee will work. We've greeted them at work at sunrise and said goodnight to them at dusk.

An orange-belted bumble bee foraging on a raspberry blossom.

Solitary Bees

Walking through the garden in late January with the sun shining bright and the temperature in the mid-teens, we see few signs of life other than two crows in the top of a spruce tree, a mixed flock of pine siskins and chickadees at the porch feeders, and a red squirrel perched atop a tall cedar stump. And then we notice the native bee nest box mounted about four feet off the ground on one of the grape arbor posts. It was easy to ignore during the garden season when it was surrounded by grape leaves the size of dinner plates, but now it is in plain sight, facing east. We made it a few years ago from an old 2 x 4, drilling one of its narrow faces with 3½-inch-deep holes, some 3/32-inch and others ⅜-inch in diam-eter, and it is this side that now faces the low-angled sun. Several of the drilled cavities are sealed off at the entrance with a substance that looks like dried mud.

This solitary bee nest box has some of its cavities filled with adult solitary bees waiting for spring.

There is life behind each of those mud walls. Each sealed cavity represents a row of cells separated by walls of mud, and within each cell sleeps a soli-tary bee, perhaps a mason bee (*Osmia* sp.), waiting for a thermal signal that it is time to emerge. Rather than construct elaborate colonies as bumble bees do, each solitary bee lives its life alone.

Many species of solitary bee spend the winter as adults, each snuggled within a cocoon and burning stored fat to stay warm, waiting for the daytime tem-peratures to approach 60° F. About 30 percent of native bee species will make their nests in old beetle tunnels and other cavities found in snags and fence posts. These natural nesting sites have become scarce in small gardens, and thus nest boxes, like the one in our garden, have taken their place.

Should the weather stay cold for too long, the bees could die of starvation. Alternatively, an early spring warm spell could trigger emergence of the bees at a time when pollen sources are scarce or when cold weather could return, both potentially lethal conditions.

Male bees are typically the first to emerge in spring, leaving the nest when the apple trees begin to bloom. They stay close to the nest, waiting for the females to emerge. Mat-ing occurs immediately, and the female begins to forage, waiting for her ovaries to mature before seeking out a suitable nest site.

A nearby source of silty or clayey mud with the correct moisture content is also needed for building walls within the nest cavity. And so the female bee may inspect several potential sites before settling in. Once the decision is made, she performs an aerial dance, imprinting major visual features to find her nest when returning from foraging.

She starts her nest construction by collecting mud and building a back wall for the first partition. Working tirelessly from dawn to dusk, she then begins foraging for pollen from flowers that are near the nest, visiting approximately 2,000 flowers over 25 trips to provision the first cell. She nourishes herself with nectar from the same blossoms. Once she has packed enough pollen in the first cell, she backs into the hole and lays one egg directly on the lump of pollen, then collects more mud to seal off the cell. This new wall also serves as the back wall of the next cell. This process continues over several days until she has filled the nest cavity with capped cells.

Carrying sperm in her body, the female bee can determine the gender of each egg by fertilizing it or not. Unfertilized eggs develop into male bees, while fertilized eggs become females. Female eggs are laid at the back of the nest cavity, male eggs towards the front, adhering to a sex ratio of about three males to every one or two females.

After filling the nest cavity, the female plugs the entrance hole with a mud wall that is thicker than the internal partitions, a barrier against intrusion by a woodpecker looking for a meal, although it does not always work. She then looks for another suitable nest cavity to begin the process anew. She works her entire life in this manner, a span of four to eight weeks, filling an average of four nest cavities with about eight eggs per cavity. Over the course of her life, she visits approximately 60,000 blossoms, a testament to her productivity as a pollinator in the garden.

A solitary bee foraging for raspberry nectar and pollen.

By early summer, each bee larva has consumed all of its pollen provisions and begins spinning a cocoon around itself, entering the pupal stage. The transformation from pupa to adult occurs within the cocoon, and as cold weather approaches, each bee enters a diapause, a state of suspended development, until spring arrives.

Of the 4,000 or so species of bees in North America, more than 90 percent lead solitary rather than social lives, each female constructing and provisioning her own nest without the help of others of her kind. The diversity among these solitary bee species is mind-boggling. While about 30 percent build their nests in wood cavities, 70 percent construct tunnel-like nests in the ground. These earthen nests range from single short tunnels to complex,

A polyester bee, *Colletes inaequalis*, foraging on mountain bluet (*Centaurea montana*).

branching tunnels, and many ground-nesting species, like the polyester bee (genus *Colletes*), secrete substances to construct waterproof linings for their egg cells.

Like mason bees, solitary leafcutter bees (*Megachile* spp.) also nest in wood cavities, but they use pieces of leaves or flower petals instead of mud to seal the ends of each cell. Using their mandibles (jaws), they cut the plant pieces into specific shapes and sizes to line the entire cell as well as sealing the ends.

Along with bumble bees, solitary bees are primary pollinators in our garden. Honeybees show up en masse only when the Shirley poppies are blooming and remain totally focused on them. Solitary bees, however, visit the blossoms of many different garden plants in the same day.

Solitary bees are among a gardener's best friends, and all the gardener has to do is provide them with year-round forage and a place to live. You can accomplish the former by planting a variety of flowering plants to ensure that the bees will have a summer-long source of pollen and nectar, plants that are presented in Chapters 8 through 10. Also, let dandelions bloom in your garden, providing an early source of pollen. And put up nest boxes, attaching them to arbor posts and fence posts, always facing the rising sun.

Honeybees

Honeybees are rare visitors to our garden for much of the year, but when the Shirley poppies bloom in late May, every flower hosts at least one honeybee, and many have several. These poppies are volunteers, their origin traceable to a dusting of seeds sown years ago, and now every open garden spot has a few of these tall, straight-stemmed plants, each bearing a blossom with translucent pink petals surrounding a heart of pollen-loaded stamens. They set the table for honeybees, a non-native social bee that prefers to forage mass plantings of a single plant.

Unlike solitary bees and bumble bees, social bees—like a colony of honeybees—have a perennial life cycle. The honeybee colony survives the winter, and other dearths of forage, by feeding on stored honey, the bees shivering together in a tight mass to keep warm.

A honeybee colony grows much larger than that of the bumble bee, often exceeding 50,000 workers, with a queen laying up to a thousand eggs per day. Maintaining a colony of this magnitude requires workers to fly much longer distances for nectar and pollen than bumble bees or solitary bees. Thus, in searching for provisions, honeybees much prefer large expanses of the same plant, such as acres of lowbush blueberries or fields of wildflowers.

A honeybee approaching the landing strip in a Shirley poppy blossom.

I'm not sure why honeybees visit our garden en masse only for the poppies. The poppies are more numerous than surrounding plants, but their numbers pale by comparison with the blossoms in a field of clover or an orchard of apple trees. Perhaps poppies offer a quantity of nectar or pollen that is irresistible. Once the poppy bloom is over, most of the honeybees go elsewhere, leaving the garden to the bumble bees and solitary bees.

Butterflies and Moths

It is in a gardener's nature to lean on a rake handle and watch a butterfly float over the garden fence, alighting on a nearby blossom to sip nectar. In midcoast Maine, where bleak winters can be nearly six months long, the first butterfly of spring is a true harbinger of the long gardening days ahead, as good a reason for celebration as we can imagine. In all their diversity of sizes, colors, and life histories, butterflies, both the adults and their caterpillars, add a dimension of wildness to the garden and a sense of wonder. They are emblems of a sacred world that deserves our devotion.

Butterfly watching is an integral part of gardening. We delight in watching them sip nectar from the flowers of plants grown expressly for their use, and we strive to learn the name of each species, often a daunting task. Reeser is still laboring over photographs of fritillaries taken in past years, wading through field guide images of similar species and trying to pin down the identity of each unknown.

Adult butterflies are conspicuous incidental pollinators. They survive entirely on nectar, which they sip with long tongues, often avoiding contact with the flower's pollen-loaded anthers. Nevertheless, they do move enough pollen around to contribute to reproduction in some plant species.

Attracting Butterflies to Your Garden

You can increase the number and variety of butterflies in your garden by providing food for adult butterflies and caterpillars. Adults of many butterfly species will nectar on a wide variety of flowering plants in your garden, but you will see more species if you also grow the larval hosts, the plants on which caterpillars feed.

Some species, such as the Eastern yellow swallowtail and white admiral, rely on native trees as larval hosts (see the accompanying butterfly species discussions), and you are more likely to see the adults of these butterfly species if one or more larval host trees are nearby. The red admiral butterfly, however, lays its eggs on the foliage of nettles, and the monarch butterfly must have access to milkweed. A truly functional butterfly garden will include as many larval host plants as possible.

Most adult butterflies feed on the nectar of flowers, preferring flat-topped clusters of red, orange, yellow, pink, or purple blossoms with short floral tubes.

(continued on page 56)

(continued from page 55)

The successful butterfly garden will provide a wide variety of such flowering plants with overlapping bloom periods. Such a list might include mints (*Mentha* spp.), milkweeds (*Asclepias* spp.), Joe-pye weed (*Eutrochium purpureum*), and non-invasive species of thistle (*Cirsium* spp.). A search of the Internet for butterfly nectar plants for your region of the country will greatly expand this list, and in Chapters 8, 9, and 10 we present several plants that function as nectar sources for butterflies in our garden.

In addition to food, butterflies need a source of water. Rather than drinking from open water, they obtain moisture and essential minerals such as sodium from damp areas around water, a practice called "mud puddling." Males of some species congregate in large numbers on the mud near small rain pools. Such gatherings are called "puddle clubs."

An area of damp soil provides moisture for a puddle club of Eastern tiger swallowtails.

It is easy to provide a spot for mud puddling in your garden. One approach is to appropriate a pedestaled bird bath, fill it with gravel or sand, add a little salt, and keep it moist. The elevation of the puddling site offers some protection from the neighbor's cat. Burying a bucket in the soil and filling it with gravel or sand will also suffice, if predators are not an issue.

Finally, don't be surprised if you find butterflies puddling in the manure pile or your dog's favorite spot to urinate. Both are excellent sources of moisture and essential nutrients.

The stages in the life history of the monarch butterfly (*Danaus plexippus*), described in detail in Chapter 1, serve as a general model for the life cycles of butterflies and moths: egg, larva, pupa, adult. Eggs are laid on or near a preferred larval host plant, such as milkweed in the case of monarchs. From each monarch egg hatches a tiny black-, white-, and yellow-banded caterpillar that feeds voraciously on the host plant for about two weeks, growing longer and fatter each day, until it transforms into a pupa encased in a chrysalis. It is during

While monarch caterpillars must have milkweed, adult monarch butterflies will nectar on a variety of flowering plants, including the swamp milkweed shown here.

this pupal stage, also about two weeks in duration for the monarch, that the amazing transformation to a winged adult takes place.

There are, of course, variations in the timing of the stages for each species. Monarchs, the best known of the migratory butterflies, overwinter as adults in the oyamel fir forests of Mexico before embarking on a multi-generational trek, laying eggs on milkweeds as they travel north and east. A handful of other species overwinter as adults in areas of the country with frigid winters, holing up in the cracks and crevices of rocks and trees. This group includes the mourning cloak (*Nymphalis antiopa*), Eastern comma (*Polygonia comma*), green comma (*P. faunus*), question mark (*P. interrogationis*), and the Milbert's tortoiseshell (*Aglais milberti*). Across the country, these are the first butterflies of spring, the first caterpillars to feast on new foliage. Wherever you live in the U.S., a walk in the winter woods is likely to bring you close to one or more of these species.

Red admiral butterflies (*Vanessa atalanta*) also migrate, moving northward from overwintering areas of the deep south (North Carolina southward) to appear in Massachusetts during the first week of May, later in more northern locations. We've noticed that the wings of early arrivals to our garden are often tattered, an indication of their long northward trek. Adults from spring matings in northern areas begin to appear in mid-summer and repeat the

This adult red admiral butterfly is nectaring on goldenrod.

reproductive cycle to produce a third generation of adults, which are seen from late August to October. Some butterflies from this third generation migrate south as temperatures drop.

Nettles, including the stinging nettle (*Urtica dioica*) and false nettle (*Boehmeria cylindrica*), are the larval host plants for red admirals. In our garden we have seen red admirals nectaring on a variety of flowering plants, including spring dandelions, chives, and late summer goldenrod.

One of the most beautiful butterflies to grace our garden each summer is the white admiral (*Limenitis arthemis*), named for the broad white median bands on its black wings, the hindwing marked with a marginal row of blue dashes and a submarginal row of red dots. The reddish-brown undersides of the wings are painted with the same white median bands. (There is another form of this same species called the red-spotted purple butterfly, and the two variants hybridize where their ranges overlap.)

The list of larval host plants for white admirals includes many of the tree species that surround our garden, including red oaks, yellow birches, willows, aspens, and serviceberries. The adults feed on sap flow and rotting fruit; we often see them foraging on overripe blueberries as well as aphid honeydew and the nectar from small white flowers, including spireas, viburnums, and summersweet clethra. A pink-flowering form of *Clethra alnifolia* keeps them in our garden through the summer.

Adult white admiral butterflies, such as this one, will feed on the juice of fruits such as these blueberries.

The white admiral survives the winter as a small immature caterpillar enclosed within a leafy shelter on one of its preferred host trees. The larva chooses the leaf that will be its winter

This female Eastern tiger swallowtail is nectaring on *Lobelia erinus*.
It is not often that we see them this close to the ground.

home in late summer, firmly attaching it to a twig with threads of silk to keep it from falling off the tree in autumn. When ready to pupate, the inch-long caterpillar aligns itself with the midrib of the leaf blade, chews off the end and most of the sides of the leaf, then pulls what remains around its body, forming a small tube held together with more threads of silk. The young larva sleeps through the winter in its leafy cocoon, protected from subzero temperatures by remaining in a state of deep diapause, and completes its larval growth in spring.

The Eastern tiger swallowtail (*Papilio glaucus*), easily recognized by its bright yellow wings, the forewings marked with four black "tiger stripes," is a regular visitor to our garden, drawn there by several plants, including pots of annual blue lobelia (*Lobelia erinus*) scattered about the garden. Males have a few orange and blue spots near the tail, while females have more blue on the hind wing.

Female tiger swallowtails occur in two forms: yellow, like the males, or black with blue spots but no yellow. The dark form mimics another butterfly, the pipevine swallowtail, which has a very disagreeable taste and thus is shunned by most predators. Black female tiger swallowtails that coexist with large populations of pipevine swallowtails experience reduced predation.

Favorite larval host plants of Eastern tiger swallowtails include tulip poplars (*Liriodendron tulipifera*), sweet bay magnolia (*Magnolia virginiana*), willows (*Salix* spp.), American hornbeam (*Carpinus caroliniana*), red maple (*Acer rubrum*), spicebush (*Lindera benzoin*), American elm (*Ulmus americana*), sassafras (*Sassafras albidum*), and black cherry (*Prunus serotina*).

Eastern tiger swallowtails can often be seen puddling, with young males congregating in large groups on mud, damp gravel, or puddles to extract sodium ions and essential amino acids. Solitary females also engage in this activity.

Other butterfly visitors to our garden include Northern crescents (*Phyciodes cocyta*), silver-spotted skippers (*Epargyreus clarus*), Atlantis fritillaries (*Speyeria atlantis*), and banded hairstreaks (*Satyrium calanus*). These species will be pictured and discussed in later chapters.

A primrose moth at dawn, sipping nectar from a primrose flower.

Far less conspicuous than butterflies are the thousands of North American moth species, their muted colors and nocturnal lives keeping most of them out of sight. Some do not feed as adults and thus are not pollinators, and most of the moths that do feed on plant nectar are, like butterflies, considered incidental pollinators.

The exceptions to this rule involve a few specialized plants that depend on moths for their survival. For example, the evening primrose (*Oenothera biennis*), a common wildflower along the lane that leads to our garden, depends upon the primrose moth (*Schinia florida*) for pollination. The moth must crawl headfirst into the middle of the flower in order to reach the nectar through a proboscis half the length of its body. As the moth moves around, it transfers pollen from the anthers of previously visited flowers to the stigma. In exchange for this service, the female moth lays her eggs within the flowers so that her caterpillars can feed on some of the plant's developing seed pods. This mutualism benefits both species, enhancing the genetic diversity of primrose populations through cross pollination. The primrose moth's bright pink forewings make it one of the most colorful of North American moths.

Discovering Moth Diversity after Dark

We are reminded of the diversity of moths in and around our garden when we forget to turn off the outside lights on warm nights in late June, waking at daybreak to a porch wall covered with moths of all sizes and patterns. The moth species presented here represent a small fraction of this diversity. We do not recommend this as the best approach to moth watching, as it leaves moths exposed through the day to predators. A better technique is to hang a white sheet between two trees at night and backlight it with a lantern. When you have finished moth watching, turn off the lantern, and the moths will disappear into the night.

The waved sphinx moth, *Ceratomia undulosa*, has a wing span of 3 to 4 inches and a range of color from almost black to light yellowish-brown. Larval hosts include ash (*Fraxinus* spp.), privet (*Ligustrum* spp.), oak (*Quercus* spp.), hawthorn (*Crataegus* spp.), and fringe tree (*Chionanthus virginicus*). The adults probably do not feed. This moth can be found from Maine west to Alberta, western North Dakota and Colorado, and south to Florida, the Gulf Coast, and Texas.

Drepana arcuata, the arched hooktip moth, is a resident of boreal forests from Newfoundland to Vancouver Island, south to South Carolina and California. Larval hosts include alders (*Alnus* spp.) and paperbark birch (*Betula papyrifera*).

The Virginia tiger moth, *Spilosoma virginica*, can be found throughout the eastern half of the United States and along the West Coast. Larval hosts include a large variety of herbaceous plants, including grasses, as well as shrubs. (A photograph of the larva, the yellow wooly bear caterpillar, can be found in Chapter 6.)

This unusual moth is the blinded sphinx moth, *Paonias excaecata*, shown here resting on a porch-side Virginia creeper vine. It can be found across most of the United States (except Nevada) and southern Canada. The pink underwings, each with a prominent dark eyespot, are hidden in the resting stage. Larval hosts include basswood (*Tilia* spp.), willow (*Salix* spp.), birch, hawthorn, poplar, oak, and cherry (*Prunus* spp.) The adult does not feed.

The Northern pine looper moth, *Caripeta piniata*, is a New England moth that depends entirely on pines (*Pinus* spp.) as larval host.

Xanthotype urticaria, the false crocus geometer, is a common moth from New England west to the Mississippi River and south to the Gulf States except Texas. Its wide range of larval host plants include red-osier dogwood (*Cornus sericea*), ground ivy (*Glechoma hederacea*), catmint (*Nepeta* spp.), rhodora (*Rhododendron canadense*), and goldenrods (*Solidago* spp.).

The confused eusarca, *Eusarca confusaria*, can be found throughout eastern North America, including Nova Scotia, south to Florida and as far west as Texas and Saskatchewan. Throughout its range it frequents meadows, fields, and roadside verges where its larval host plants (including aster, clover, dandelion, and goldenrod) grow.

The largest moth in our garden is the polyphemus moth, *Antheraea polyphemus*. With a wingspan of 4 to 6 inches, it is one of the largest and most widely distributed silk moths. Its range extends from southern Canada to Mexico and includes all 48 contiguous states except Arizona and Nevada. Larval hosts include oaks (*Quercus* spp.), willows (*Salix* spp.), maples (*Acer* spp.), and birches (*Betula* spp.). Those beautiful bold eye spots are effective in warding off would-be predators.

The diversity of moths in and around your garden is as expansive as that of birds and flowers, yet most moths remain undiscovered, living their lives in treetops and tall grasses. The diversity of bird life in the garden, however, is directly linked to this unseen world, since most songbirds rely on moth caterpillars to feed their young.

Not all moths are nocturnal creatures. On late summer afternoons we watch bumble bee moths (*Hemaris* spp.) hovering like hummingbirds in front of the long white tubular flowers of annual tobacco (*Nicotiana alata*), sipping nectar with their long proboscises. Mimics of bumble bees, a trait which allows them to avoid many would-be predators, these moths are extremely fast fliers, reaching velocities of more than 30 miles per hour. Lacking the scales common to most butterflies and moths, their wings are nearly clear, giving them the alternative common name of "clearwings."

In addition to flowering tobacco, bumble bee moth adults nectar on a variety of plants, includ-

A bumble bee moth nectaring on *Lobelia erinus*.

ing thistles, lilacs, orange hawkweed, snowberry, and dwarf bush honeysuckle. They lay their eggs on snowberry (*Symphoricarpos albus*), dwarf bush honeysuckle (*Diervilla lonicera*),

The Virginia ctenucha moth.

and dogbane (*Apocynum* spp.), the first two of which are among the best of native shrubs for an ornamental garden. The eggs hatch after about a week and the caterpillars, often called hornworms, feed on the host plants for about a month, then pupate on the ground within a sturdy cocoon covered with leaf litter. After several weeks, the adults emerge and lay another generation of eggs. Second-generation larvae undergo metamorphosis during the winter.

With its metallic-blue body, orange head, and dark gray-brown wings, the Virginia ctenucha (*Ctenucha virginica*, the first "c" silent) is one of the most colorful diurnal moth species visiting our garden each summer. It is known as a food plant specialist, the larvae feeding solely on grasses, sedges, and irises. Adults sip the nectar of a variety of plants, including goldenrod. Its common name belies its distribution, as it is typically a northern species with Virginia as it southernmost range.

An adult ailanthus webworm moth nectaring on goldenrod.

Thought to be native to south Florida and the American tropics south to Costa Rica, the ailanthus webworm moth (*Atteva aurea*) cannot survive cold winters, and yet there it was, nectaring on goldenrod in our summer garden, a slender moth with bright orange wings marked with white spots bordered in black, forming a pattern of tiny stained-glass windows. A little research revealed that moths of this species migrate north each year, making it as far as eastern Canada, relying on the invasive tree species called tree-of-heaven, *Ailanthus altissima*, as the primary larval host.

The Virginia ctenucha caterpillar.

Flies

When Reeser was a boy growing up on the central Georgia-Alabama border, all doors and windows were screened, and a fly swatter hung on a nail in most rooms. Some folks, like Dr. Lenoir, head of the small biology department where Reeser studied as an undergrad, eschewed the swatter in favor of snatching a housefly from the air with his hand, a feat he would accomplish from his chair without interruption of discussion, then throw it with sufficient force against the nearest wall.

Until we started paying much closer attention to the life in our garden, such memories formed the substance of our understanding of flies. We had no real sense of the diversity within the insect order Diptera, nor of the role of some fly species as both pollinators and predators of aphids, caterpillars, and other garden herbivores. All we had to do was stop and look, and we began to see flies in a totally different way.

Hoverflies

Among the most frequent visitors to flowers in our garden are adult hoverflies, also called flower flies or syrphid flies, the latter name in reference to their family, the Syrphidae, a group of about 6,000 species within 200 genera. The common name of hoverfly comes from their habit of hovering over flower heads before alighting to feed. You will find them feeding on the nectar and pollen of white and yellow flowers, including the white flower clusters of Queen Anne's lace (*Daucus carota*) and mapleleaf viburnum (*Viburnum acerifolium*), the single white blossoms of crabapples, and the golden flower clusters of yarrow (*Achillea* spp.). They are also attracted by odors, including the sweet-smelling spikes of sum-

A small hoverfly (possibly *Toxomerus* sp.) nectaring on blue lobelia.

mersweet clethra (*Clethra alnifolia*) and the nectar-rich blue flowers of annual plants such as lobelia (*Lobelia* spp.) and bachelor's buttons (*Centaurea cyanus*).

Hoverflies bear little resemblance to houseflies except for the presence of only two wings, a characteristic that separates all Dipterans from the four-winged bees and wasps (Hymenoptera). Some hoverflies mimic the bold warning colors of bees and wasps in an effort

A hoverfly (*Spilomyia fusca*) that mimics the bald-faced hornet.

A hoverfly nymph feeding on aphids.
(Photo courtesy of Kate Redmond.)

to ward off potential predators, but they can be distinguished by their single pair of wings and their stubby antennae, which are much shorter than those of bees or wasps.

Pollinating hoverflies are typically not as hairy as bees, which makes them less efficient pollinators. Some species compensate for this, however, by making more frequent visits to flowers. Certain hoverfly species are important pollinators for specific plants in natural ecosystems, while others are occasional pollinators of vegetable garden plants.

Hoverfly larvae are either saprotrophs, feeding on decaying plant and animal matter in the soil, or insectivores, feeding on aphids, thrips, and other plant-sucking insects. In both cases, they perform a valuable garden service. Hoverflies in the genus *Volucella* are unique in that they use their mimicry to enter the nests of bees, where they lay their eggs. The larvae act as nest cleaners, feeding on dead bees and detritus.

Tachinid flies

Flies in the family Tachinidae, commonly called tachinid flies, are the most important form of parasitoid fly for the biological control of garden herbivores. (Unlike a "parasite," which seldom kills its host, a "parasitoid" ultimately kills and consumes its prey.) They resemble houseflies except for the very stout bristles at the tips of their abdomens. There are over 1,300 known species of tachinid flies in North America.

Tachinid larvae are internal parasitoids of a large variety of immature insects, including the larvae of beetles, butterflies, moths, and sawflies, and the nymphs of earwigs, grasshoppers, and true bugs. As a group, they control a wide variety of garden herbivores, including cabbage loopers, Japanese beetles, army worms, cutworms, tent caterpillars, squash bugs, Colorado potato beetles, and many others. The adults

An adult tachinid fly, *Belvosia borealis*, nectaring on Queen Anne's lace.

of some tachinid species glue their eggs to the host larvae, while others lay eggs on the foliage where the host larvae will eat them. Still other species inject their eggs directly into the host's body.

To date we have identified three species of tachinid flies in our garden. The larvae of one of these, *Belvosia borealis*, found foraging as an adult on Queen Anne's lace, are parasitoids of moth larvae that feed on catalpa, ash, privet, and lilac. The larvae of *Hystricia abrupta*, a common tachinid that as an adult we find foraging on the flowers of summer-sweet clethra, are parasitoids of tussock moth larvae and fall webworms.

An adult tachinid fly, *Hystricia abrupta*, nectaring on summersweet clethra.

Perhaps most important to gardeners is the work of a small tachinid, *Istocheta aldrichi*, imported from Asia in 1922 and released into the wild to combat agriculturally important herbivores. The larva of this tachinid is an internal parasite of the adult Japanese beetle. Each adult female fly produces up to 100 tiny eggs over a two-week period, gluing them to the thorax of any adult Japanese beetles it encounters. Upon hatching, each maggot bores into the beetle's body, killing it before it has a chance to reproduce. Early each summer, as we knock Japanese beetles from grape leaves into a pail of soapy water, we quickly extract any that harbor the lethal eggs, tossing

A Japanese beetle with a single *Istocheta aldrichi* egg on its thorax.

them onto the ground so that the fly larvae can finish them off, thus completing the tachinid fly's life cycle.

Keep a watchful eye this coming garden season. If you find a Japanese beetle with one or more small whitish dots just behind its head, don't destroy it! Let it live out its short doomed existence so that the tachinid eggs will hatch and the larvae will consume the beetle on their way to becoming adult flies.

Reports on the effectiveness of tachinid fly parasitization of Japanese beetles in northern New England range from 20 to 40 percent. Sounds encouraging, but hold on, there are some interesting wrinkles preventing the fly from becoming the be-all and end-all. First, the presence of the tachinid fly depends on the presence of the adult fly's major food source, aphid secretions on Japanese knotweed (*Fallopia japonica*), a non-native invasive plant that many of us are trying hard to eliminate. So, to combat the Japanese beetle we need to encourage an Asian fly which depends for its existence on an invasive plant species from Japan.

Also, the tachinid fly's life cycle is not well synchronized with that of the beetle. The flies emerge several weeks before the beetles and thus lay eggs only on the first emerging beetles, then disappear before the peak of beetle emergence. Still, we think most gardeners will agree, let's take all the help we can get!

If you take the time to search them out, you too will come to understand that flies are much more than targets for swatters and the swift of hand. They are pollinators, predators, and recyclers of organic matter. They are creatures that help us succeed as gardeners. Most important, they are part of the garden's wildness.

Pollinating Beetles

Beetles are infamous in the minds of most gardeners, their mere mention conjuring up memories of Japanese beetles devouring grape foliage, flea beetles shot-holing tomatillo leaves, cucumber beetles, Colorado potato beetles, asparagus beetles, Mexican bean beetles, lily leaf beetles, corn rootworm beetles, viburnum leaf beetles, vine weevils, Asian longhorn beetles, and emerald ash borers, to name a few serious offenders. We rotate crops to elude them, use row covers to exclude them, and plant trap crops to divert them. We become their primary predator, hand-picking them at dawn when they are too sluggish to escape, tossing them into soapy water. We search for and destroy their eggs. And when every non-chemical effort fails, we give up in despair, tossing a once-favorite garden plant onto the compost heap.

In North America there are approximately 25,000 species of beetles. The eastern North American component of this total, approximately 14,000 species, equals one-fifth of all plant and animal species in this part of the world. What are all these beetles *doing* in our gardens?

Some, it turns out, are pollinating garden plants. By their sheer numbers, beetles are the largest group of pollinating animals, responsible for pollinating 88 percent of the estimated 240,000 plant species on Earth. In the U.S. and Canada, 52 native plant species are known to be pollinated by beetles, including asters, sunflowers, roses, butterfly weed, goldenrods, and spireas. Known as "mess-and-soil" pollinators, beetles move pollen around as they eat exposed floral tissues such as petals and stamens, often copulating and defecating as they go about feeding. In plants that are pollinated by beetles, the all-important ovules are protected by sturdy tissues that resist invasion.

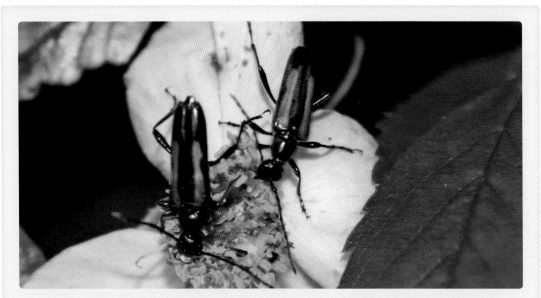

Two adult flower longhorn beetles, *Strangalepta abbreviata*, foraging on a native rose blossom. Will anything remain of the flower when they are done eating the pollen, stamens, and petals?

Indeed, beetles were the first pollinators. Long before bees came on the scene, beetles were munching on cycads and primitive flowering plants, collecting pollen on their bristly bodies as they fed. Present-day beetles still show a preference for pollinating descendants of those ancient plants, including magnolias and water lilies. Many of these plants, like the sweetbay magnolia (*Magnolia virginiana*), attract beetles by producing flowers with a fruity or fetid fragrance.

The most abundant pollinating beetles in our garden are several species of flower long-horn beetles of the Cerambycidae, a family of some 20,000 species worldwide. The common name points to the long antennae, in some species longer than the beetle's body. Most are slender creatures, their outer wing cases marked with distinctive spots or stripes.

Flower longhorn beetles prefer flat, open clusters of blossoms such as the umbels of Queen Anne's lace and other members of the carrot family. Occasionally we also see them on flowers of the wild rose as well as goldenrod and other members of the aster family. Watching these diurnal beetles gorge on the pollen, stamens, and petals of a garden flower, one has to wonder how much pollination is happening. Will anything remain of the flower when they are done? But if you look closely, you discover that much of the beetle's body is covered with pollen that can be brushed on a nearby pistil in passing.

Evodinus monticola—a flower longhorn beetle found foraging in our garden on crabap-ple flowers, the globose flower clusters of globe thistle, and the pendulous blueberry-like blossoms of enkianthus—is a specialist pollinator of bunchberry (*Cornus canadensis*), a native groundcover dogwood. The tiny flowers that make up the bunchberry blossom release their pollen in an explosion triggered by the treading of the heavy foraging beetle. Much of the pollen, embedded deep within hairs on the beetle's body, is then transferred to pistils in nearby flower clusters.

An adult flower longhorn beetle, *Evodinus monticola*, foraging on globe thistle.

Viva the Pollinators

On any summer day, if you spend sufficient time searching and observing, you will discover numerous examples of pollinators at work: a bumble bee disappearing into the throat of a penstemon flower, a tiny blue solitary bee crawling across a bright yellow dandelion clock, pollen-laden honeybees foraging within the translucent petals of a poppy blossom, a gang of flower beetles munching on the pollen of a wild rose, a red admiral butterfly sipping nectar with its long proboscis. Just before dark, a sphinx moth, large enough to be mistaken for a hummingbird, hovers in front of a flowering tobacco blossom to sip the fragrant nectar.

They're making a living, and they're doing vital work. Let's hear it for the pollinators.

Monarch Butterfly (*Danaus plexippus*)

Chapter 6

Garden Herbivores

"I cannot overemphasize how important insect herbivores are to the health of all terrestrial ecosystems. Worldwide, 37 percent of animal species are herbivorous insects. These species are collectively very good at converting plant tissue of all types to insect tissue, and as a consequence they also excel at providing food—in the form of themselves—for other species. In fact, a large percentage of the world's fauna depends entirely on insects to access the energy stored in plants."
—Douglas Tallamy, *Bringing Nature Home*

Herbivorous insects are species that at some stage in their life cycles feed on plants. Those that feed on vegetables attract a disproportionate share of the gardener's attention, and they include Japanese beetles, flea beetles, cucumber beetles, Colorado potato beetles, asparagus beetles, Mexican bean beetles, lily leaf beetles, corn rootworm beetles, viburnum leaf beetles, vine weevils, and strawberry clippers. Some well-known butterflies and lesser-known moths are herbivores as larvae (caterpillars) and either nectar feeders or non-feeders as adults. Insects that suck the sap from plant stems, including species of aphids, whiteflies, and true bugs, are also herbivores.

At one time or another, we have discovered each of the above-named herbivores on our garden plants. On a few occasions the population of a vegetable herbivore has reached truly damaging levels. One summer, flea beetles riddled the leaves of our just-planted pineapple tomatillo seedlings. Another year, cucumber beetles ran rampant through the cucurbits, and we can't forget the summer that our strawberry harvest was cut in half, literally, by strawberry clippers, tiny weevils (a type of beetle) that clip off the flower buds. In each of these cases and others, we have resisted using any form of chemical control, including plant-derived "biorational" chemicals such as neem oil. Few chemicals, synthetic or natural, can discriminate between what some misguided writers call "good bugs" and "bad bugs." Control of herbivores is best left to the garden's population of predatory insects and, when necessary, to hand-picking by the gardener.

All insects are beneficial; all are "good bugs." In order for your garden to have a healthy population of herbivore predators, there must be a constant population of herbivores. Such is the nature of the garden food web.

Caterpillars

"Caterpillar" is a common term applied to the larval stage of any butterfly or moth, insects belonging to the Order Lepidoptera. Most but not all caterpillars are herbivores. Some are insectivores, and some feed on animal products. (Clothes moth caterpillars, for example, feed on wool.)

Most garden caterpillars are specialist feeders, and the plants on which you should expect to find a particular species of caterpillar are called its "larval host plants," the number of which range from a single plant species to several species within one or more genera. Most butterflies confine their feeding to a narrow range of related larval host plant species: Baltimore checkerspots on turtlehead; black swallowtails on dill, fennel, parsley, and rue; Eastern tiger swallowtails on tulip tree, wild cherry, and lilac; field skippers on grasses; gulf fritillaries on passion flower; monarch butterflies on milkweed; mourning cloaks on willow, aspen, and elm; pipevine swallowtails on pipevine; silver spotted skippers on locust and wisteria; spicebush swallowtails on spicebush and sassafras; viceroys on willow and cotton-wood; and Western tiger swallowtails on wild cherry, sycamore, and willow. Thus the true butterfly garden or its surroundings should contain a large variety of larval host plants.

The best-known association of a lepidopteran species with larval host plants of a single genus is the monarch butterfly and milkweed (*Asclepias*). The loss of milkweed due to herbicide use in agricultural fields across the monarchs' annual migration routes is threatening their survival as a species. Fortunately, gardeners are helping to mitigate this threat by planting *Asclepias* species in their gardens. (See Appendix 2, "Native *Asclepias* Species for the Garden Insectary," for milkweed species native to your state.)

Another regular, if uncommon, caterpillar in our garden is the brown-hooded owlet moth larva (*Cucullia convexipennis*). Native to the northeastern U.S. and adjacent areas of Canada, this

A brown-hooded owlet moth caterpillar.

colorful caterpillar appears during the first week of September, feeding on goldenrod leaves. While we find it only on goldenrods, it is also reported to feed on asters, including an aster species native to China and Korea that has become naturalized in North America.

We see less than a handful of these owlet moth caterpillars each year and wonder if their bright coloration makes them an easy mark for predators. Another possibility is that there are never many of these larvae, and their blend of vivid colors flashes a warning of toxicity to potential predators. If the latter, the adult moth uses a different survival strategy, relying on the camouflage of its dull brown coloration to avoid predators.

Tussock moth larvae, hairy caterpillars often found crawling across porch walls and steps, are well represented in our summer garden. Many species have patterns of alternating bristles and hairs, and some have shorter urticating (stinging) hairs that cause painful reactions on contact with the skin. For example, the hickory tussock moth caterpillar

The hickory tussock moth caterpillar.

Young milkweed tussock moth caterpillars. (A photograph of the mature stage of this caterpillar appears in Chapter 2).

(*Lophocampa caryae*) is a stinging species, and we take care when escorting these black-and-white caterpillars from the porch to the nearest host plant. Larval host plants for this species include ashes, elms, hickories, maples, oaks, and other trees.

A favorite among the tussock moths is the milkweed tussock moth, *Euchaetes egle*. We say this with some exasperation, since the first year they appeared in our garden we watched a horde of the caterpillars completely consume the leaves of a new planting of swamp milkweed intended for the future benefit of monarch butterfly larvae. Still, the milkweed tussock moths were a delight to watch as they grew from tiny, nearly hairless young larvae to inch-long creatures that looked like Cousin Itt of Addams Family fame, all within less than a month's time. Once grown, they skeletonized a plant's leaves in a matter of hours and eventually reduced the entire stand of milkweeds to slender leafless stalks. This happened late enough in the season to avoid serious permanent damage to the perennial milkweeds. The following year the milkweed plants were larger, tussock moth numbers were down, and there were plenty of leaves to feed everyone, including several monarch caterpillars.

Winner of the award for "Best Dressed Tussock Moth Caterpillar" is the white-marked tussock moth, *Orgyia leucostigma*. With its bright red head, yellow- and white-striped body with a black stripe down the middle of the back, bright red defensive glands on its rear end, four white toothbrush-like tufts along its back, and a dark tuft of hair on its hind end, there is no way this caterpillar is going to hide among the foliage. Clearly its colorful markings are a warning: touch me and pay a steep price. Indeed, brushing against the hairs causes allergic reactions in many humans, yet some birds are able to eat these caterpillars. White-marked tussock moth larvae feed on plants in over 100 plant genera. Common larval host trees include apples, birches, black locusts, cherries, elms,

A white-marked tussock moth caterpillar.

A banded tussock moth caterpillar.

firs, hackberries, hemlocks, hickories, larches, oaks, roses, spruces, chestnuts, and willows. In our garden we have found them feeding on highbush blueberries and grapes.

A yellow woolly bear caterpillar feeding on a summer squash leaf.

The banded tussock moth caterpillar (*Halysidota tessellaris*) is a regular herbivore in our garden, often found feeding on the leaves of blueberries and grapes. Like the white-marked tussock moth, it also feeds on the leaves of a wide variety of trees, including alders, ash, birches, oaks, walnuts, and willows.

While tussock moth caterpillars are abundant in our garden, many other moth and butterfly larvae also abound. A favorite of ours among the moth caterpillars is the aptly named yellow woolly bear caterpillar (*Spilosoma virginica*). Not much of a specialist, its diet consists of many low-growing plants, including grasses and clover, as well as vegetable garden plants such as summer squash.

Canopy Trees, Caterpillars, and Chickadees

Most gardeners are delighted to see a butterfly sipping nectar from a flower in their garden, a delight that may be accompanied by a sense of accomplishment: "My garden is a butterfly garden!" Yet many of these same gardeners become alarmed by the sight of a caterpillar chewing the leaves of a garden plant, a sight that sends some to the garden shed for a chemical solution.

A chickadee in a birch tree.
(Photo by Phil Juvet)

There is no such thing as an "adults only" butterfly garden. While occasional visits by passing butterflies do occur, a female butterfly is not likely to linger in a garden unless there are plenty of larval host plants for caterpillars to eat until they pupate. If she finds these plants, she will deposit eggs on them, and perhaps stay awhile to sip nectar from the garden's flowers.

A recent experience with monarch butterflies serves as a good example. In our first twelve years of gardening together, monarchs were absent from our garden. Then, in early June 2014, we planted several seedlings of a tropical annual milkweed (*Asclepias curassavica*), some in the ground and others in a large tub. A month later, two monarchs fluttered over the garden fence, and two weeks after that, two dozen tiny caterpillars were munching away on milkweed leaves. Lesson learned: plant the larval host and they will come. (Research scientists stress that this tropical milkweed should not be planted in regions of the country with mild winters. Large populations of overwintering *A. curassavica* in these areas may entice monarchs to forego migration, creating an increased likelihood of infection with a protozoan disease that cripples and kills the monarchs. Gardeners in mild-winter regions should rely on native perennial milkweeds to attract monarchs. See Appendix 2 for native milkweeds in your state.)

In short, the gardener must welcome munching caterpillars. A portion of any butterfly garden, the larval host plants, will be grazed, and by the end of the garden season may be reduced to leafless stems.

Well, says the gardener who would rather not host caterpillars, my garden will be a songbird garden, filled with the calls of chickadees, warblers, cardinals, thrushes, and other songbirds. No way! Songbirds will not nest in and around your garden unless you can offer them an abundance of caterpillars. For example, each pair of chickadees, which raise their young exclusively on lepidopteran larvae, requires between 6,000 and 10,000 caterpillars for a single clutch of fledglings. The same picture can be painted for other songbirds: insects, notably butterfly and moth larvae, are a major component of each nestling's diet.

Where do all these caterpillars come from? Perhaps a better question would be: what kind of garden can produce caterpillars in such abundance? The answer: a garden planted with a wide variety of plants, woody and herbaceous, that are known larval hosts for butterflies and moths. *(continued on page 78)*

Oak leaves in October, ragged from the chewing of caterpillars, are an indicator of high garden biodiversity.

(continued from page 77)

Native canopy trees and shrubs are important larval hosts, especially for moth species. In his groundbreaking book *Bringing Nature Home*, entomologist Douglas Tallamy ranks oaks (*Quercus* spp.) at the top of the list of woody plants that function as lepidopteran larval hosts. According to Tallamy, the 80 *Quercus* species in North America host 534 species of moths and butterflies, including at least 20 species of dagger moths, 18 underwings, 8 hairstreaks, 44 inchworms, and 15 giant silk moths. Willows (*Salix* spp.) share a second place ranking with cherries and plums (*Prunus* spp.), each group hosting 456 species of moths and butterflies. Birches (*Betula* spp.) are another important group, hosting 413 species, while poplars and cottonwoods (*Populus* spp.) serve as hosts to 368 species. Other woody larval host plants include crabapples (*Malus* spp.), blueberries (*Vaccinium* spp.), maples (*Acer* spp.), pines (*Pinus* spp.), and spruce (*Picea* spp.).

A mature tree can host thousands of caterpillars, and these larvae are what bird food looks like. Not all caterpillars, however, are palatable to each species of bird. Chickadees, for example, feed mainly on spruce budworms, tent caterpillars, and other small larvae. Only gardens that are planted with a large variety of larval host plants, mostly trees and shrubs, can sustain a large variety of songbirds in the nesting season. We offer additional advice on which plants function best as lepidopteran larval host plants in Chapters 8 and 9.

In late summer, when the leaves of deciduous trees are riddled with holes from caterpillar feeding, the gardener may worry about permanent damage. In fact, healthy trees and shrubs can withstand considerable loss of leaf area over the growing season without harm, while birds and other predators work to reduce herbivore populations.

Caterpillars are important links in the garden food web. Not only are they the principal food of summer songbirds, they are the principal prey of many predatory insects, including hoverflies, wasps, and beetles—insects that keep garden herbivore populations at tolerable levels. Many gardeners who spend time in the garden looking for caterpillars find them among the most beautiful of garden creatures.

Aphids and Other Hemipterans

The insect order Hemiptera contains several sap-sucking herbivores, including aphids, whiteflies, cicadas, leafhoppers, treehoppers, scale insects, and true bugs, all familiar to observant gardeners. By far the most represented members of this group in our garden are aphids, also known as plant lice. Aphids seek out the new leaves and tender stems of garden plants, pierce the epidermal tissues, and suck the nutrient-rich sap. A few aphids rapidly become a herd, standing room only on your favorite herbaceous perennial or shrub.

I have known otherwise rational gardeners to bring out the big guns from the chemical shelf when they spotted a cluster of aphids. Some of the most toxic insecticides—including nicotine sulfate, malathion, diazinon, and dimethoate—have been used to kill aphids, with untold collateral damage to populations of beneficial insects and other garden life.

In fact, aphids are evidence of a healthy garden ecosystem, and they play an enormously important role in transferring solar energy from plants to animals. Healthy garden ecosystems are homes for a variety of aphid predators, including ladybird beetles, lacewings, parasitic wasps, and syrphid flies (also known as hoverflies or flower flies). Some of these predators may also benefit the gardener by preying on other garden herbivores, such as caterpillars. In order to maintain populations of these beneficial insects about the garden, there must be a steady supply of their prey, including an abundance of aphids.

Oleander aphids tapped into the sap of milkweed plants.

In the U.S. alone there are more than 1,400 aphid species, each feeding in summer on one plant species or a group of related plant species. Colonies grow rapidly as females give birth to live young, all female; males enter the picture, if at all, only when it is time to produce eggs for overwintering. In a typical colony, some of the female aphids will be winged, others wingless.

Aphids have complex life cycles that maximize acquisition of nutrients from their plant hosts. They become so numerous each summer because they are able to use plant resources efficiently, exploiting host plants with few measurable effects, particularly if the plants are not water stressed. I often find aphid colonies literally covering the stems of garden plants, yet the plants continue to grow normally. And typically the aphid colony has been infiltrated by one or more aphid predators bent on reducing the colony's numbers.

While details differ, the typical aphid life cycle begins with tiny eggs laid in autumn on the twigs or branches of deciduous trees. The eggs hatch in spring, releasing a generation of "stem mothers" that move to the emerging leaves of the tree, where nitrogen is most abundant. These wingless females are both viviparous (giving birth to live young) and parthenogenic (giving birth without mating). One adult female aphid can produce five nymphs per day over a 30-day period, all clones of the stem mother.

The nymphs go through five instar (molting) stages to become adult females, a process that takes about 30 days. As the nitrogen levels in the tree's leaves decline, winged females are produced that fly to summer host plants, typically herbaceous perennials with stems and leaves that are high in nitrogen. Colonies grow through the summer, often numbering in the hundreds, even thousands, on a single plant.

At the end of summer, triggered by reduced nitrogen levels in the summer host plants, winged females and winged males are produced. After mating, the females fly to the winter host tree species to lay eggs.

One interesting life cycle variation can be found in *Aphis nerii*, the oleander aphid, also called the milkweed aphid. A bright yellow aphid with black appendages, this Mediterranean species has spread throughout the world. In North America it is an obligate parthenogenic species in which males do not occur. Winged females are produced when colonies become overcrowded and when it is necessary to change host plants. Females overwinter on host trees.

In summer, when we find a ladybird beetle larva in the midst of an aphid colony; or aphid exoskeletons punctured with the emergence holes of adult wasps; or a chickadee, warbler, robin, or Northern flicker plucking aphids from garden plants, we feel that all is right in the garden world. In winter we can stand at the window and watch chickadees pecking aphid eggs from rhododendron branches.

Entomologists agree that aphids rarely do enough damage to warrant intervention by the gardener. In exceptional situations, when predators cannot keep up with a heavy infestation on young plants, mechanical controls will work. The gardener can dislodge them with a strong stream of water. Once knocked to the ground, aphids have a difficult time climbing back to the stem tip.

Aphids, Ants, and Sooty Mold:
A Lesson in Garden Ecology

One June morning, while leaving the porch by the back steps, we spotted a cluster of blue aphids on the tip of a red elder stem. At least a hundred aphids completely encircled the stem, tapping the sugar-rich sap just beneath the surface, while several winged females prepared to migrate and establish new colonies on nearby plants.

A dozen or so black-and-red ants worked at one end of the colony, milking the aphids for honeydew by stroking them with their antennae. Honeydew, excreted by the feeding aphids and rich in plant sugars, is valued by ants as a high carbohydrate food.

Drops of honeydew missed by the ants had accumulated on leaves below the aphids and started a colony of a fungus, commonly called sooty mold, on the upper leaf surfaces. The mold blocks sunlight from the leaf surface, rendering the few affected leaves useless in photosynthesis.

On the other end of the aphid colony, a ladybird beetle larva was devouring an aphid. In the absence of the ants, there might have been more of these larvae, but the ants protected their herd of aphids from predation by killing and eating the lady beetle larvae, a good source of needed protein.

Aphids and aphid-farming ants, predaceous beetle larvae and a sooty mold, characters in a drama unfolding within the terminal six inches of a single elderberry stem, a lesson in garden ecology delivered on the back steps. A week later, the stage was empty, all the players gone, and the elderberry was no worse for wear.

Treehopper Nymphs and the Ants That Protect Them

One summer day, while working next to a bed of tall sunflowers, Reeser noticed a lone ant crawling across a leaf. What was the ant doing six feet off the ground? He turned the leaf over and, sure enough, there were two other ants at work, tending a herd of tiny insects.

Ants herding treehopper nymphs on the underside of a sunflower leaf.

The ants seemed to have divided the herd into two groups, and each ant was stroking one of their charges with its antennae. We turned over other sunflower leaves and found more of the same.

While we often find ants "milking" aphids for honeydew, these little insects were clearly not aphids. Excited by the prospect of adding yet another species to our growing list of garden biodiversity, Reeser grabbed his camera and began shooting, hoping the photos would be useful in solving the mystery. He pored through Internet images of nymphs, assuming the unknown insects were immature stages in the life cycle of a species closely allied with aphids. Persistence paid off, and he finally found an image that looked exactly like the creatures in his photographs. The mystery nymphs were treehoppers, *Entylia carinata*.

Like aphids, treehopper nymphs and adults typically do little damage to garden plants. While they are often found on oaks, walnuts, black cherries, and other tree species, *E. carinata* also feed on several herbaceous garden annuals and perennials, including Joe-pye weed, calendulas, artemisias, achilleas, rudbeckias, goldenrods, and, of course, sunflowers. We grow several of these perennials in our garden, but we had not previously run across *E. carinata*, no doubt because we were spending insufficient time turning over leaves.

Herbivores Revisited

Watch carefully as you work in the garden and you will understand the relationship between gardening success and the intricate balance of insect herbivores and their predators. You might encounter a hoverfly larva hunting aphids, or a Japanese beetle with tachinid fly eggs attached to its thorax. Turn over a leaf, and there is a harvestmen devouring a leafhopper. Or perhaps one day you will catch a glimpse of a chickadee entering its birdhouse carrying a caterpillar in its beak.

Insect herbivores are fundamental links in transferring energy from plants to the rest of garden life, and thus they are critical to success in creating functional garden ecosystems. Garden animals that depend on insect herbivores include songbirds, amphibians, reptiles, rodents, and small mammals as well as spiders, harvestmen, and the larvae of predatory and parasitoid wasps. As examples, the caterpillars of moths and butterflies are primary food sources for songbirds, predatory wasp larvae, and parasitoid fly larvae, while beetles that feed on garden plants become food for birds, frogs, toads, snakes, and rodents.

Remove herbivores from the food chain with poisons, and the garden will surely fail as a healthy ecosystem. Herbivore predators, such as birds and predatory insects, will disappear, setting the stage for an herbivore population explosion. It is far better to tolerate a moderate degree of herbivory in exchange for a resilient garden ecosystem.

Monarch Butterfly Caterpillar
(*Danaus plexippus*)

Chapter 7

Garden Predators

"If all mankind were to disappear, the world would regenerate back to the rich state of equilibrium that existed ten thousand years ago. If insects were to vanish, the environment would collapse into chaos."
—E.O. Wilson

Predatory insects live all or parts of their lives hunting other insects for food to sustain themselves, their offspring, or both. Many species, such as the great black wasp (*Sphex pensylvanicus*) discussed in Chapter 2, spend their adult lives as both nectar feeders and hunters, capturing live prey such as caterpillars, grasshoppers, and cicadas to feed their larvae. Chapter 5 described the dual roles of pollinator and predator served by hoverflies and tachinid flies. This chapter focuses on the dual role of garden wasps as predators and parasitoids, and on the importance of beetles, spiders, and harvestmen as garden predators.

Predatory insects are vital to the garden ecosystem. They control herbivore populations, thus allowing garden plants to flourish. Many garden predators are also incidental pollinators.

Predatory and Parasitoid Wasps

We admit to being intimidated by the large wasps that frequent the garden in summer: the bald-faced hornets that forage nectar from raspberry blossoms or the yellow jackets that swarm over ripe fruits. They seem docile when so preoccupied, yet we recall incidents from youth when too much interest in these creatures resulted in painful stings. So we give these social wasps a wide berth, thankful that their nests remain undiscovered. The solitary hunting wasps, such as the great black wasp featured in Chapter 2 or the smaller sand wasps discussed below, are less intimidating to us, largely due to a lack of negative experiences with them. Most of the parasitoid wasps encountered in the garden are small and harmless, allowing close scrutiny without incident. (Unlike a parasite, which seldom kills its host, a parasitoid ultimately kills and consumes its prey.)

Wasps are close relatives of bees and, from an evolutionary standpoint, were here first. Bees are wasps that adopted a vegetarian diet, their hairy bodies enabling them to collect pollen. Many wasp species are smooth-bodied and thus do not collect large amounts of pollen from the flowers they visit, and even those with hairs lack the branched, pollen-trapping hairs of bees.

Like butterflies and moths, wasps are "incidental pollinators," moving around a few grains of pollen as they forage, perhaps dropping a grain on a stigma in the process. Unable to reach the nectar of many flowers due to their relatively short tongues, they favor flowers with shallow nectaries. In our garden we find them on goldenrod, raspberry, and plants of the carrot family, including Queen Anne's lace.

The wasp species discussed in this section are either predators as adults—capturing caterpillars and other insect larvae to feed their larvae—or they are parasitoids, laying their eggs in or on an insect host. In the latter instance, after the eggs hatch, the carnivorous larvae feed on the insect prey captured by their mothers; once the larvae become adults and are less reliant on a high protein diet, they switch to a high carbohydrate diet fueled by nectar and rotting fruit.

Beneficial wasps, including those that pollinate plants and those that control garden herbivores by predation or parasitism, far outnumber the few species that create problems for humans. They are among the gardener's best friends, and they deserve our protection.

Predatory Wasps

At the forefront of controlling herbivores in our gardens are the various predatory wasps, hunters of immature insects including caterpillars and other larvae. Common names associated with these wasps include sand wasp, digger wasp, mud wasp, hunting wasp, caterpillar-hunter, and cicada killer, all indicators of life styles found among various species in this group. Most nest in the soil or mud, and most adults are solitary hunters of other insects, feeding their prey to their larvae. The great black wasp (also called "cicada killer"), *Sphex pensylvanicus*, was discussed in Chapter 2. Also well represented in our garden are thread-waisted wasps, so named for the thread-like anterior end of the abdomen.

Ammophila procera, one of several species of thread-waisted wasps, serves as a good example. *A. procera* is distinguished by a long black abdomen that is very slender except for a terminal bulbous portion, a bright red band that encircles the abdomen, and a thorax that is black with silver bars on the side. *A. procera* is smaller than the great black wasp and much less intimidating.

Ammophila procera nectaring on a coreopsis flower.

A. procera is a species of sand wasp and favors gardens with sandy soils. Like the great black wasp, the female is a nectar feeder and can be found foraging on a variety of garden flowers. She provisions her underground nest cavities with caterpillars and other insects, one paralyzed host for each egg.

One summer afternoon our work in the vegetable garden was interrupted by the rare opportunity to watch a female *A. procera* drag a captured and paralyzed green caterpillar over one of the garden beds and across a granite rock, then jump through the mesh of the deer fence. Reeser grabbed his camera as soon as we saw her and was able to shoot several frames, only one of which was focused well enough to include here. The problem was her speed! The caterpillar was much longer than the wasp and must have weighed a great deal more, yet the wasp dragged her load 10 feet in about 10 seconds, her wings constantly fluttering to increase her velocity. By the time Reeser could run to the other side of the fence, she had disappeared, perhaps to her underground nest.

Ammophila procera dragging a captured caterpillar back to her underground nest.

Eremnophila aureonotata, a sand wasp, foraging on goldenrod.

A third species in this group, *Eremnophila aureonotata*, is also common in our garden, often seen foraging on goldenrod. It is a striking creature, blue-black with silver markings on its thorax. The female is a caterpillar hunter specializing on the larvae of moths and skipper butterflies.

Parasitoid Wasps

Perhaps the most unusual wasp we have encountered in our garden is *Pelecinus polyturator*, the American pelecinid wasp. The first time we saw one in flight, we mistook her for a damselfly. She glided slowly through the air on her short wings, sporting long antennae and a curved black abdomen that was five times the length of the rest of her body.

While the adult pelecinid is a nectar feeder, its larva is a parasitoid, living off the paralyzed body of its host, the underground grub of a Japanese beetle or June beetle, killing it in the process. It begins with the female wasp exploring the soil with her long abdomen to determine the presence of the grub. She then deposits an egg directly into the beetle larva and moves on. When the egg hatches, the wasp larva feeds on the grub's tissue until it is ready to pupate.

Male pelecinids are so rare in certain regions of the species' range that the females have adapted the means

An American pelecinid wasp resting on a leaf.

An unidentified ichneumon wasp nectaring on wild aster.

to reproduce without them, a process called parthenogenesis. In areas where males are more numerous, they do take part in reproduction.

Another group of parasitoid wasps that visit our garden are ichneumon wasps, solitary insects that vary in length from a tenth of an inch to five inches. They are slender, the females often with long ovipositors. Ichneumon wasps are used commonly as biological control agents for the herbivores of commercial crops.

Like pelecinid wasps, some ichneumon species prey on beetle larvae in the soil, while others lay their eggs in the larvae of wood borers. In the latter case, the female is equipped with a saw-like ovipositor that she uses to drill a hole in the bark to reach the larvae.

Sometimes it is difficult to tell a wasp from a bee. Reeser spent many hours trying to identify from a photo what he assumed to be an emerald green solitary bee foraging on Queen Anne's lace, before finally discovering that it was one of 230 species of cuckoo wasps, so called because they lay their eggs in the nests of other solitary wasps or bees,

An adult cuckoo wasp (*Hedychrum* spp.) foraging on Queen Anne's lace.

consuming the host's provisions and often the host's larvae. He had overlooked one of the key features that distinguish bees and wasps, the lack of hairs on the latter.

Predatory Beetles

Some beetle species help control garden herbivores. Ladybird beetles are among the most familiar of predaceous beetles, their abundance in the garden recognized as a sign that all is well. Adults tend to focus on eating aphids, while the larvae are more generalistic, preying on insect eggs, beetle larvae, and the adults of aphids, scale insects, mealybugs, mites, and whiteflies. Each ladybird beetle larva can consume about 25 aphids per day, while an adult ladybird beetle can eat about 60 aphids each day.

Ladybird beetles are well-known predators because of their diurnal habit. Much of the good work that other beetles perform in our gardens happens during the night and thus goes unnoticed. Various species of nocturnal ground beetles, often called carabids

An adult ladybird beetle inspecting her cluster of eggs on the underside of an enkianthus leaf.

in reference to their family, the Carabidae, are carnivores, scampering about the garden under the stars in search of caterpillars, grubs, other beetles (including those that eat garden plants), fly larvae and pupae, aphids, earthworms, slugs, snails, earwigs, and other garden herbivores. Other carabid species are granivores, feeding on weed seeds in the soil. Still others are omnivores, eating both seeds and insects. Whatever its food preference, a ground beetle can eat its weight in insect prey and/or seeds every day.

You can find nocturnal carabids during the day if you go looking for them, turning over stones and old logs, lifting a potted plant, or digging at the base of bunch grasses where they seek shelter. They love to spend the day tucked beneath the foliage of any low ground cover. You will also run into them while turning the compost heap, one of their favorite hunting grounds, or when raking aside the leaf litter mulch covering a garden bed.

There are more than 2,000 species of carabids in North America. As a group, they vary in shape and color, most being shiny and dark, others metallic or patterned, and they range in size from one-third to two-thirds of an inch long. Many can be recognized by unique color patterns or body shapes that speak to their role in the garden food web. The snail-eating beetle (*Scaphinotus andrewsii*), for example, is equipped with long, slender mandibles that allow it to reach deep into the shell of a snail, while the six-spotted tiger beetle (*Cicindela sexguttata*), a diurnal species, has a brilliant metallic-green body that allows it to blend in with its surroundings, avoiding its predators while stalking its prey. Most carabids are swift of foot, preferring to outrun their prey rather than flying, and some species have lost the ability to fly.

A carabid beetle searching for prey.

The most common garden carabids belong to a group called "common black ground beetles" (CBGB), of which there are over 1,100 species worldwide. They share a common life cycle, breeding in late summer, with females laying eggs just below the soil surface.

Larvae hatch and spend the winter in the soil, emerging in early spring to feed and then pupate. Adults emerge in summer. Some adults may also overwinter.

CBGBs are at the center of a complex segment of the garden food web. As mentioned earlier, they prey on a host of garden herbivores (including army worms, cutworms, corn rootworms, potato beetles, and cucumber beetles), earthworms, slugs, and snails, while they are preyed upon by an equally large and diverse group of predators that includes other beetles (such as the six-spotted tiger beetle), wolf spiders, garden snakes, toads, frogs, birds (including robins, turkeys, red-winged blackbirds, blue jays, and mourning doves), shrews, skunks, and red fox.

A six-spotted tiger beetle searching for prey.

To those of us who garden for wildness, it is clear that beetles are important members of the garden food web. Many species are essential in limiting populations of garden herbivores, while others function as pollinators. We can increase the populations of beneficial beetles in our gardens by minimizing disturbances of the soil where beetle larvae live, and we can create beetle habitat by leaving a few rotting logs on the garden perimeter and mulching garden beds with leaf litter. We can spend summer nights watching ground beetles at work and thereby gain a greater appreciation for their existence.

Garden Spiders and Harvestmen

If there is any truth to the old saying that you are never more than three feet from a spider, it would be when you are in a garden in tune with nature. Even when you are not looking for them, spiders and their arachnid relatives, harvestmen, appear when you are weeding, harvesting, admiring that just-opened blossom, or when you reach into the garden toolbox for a spool of jute twine.

A harvestman waiting in the shadows of sunflower leaves.

Although not true spiders, harvestmen are equally important members of the garden food web. They are easily distinguished from spiders by their fused body regions (spiders have an abdomen that is separated by a constriction from the rest of the body). Also, harvestmen have a single pair of eyes, while spiders have three to four pairs.

A harvestmen basking in the sun atop a bachelor's button flower.

Like spiders, harvestmen eat aphids, caterpillars, leafhoppers, beetles, flies, mites, small slugs, snails, earthworms, spiders, and decaying plant and animal matter. On sunny late June days, we find them perched on bachelor's button flowers, waiting for a pollinating bee to come near, and on the undersides of sunflower leaves, hidden from their prey. But they are most active at night, actively searching out their victims.

In turn, harvestmen are preyed upon by birds, toads, salamanders, and frogs. We often find a harvestman missing one or two legs, likely lost in a narrow escape from one of its predators. Missing legs will not grow back, but the harvestman seems to get along quite well on its remaining six or seven.

Many people, even some gardeners, have an irrational fear of spiders. Of the 40,000 known species (3,400 in North America), only three are poisonous to humans: the black widow, brown recluse, and hobo spiders. In fact, most garden spiders do not have strong enough fangs to pierce human skin or venom poisonous enough to affect humans.

The most numerous land predators on Earth, spiders and harvestmen are also among the most important garden predators. They are very effective in controlling insect herbivores, even more so than birds or bats. Many spider species survive the winter as adults and

This nursery web spider was not interested in the raspberries except as a perch from which to hunt and capture prey.

reduce herbivore populations at the beginning of the growing season, before other predators emerge.

Most spiders and harvestmen are generalist predators and eat their share of beneficial insects, including pollinators, as well. Because of this generalist eating habit, they are rarely successful in controlling a large outbreak of an herbivore like the cucumber beetle.

We are accustomed to finding spiders in the garden, but every once in awhile the unexpected spider will startle one of us. Such was the case when Marjorie reached up to harvest a pair of ripe raspberries and almost grabbed a nursery web spider (*Pisaurina mira*) that was sprawled across both fruits, waiting for a likely prey to come close. It lingered there while we continued our garden work. As we closed the garden gate behind us, Marjorie lamented, "I really wanted those two raspberries!"

The female nursery web spider constructs a web only when her eggs, held within an egg sac, are ready to hatch. She hangs the egg sac within the web where the young spiders live under her protection until they are able to fend for themselves.

Also among the true spiders in our garden are crab spiders, named for their sideways, crablike walk. We find them in open flowers, either lying in wait to capture their prey or consuming a captured butterfly, bee, or fly. Crab spiders are capable of changing their color to white, yellow, or pink over several days to make them better camouflaged within a blossom.

A crab spider (*Misumena vatia*) and its prey on a dandelion flower.

Spiders commonly known as orb web weavers spin elaborate webs in the garden. These spiral webs are architectural wonders designed to extend the spider's sensory system and trap or slow down prey with a minimal amount of energy expended in silk production.

A giant lichen orbweaver spider, easily mistaken for a lichen.

One summer Reeser found a giant lichen orbweaver spider (*Araneus bicentenarius*) resting on a small sandstone caricature mounted on one of the garden fence posts, a human face with a glum expression. At first glance he thought a lichen had started growing in one of Mr. Glum's nostrils, for it looked exactly like the lichens found on old cemetery headstones or on tree trunks. Then he noticed the lichen's legs. Two days later it was still there, having moved only an inch or two to one of the eyelids. On the third day it had moved again, this time beneath an overarching brow in order to stay out of the rain. Rather than serving as camouflage, the lichen-like appearance of this spider made it more conspicuous. And where was its elaborate web? A garden mystery….

Enoplognatha ovata lineata waiting for its prey to come near. Look closely and you can see the fine threads of its web.

In late June, when tree hoppers are laying eggs on the undersides of sunflower leaves and ants crawl across leaves and stems in search of honeydew, a small spider,

Enoplognatha ovata redimita, lying in wait.

no more than a quarter inch long, takes up residence in the cluster of terminal leaves. Nearly every sunflower plant in the garden hosts one of these spiders, commonly called the cobweb spider (*Enoplognatha ovata*). On close inspection, you can see the fine threads of its web glistening in the sunlight. The spider's translucent legs are nearly invisible as well, its abdomen creamy white with either two rows of paired black dots (*E. ovata lineata*) or two bright red lines (*E. ovata redimita*), two forms of the same species. *E. ovata* belongs to the same family as the deadly black widow spider and, indeed, its venom is poisonous, although not potent enough to harm humans. The trapped ant's fate, however, is sealed. The same fate awaits other insects that venture too near, including bees and other pollinators.

In the garden, as in any functional ecosystem, everybody is somebody's lunch. So who preys on spiders and harvestmen? Invertebrates such as centipedes and mantids and vertebrates including toads, wood frogs, skinks, nuthatches, chickadees, warblers, skunks, and shrews are some of the creatures known to eat arachnids.

For the gardener in tune with nature, little additional work is needed to increase the garden's populations of spiders and harvestmen. Organic mulches such as grass clippings or shredded leaves provide protection as well as the humidity that spiders must have. Apply these mulches early in the garden season when the

Spiderlings of *Araneus diadematus*, the cross orbweaver spider. We spotted this congregation of young spiders on a dewy morning in late June, clumped together beneath a web on a rhubarb leaf. Before the day was done, they had dispersed.

spiders are dispersing. Leave some areas of the garden covered with a little plant debris at the end of the gardening year to provide winter habitat. And don't be too tidy. Leaving a pot upturned or a tree stump to rot will provide microhabitats for garden arachnids.

Whether you go about your gardening with little thought to spiders and harvestmen or take the time to search them out, rest assured that they are there, filling an important niche in the garden food web. Whenever you are in the garden, you are never more than three feet away from a beneficial spider or harvestman.

The Gardener as Predator

There are times when the gardener becomes the chief predator of insect herbivores. Examples of gardener-as-predator include daily perusal of grape vines for Japanese beetles, a pail of soapy water in hand, and early morning inspections of tomatillo leaves to squash torpid flea beetles.

In our garden, we get help controlling the early-emerging Japanese beetle population from a small tachinid fly (*Istocheta aldrichi*), an introduced parasitoid that lays from one to several eggs on the thorax of any Japanese beetle it can find. Upon hatching, the maggots bore into the beetle's body, killing the beetle before it has a chance to reproduce. If we find a beetle with one or more small white eggs just behind its head, we rescue it from the soapy water and toss it into the grass to live out its short doomed existence. Within a few hours the fly eggs will hatch and the tachinid larvae will consume the beetle on their way to becoming adults.

How effective is the introduced predator? In early August, more than half of the beetles we find on our grape plants bear white eggs on their thorax, but the late summer emergence of Japanese beetles is another story. By mid-August the tachinid fly has disappeared, and Japanese beetle populations soar. Miss one day of scouting with the pail, and entire grape leaves are reduced to tatters. Stay with it, however, and hand-picking will keep Japanese beetle damage to a tolerable level.

In addition to functioning as primary predator of Japanese beetles, we have met the sunrise in the garden with pail in hand, picking torpid cucumber beetles from cucurbit foliage and flowers. We've covered the potato crop with row cover material to exclude the Colorado potato beetle. (For more on using row covers, see the sidebar in Chapter 11, "Floating Row Covers Foil Herbivores in the Vegetable Garden.") We've hand-picked lily leaf beetles and fed handfuls of slugs to a neighbor's chickens. In every case, however, we have given the garden's food web a chance to deal with such problems. In most years, a few cucumber beetles (or other herbivores) show up, and a few days later they are gone.

Pelecinid Wasp (*Pelecinus polyturator*)

Chapter 8

Functional Understory Trees and Shrubs

"Let's imagine a goal: that at some time in the future, the value of a property will be perceived in part according to its value to wildlife. A property hedged with fruiting shrubs will be worth more than one bordered by forsythia. One with dry-stone walls that provide passageways for chipmunks will be valued higher than one whose walls are cemented stone. Buyers will place a premium on lots that provide summer flowers and fall crops of seed….
Oh, brave new world!"

—Sara Stein, *Noah's Garden: Restoring the Ecology of Our Own Back Yards*

Wherever you garden, there are native deciduous trees, species that top out at 30 feet or shorter, that you can plant in the dappled sunlight beneath taller canopy trees. These understory trees, together with a variety of native shrub species, form the bones of a *functional garden*—that is, a garden that nourishes wildlife. When flowering in spring or summer, many of these trees and shrubs provide pollinators and other insects with essential nectar and pollen. Later in the year, some provide lipid-rich berries that sustain migrating birds on long flights and allow resident birds to endure cold winters. The best understory trees and shrubs do both.

From May through October, we measure our success in fostering garden biodiversity by the pollinators, herbivores, and predators we find on the understory trees and shrubs we've planted over the years. Most of these woody plants are native to our state of Maine; many of these have native ranges that extend westward to the Mississippi River and beyond, and southward to states bordering the Gulf of Mexico. Based on our observations, we believe that the species described in this chapter are every bit as important as canopy trees in fostering garden biodiversity.

Much as oaks, willows, cherries, and birches top the list of trees that serve as host plants for lepidopteran larvae, certain understory trees and shrubs are more important than others when it comes to providing nectar and pollen for insects and fruits for birds. While the species within a genus may vary from state to state, the importance of the genus to wildlife remains constant everywhere. As an example, all species in the genus *Cornus* (dogwoods) are important wildlife plants wherever you garden.

River birch, recognized by its peeling bark, while not considered native to Maine, is highly functional in coastal Maine gardens.

In this chapter we present functional understory trees and shrubs that we consider among the best for supporting a wide variety of birds, insects, and other wildlife. We describe their garden assets and for many we include a short essay to provide a more complete picture of garden worth and wildlife value. Appendix 3, "Recommended Understory Trees and Shrubs by State," describes many other species, using U.S. Department of Agriculture range maps to show where in North America each species is native.

In general, locally native plants, those that have co-evolved with the local fauna, are the best choices for creating a biodiverse garden. The question is how to define "locally native." Some authors define nativity on a regional basis (New England, Southeast, Pacific Northwest, etc.), but this approach invites use of a species that is native to only one or two states. And state boundaries are arbitrary where plants are concerned. For example, river birch (*Betula nigra*) is not generally considered native to Maine, but it can be found in New Hampshire within a grouse's flight of the Maine border. Must we therefore abstain from using it in a Maine garden? (There are unconfirmed reports of river birch growing in the wild on the Maine side of the border.) No system of defining nativity is perfect, but for the purposes of this book we have chosen to define nativity at the state level, using native range maps produced by the USDA.

Because annual low temperatures vary considerably from north to south within some states, we include USDA hardiness zones for each plant species in order to help gardeners decide if a particular species will grow in their garden. Maine, for example, has four hardiness zones (USDA Zones 3 through 6), allowing gardeners in southern Maine to grow many native plants that would not survive the winters of northern Maine. (You can determine the hardiness zone for your garden by entering your ZIP code in the USDA Interactive map at http://planthardiness.ars.usda.gov/PHZMWeb/InteractiveMap.aspx.)

Height and width measurements are typically given as ranges, the actual dimensions of a species in any garden being dependent on light and soil conditions. Information on wildlife use is based on our review of numerous authorities, many of which are listed in the Suggested Reading section, and on our own observations of the plants in our garden and in gardens we have visited over the years.

Acer (Maples)
Mountain Maple (*A. spicatum*)

USDA Hardiness Zones: 3 to 7
Height: 20 to 35 feet
Width: Multi-trunked plants, may be wider than tall.
Sunlight: partial shade
Soil: moist, cool, acidic (pH less than 6.8)
Flowers: long, erect, spike-like clusters of small greenish-yellow flowers; spring
Fruits: winged samaras
Autumn color: mottled orange to bright red
Wildlife use: Solitary bees appear to be the primary pollinators. Ruffed grouse feed on winter buds, while deer browse the foliage.

Known as mountain maple in the Great Smokies of Tennessee and North Carolina, where it grows as a thirty-foot tree, *A. spicatum* is often reduced by deer and moose browsing to a large, multi-stemmed shrub in New England forests, hence the alternate common names of moose maple and low maple. Yet another common name, water maple, refers to its mountain habitat, described by Donald Culross Peattie as "the neighborhood of white and singing water."

We have encountered examples of both growth habits, tree form and shrubby. Reeser's introduction to the species was a lovely small tree growing in the shade of tall pines at a site near Boothbay, Maine, where he and a graduate student were collecting data for a research project. It was near dusk and the small maple was in full flower.

He was so enchanted by the tree that he returned later with the intent of collecting seed, only to find the tree nearly destroyed by timber harvesters dragging pine logs out of

USDA Range Map - *Acer spicatum*

the woods. One of the original three trunks survived long enough to mature a handful of seeds on its branches. He collected these seeds and successfully produced seedlings, one of which has been growing in our garden for 15 years. Despite the regular appearance of deer in our garden, this tree now stands 20 feet tall.

Mountain maple deserves to be more frequently grown in shady gardens. In June, its shoot tips are graced with long-stemmed upright spikes of chartreuse flowers that glow like candles in the understory. Small two-winged samaras (seeds) ripen over summer to red or yellow before they are carried off on autumn winds as the leaves turn to yellow, orange and scarlet. In shrubby forms, bright red young twigs poke through the winter snow.

Mountain maple is easily grown from seed, either sown outside in fall or stratified in the refrigerator for three to four months followed by spring sowing. Considering the scarcity of this species in nurseries and garden centers, growing your own from seed may be the only way to bring this lovely maple from woods to garden.

Upright spikes of mountain maple's greenish-yellow flowers turn the tree's horizontal branches into candelabras.

An inhabitant of beech-maple-hemlock woods and hemlock ravines, mountain maple demands shade. Scorching of the leaves and the thin bark occurs when it is exposed to full sun, a trait which it shares with another eastern boreal maple, striped maple (*A. pensylvanicum*). A sheltered location protects the weak wood of both species from damage by wind.

Mountain maple is not tolerant of urban stresses, such as soil compaction and pollution. It is intolerant of flooding, and its shallow roots, seldom more than a few inches below the soil surface, make it susceptible to drought. On the plus side, it can be grown from USDA Zone 2 to the mountains of Zone 7, and it has no serious diseases or herbivores. Both mountain maple and striped maple are among the most resistant of all maples to attack by the gypsy moth.

Europeans have long recognized the garden worth of this small maple, first introduced to Europe in 1775 and again in 1905. Like many gardeners in the United States today, they had a penchant for the exotic. For many of us, however, there is growing interest in sustainable managed landscapes that express the uniqueness of native flora. Plants like mountain maple have come into their own.

Alnus (Alders)
Speckled Alder (*A. incana* ssp. *rugosa*)

USDA Hardiness Zones: 2 to 6
Height: 15 to 25 feet; multi-trunked
Width: 15 to 25 feet; thicket-forming
Sunlight: full sun to partial shade
Soil: mesic to wet; tolerates mucky soils
Flowers: drooping male catkins, purplish-brown with yellow pollen, slender, cylindrical; female catkins green, rounded, clustered on stalks.
Fruits: One-inch-long, woody, red-brown cones bearing winged seeds into winter.
Autumn color: insignificant
Wildlife use: Speckled alder seeds are food for songbirds, water birds, and small mammals. Songbird feeders include black-capped chickadees, redpolls, pine siskins, and American goldfinches. Birds commonly found nesting in alder thickets include yellow-bellied and alder flycatchers, yellow warblers, common yellowthroats, Wilson's warblers, red-winged blackbirds, swamp and white-throated sparrows, and American goldfinches. Alders are also host to several species of butterflies and moths, including the green comma butterfly (*Polygonia faunus*).

USDA Range Map - *Alnus incana* ssp *rugosa*

Named for the white, raised lenticels on its bark, speckled alder is a good example of the subtle beauty of native shrubs. A large understory shrub (15 to 25 feet tall and wide) with a rounded crown and multiple crooked and leggy trunks, it can be found growing in colonies along the banks of streams and ponds, in low wet openings in the woods, in swamps and bogs. And this is where it should be grown in gardens, naturalized in wet areas with red maple (*Acer rubrum*), buttonbush (*Cephalanthus occidentalis*), willows (*Ilex* spp.), winterberry (*Ilex verticillata*), mountain holly (*I. mucronata*), nannyberry viburnum (*Viburnum lentago*), silky dogwood (*Cornus amomum*), and gray birch (*Betula populifolia*). While extremely tolerant of flooding, speckled alder is intolerant of shade and should be planted in open areas.

White raised lenticels on the bark give speckled alder its common name.

Speckled alder is an aggressive colonizing wetland shrub without brilliant spring or summer flowers, without showy fruit or handsome fall foliage. But we love to see this plant in winter, the drooping, purple-brown, snow-capped male catkins, the previous year's small, woody, cone-like female catkins, and the coming season's smaller red female catkins all on the same winter twigs.

Alders are important members of wetland ecosystems. Before they turn woody, the female catkins produce tiny winged nuts that are a favorite food of songbirds, waterfowl, small mammals, and deer. Alder branches are frequent nesting sites for a wide variety of birds. And alders are nitrogen-fixing plants capable of adding up to five grams of nitrogen per square meter of topsoil per year. Their roots anchor the soil and prevent bank erosion.

The male catkins and cone-like female flowers of *Alnus incana rugosa*.

Amelanchier (Serviceberry)
Shadblow serviceberry (*A. canadensis*)

USDA Hardiness Zones: 4 to 8
Height: 25 to 30 feet
Width: 15 to 20 feet
Sunlight: full sun to partial shade
Soil: average, mesic, well-drained
Flowers: white, April to May, before the leaves emerge
Fruits: purplish-black, early summer
Autumn color: orange-red
Wildlife use: Shadblow serviceberry is an early spring nectar source for bees and butterflies and a larval host for several butterflies, including the viceroy (*Limenitis archippus*), striped hairstreak (*Satyrium liparops*), Canadian tiger swallowtail (*Papilio canadensis*), and red-spotted purple (*Limenitis arthemis*). Flower longhorn beetles (*Evodinus monticola*) forage among the early spring flowers for pollen. The berries are relished by cardinals, waxwings, hairy woodpeckers, thrushes, catbirds, orioles, and robins, as well as squirrels and chipmunks.

USDA Range Map -
Amelanchier canadensis

From mid-April to mid-May, serviceberries signal the true arrival of spring, the loosening of winter's grip on their pointed buds. Roadsides are adorned with these small, multi-stemmed trees in full bloom, bright white clouds come to earth.

We admit to total confusion when it comes to distinguishing the numerous species of serviceberry. Here we discuss *A. canadensis*, the shadblow serviceberry, but there are several other species, all heralds of spring, all very functional in nourishing wildlife.

A serviceberry in full bloom, a white cloud come to earth.

Some serviceberry species are understory shrubs, others small trees. We are partial to the tree-form species and grow what we believe to be *A. canadensis* in our garden. A few weeks after the flowers have faded, the fruits begin to ripen, a few at a time changing from red to dark blue. Some we pick to eat as we walk by the tree, others are snatched by a catbird or chipmunk.

The common name of "serviceberry" has its origin in cold country, I'm told. It seems that in Maine, when the fruits start to form, we know that the ground has thawed sufficiently to hold interment services for those who died during the long winter.

The delicate white flowers of serviceberries herald the arrival of spring.

Amelanchier berries ripen slowly in spring and not all at the same time.

Aronia (Chokeberries)
Black Chokeberry (*A. melanocarpa*)

USDA Hardiness Zones: 3 to 8
Height: 3 to 6 feet
Width: 3 to 6 feet; spreads by root suckers
Sunlight: full sun to partial shade
Soil: best growth in mesic, well-drained soils; tolerant of boggy soils
Flowers: clusters of five or six white, five-petaled flowers in May
Fruits: black berries
Autumn color: purple or red
Wildlife use: Primary pollinators are bumble bees and solitary bees. In winter, the fruits are eaten by grouse, pheasants, black-capped chickadees, cedar waxwings, black bears, red foxes, rabbits, squirrels, and white-footed mice. Caterpillars of the praeclara underwing moth (*Catocala praeclara*) feed on the foliage.

Blooming in early June along roadsides, in the low ground of open coniferous woods, in local swamps, and on dry sandy hillsides and rocky upland barrens, the flowers of black chokeberries fill the air with a musky sweet scent. In these wild places they seldom exceed

USDA Range Map -
Aronia melanocarpa

3 feet in height, but in the garden, growing in full sunlight with their roots in compost-enriched soil, they reach a height of 6 feet.

Suckering profusely, each black chokeberry shrub consists of multiple slender stems held stiffly erect, the upper two-thirds of each stem covered in glossy dark-green leaves frosted with white flowers in late May to early June. The five petals of each half-inch flower surround a cluster of pink anthers held high on extended filaments.

The flowers are foraged by several pollinator species. Once, in a few minutes of close observation, we recognized two species of bumble bee, two fly species, a tiny wasp of unknown identity, and several solitary bee species moving chokeberry pollen around as they went about their foraging.

From early September to late November, the shrubs bear loose clusters of glossy black berries that contain higher levels of antioxidants than any other temperate-zone fruit, including blueberries. This feature has prompted increasing interest in black chokeberries among small fruit growers in the United States and Canada. Whole berries are canned, the juice is used in making jelly or added to apple juice, and extracts of the berries are used as natural colorants in other foods.

We have read that the astringent taste of the berry (the characteristic responsible for its common name) makes it a food of last resort among winter birds. While

Chokeberry's dark-green leaves are frosted with half-inch white flowers, each with five petals surrounding a cluster of pink anthers.

many berries do shrivel on the stems, we have watched winter robins feast on ripe chokeberries when other fruits were still locally abundant.

As a landscape plant, the merits of *A. melanocarpa* have been sung since its introduction to western hemisphere gardens in the 1700s. In 1972, black chokeberry received the Royal Society's Award of Merit and was described as a "splendid shrub for naturalistic plantings, especially on the edge of woodlands." We recommend it for use in mass plantings, informal hedges, pond plantings, and as a spot of color in a mixed border.

A bumble bee foraging on chokeberry flowers.

Chokeberry fruits are eaten by gamebirds, black-capped chickadees, cedar waxwings, black bears, red foxes, rabbits, squirrels, and white-footed mice.

Chokeberry's fall foliage is another reason to plant this shrub in your garden.

Clethra (Summersweet Clethra)
Summersweet Clethra (*C. alnifolia*)

USDA Hardiness Zones: 3 to 9

Height: 3 to 8 feet

Width: 4 to 6 feet

Sunlight: best in full sun to partial shade; tolerates full shade

Soil: consistently moist, acidic, sandy; do not allow soil to dry out; tolerates heavy soils

Flowers: sweetly fragrant, white, in narrow upright clusters

Fruits: brown seed capsules that persist into winter

Autumn color: yellow to golden brown

Wildlife use: Flowers attract butterflies, bees, adult tachinid flies, and hummingbirds. Clethra seeds are eaten by birds and mammals, particularly mice.

Summersweet clethra, *Clethra alnifolia*, is a native plant success story, a favorite shrub among the many gardeners who grow it for its spicy fragrant summer flowers and golden yellow fall foliage. Commonly called sweet pepperbush for its peppercorn-like fruit, white alder for the

The white summer flowers of *Clethra alnifolia* fill the summer air with a spicy fragrance.

USDA Range Map - *Clethra alnifolia*

similarity of its foliage to that of the true alders, and "poor man's soap" because the flowers produce lather when crushed in water, summersweet clethra has been in cultivation for over 200 years. The blossoms, borne in dense narrow spikes, fill the summer air of the garden with a spicy scent for several weeks in late July and August. Following the bloom are small rounded seed capsules packed into the same dense spikes of their forebears, each capsule one-eighth inch in diameter and containing several seeds. These tan-colored capsules persist through autumn into winter, gradually darkening in color and adding textural depth to fall foliage that changes from light yellow to gold to tarnished brass.

While the species has white blossoms, many new cultivars have been introduced in recent years, including 'Hokie Pink', the cultivar that grows in our garden. And while *C. alnifolia* as a species can reach heights up to 10 feet in the garden, newer cultivars selected for compact habits top out at 3 to 4 feet.

Clethra alnifolia in autumn.

Summersweet seed capsules in winter.

Clethra alnifolia 'Hokie Pink', a pink-flowering cultivar of the species, growing in our garden.

Summersweet clethra is an essential plant in pollinator gardens, its blossoms attracting butterflies, bees, adult tachinid flies, and hummingbirds. In our garden we have noticed that both monarch butterflies and white admiral butterflies show a preference for the nectar of clethra flowers.

Late Summer Blossoms of Summersweet Nourish a Diversity of Insects

In August, when few other shrubs are flowering, summersweet clethra fills the air with the sweet scent of its blossoms, attracting gardeners and insects. We have spent many hours, camera in hand, watching the parade of insects that visit the flowers of the 'Hokie Pink' colony in our garden.

A bumble bee sips the nectar of summer-sweet clethra as it forages for pollen.

A yellow jacket (*Vespula* spp.) busies itself foraging among clethra blooms.

Sphex pensylvanicus, the great black wasp, is a frequent visitor to summersweet, relying on the nectar for energy to capture caterpillars and other prey to feed its larvae.

Hystricia abrupta is one of several tachinid fly species that rely on summersweet for energy.

A monarch butterfly (*Danaus plexippus*), just out of its chrysalis, gets its first nourishment from summersweet nectar.

A fritillary (*Speyeria* sp.) sips summersweet nectar in the summer garden.

White admiral butterflies (*Limenitis arthemis*) spend much of August sipping nectar from the clethra in our garden.

Comptonia (Sweetfern)
Sweetfern (*C. peregrina*)

USDA Hardiness Zones: 3 to 6

Height: 5 feet

Width: 3 feet

Sunlight: full sun to partial shade

Soil: sandy to loamy well-drained soils; tolerates nutritionally poor soil; can grow in very acid soils.

Flowers: brown catkins that appear before the leaves

Fruits: a bur-like husk

Autumn color: insignificant

Wildlife use: *Comptonia peregrina* is used as a food plant by the caterpillars of several moth species, including the grey pug moth (*Eupithecia subfuscata*), Io moth (*Automeris io*), and several case-bearer moths. The seeds are eaten by upland gamebirds and small mammals.

USDA Range Map -
Comptonia peregrina

Not a true fern, sweetfern's olive-green fern-like leaves have a spice fragrance when crushed.

Colonies of sweetfern, consisting of low shrubs up to 3 feet in height, grow in dry sandy soils, in old abandoned fields, and in woodland openings. Highly tolerant of shade, sweetfern grows best in poor acidic soils. Not a true fern, its long, narrow, olive-green, aromatic leaves are fern-like in appearance, often remaining dried on the plant through the winter. The narrow lobed leaves of sweetfern are covered with resin dots, the source of their spicy fragrance. During the Revolutionary War, American colonists used the leaves of sweetfern as a substitute for tea.

Many gardeners shy away from sweetfern because of its vigorous colonizing habit. That characteristic can be used to advantage, however, where a vigorous groundcover is needed.

Sweetfern makes a splendid informal hedge for garden walkways.

Cornus (Dogwoods)

Pagoda Dogwood (*C. alternifolia*)

USDA Hardiness Zones: 3 to 7

Height: 15 to 25 feet

Width: 20 to 32 feet

Sunlight: partial shade preferred; will tolerate full sun in cooler regions if the root zone is mulched and kept moist

Soil: acidic, organically rich, medium moisture, well-drained

Flowers: small, fragrant, yellowish-white, in flat-topped clusters; late spring

Fruits: blue-black berries on red stalks; mature in late summer

Autumn color: reddish-purple, often tinted with yellow

Wildlife use: Pagoda dogwood is used for cover and nesting by robins, waxwings, red-eyed vireos, scarlet tanagers, and purple finches. The ripe berries are eaten by a host of songbirds (see list below). Plants serve as larval hosts for the spring azure butterfly (*Celastrina ladon*) and as a nectar source for the unusual snout butterfly (*Libytheana carinenta*).

A must for any bird garden, the pagoda dogwood is a small understory tree reaching no more than 15 (rarely 25) feet in height with wide-spreading horizontal branches. In winter, these

USDA Range Map -
Cornus alternifolia

layered branches give the tree a pagoda-like form. From late spring to early summer, pagoda dogwood brightens a shady nook of the garden with large flat clusters of creamy white flowers. In late summer, birds feast on its purple-black berries. And in autumn, its leaves are painted yellow, red, and purple. Among the birds that eat the late summer fruits are bluebirds, brown thrashers, cardinals, cedar waxwings, flickers and other woodpeckers, catbirds, mockingbirds, robins, song sparrows, thrushes, and vireos.

Pagoda dogwood's large flat clusters of creamy white flowers brighten shady areas of the garden in late spring.

The late August fruits of *Cornus alternifolia* are eaten by a wide variety of songbirds.

The autumn foliage of pagoda dogwood is among the best to be found in understory trees.

Golden Canker on Pagoda Dogwood

Golden canker, a fungus disease of pagoda dogwoods throughout most of the eastern United States, has become more prevalent in recent years. The origin of the disease and the exact means by which it spreads is unknown. Easily recognized by the bright yellow to tan bark on infected branches, the disease can progress from the branch tips to main branches and ultimately to the trunk. Infected areas quickly die.

Infected areas often have orange spots scattered over the yellow tissue. These are the fruiting bodies of the fungus. Spores released from these fruiting bodies can infect other stems and even the main trunk, leading to dieback of affected branches or the entire above-ground portion of the tree if the infection reaches the trunk.

Golden canker on a pagoda dogwood branch.

Those of us who grow pagoda dogwoods should frequently inspect our trees for any sign of golden canker and immediately remove any infected branches. Prune 4 to 6 inches beyond the infected tissue. Between each cut, dip your pruning tool for at least 30 seconds into a solution of 10 percent bleach to avoid accidental spread of the disease. Burn all of the infected branches. There are no fungicides that are effective in controlling this disease.

Nurseries can be breeding grounds for golden canker. If shopping for a pagoda dogwood, carefully inspect the tree you plan to purchase as well as other trees around it in the nursery. Once planted in your garden, inspect the tree frequently for early signs of the canker and prune the infected areas immediately to avoid spread of the fungus spores.

Golden canker is a stress-related disease, and you can avoid or minimize infections by reducing tree stress as much as possible. If you are planting a new pagoda dogwood, choose a cool, shaded site. After planting, mulch the soil to help keep the tree's roots cool and moist. Make sure that the tree receives sufficient water, approximately 1 inch per week from rain or irrigation, particularly during periods of drought. And do not fertilize your tree unless a soil test indicates the need.

Bunchberry *(C. canadensis)*
USDA Hardiness Zones: 2 to 6
Height: 3 to 9 inches
Width: 6 to 12 inches
Sunlight: partial shade
Soil: moist, organic, acidic, well-drained
Flowers: late spring; tiny greenish-yellow flowers in clusters surrounded by four showy, oval, petal-like white bracts
Fruits: clusters of berries ripening to red in late summer, persistent until late fall unless taken by birds
Autumn color: red to purple
Wildlife use: Beetles are major pollinators. The fruits are eaten by migrating songbirds (see list below), resident songbirds, squirrels, and black bears.

Growing only 6 inches high, bunchberry is one of several plants in the mossy ground-cover of temperate and boreal forests. Together with lowbush blueberries, ferns, and other groundcovers, bunchberry helps fill in small niches where the moss languishes, creating a carpet of colors and textures. Like its tree-form relatives, the May-to-June flowers of this dogwood are in tiny white clusters surrounded by four large white bracts, giving the appearance of a single blossom. The fruits, borne in clusters (or bunches, as indicated by the common name), are coral red.

USDA Range Map - *Cornus canadensis*

The flowers of bunchberry are self-sterile and rely on insects to carry pollen from plant to plant. When the pollinator, often a beetle, lands on the central cluster of fertile flowers, pollen is expelled explosively onto its body.

As with all dogwoods, the berries are the draw for wildlife. Black bears feast on the fruits, as do squirrels, hence the alternate common names of bearberry and squirrelberry. Migrating songbirds, including robins, white-throated sparrows, and vireos are the main dispersers of the seeds in fall, dropping them after eating the fruits. Ruffed grouse have also been observed eating the ripe fruits.

Along with many other gardeners, we are lucky to have bunchberry growing wild on our property, including the cultivated garden. It grows most vigorously in partial shade, preferring soils that are moist but well drained and acidic.

Bunchberry grows alongside lowbush blueberries, ferns, and other groundcovers to create a carpet of color and texture on the forest floor.

The self-sterile flowers of bunchberry rely on beetles and other insects for pollination.

Like the tree-form dogwoods, the fruits of bunchberry are the draw for wildlife.

Diervilla (Diervilla)
Diervilla (*D. lonicera*)

USDA Hardiness Zones: 3 to 7

Height: 2 to 3 feet

Width: 2 to 4 feet; freely suckers to form large colonies

Sunlight: full sun to partial shade

Soil: mesic, well-drained; tolerates drought

Flowers: yellow, tubular, resembling flowers of true honeysuckles; late spring to early summer

Fruits: dry woody capsules

Autumn color: shades of yellow to orange, sometimes red

Wildlife use: The flowers are nectar favorites of bumble bees and the snowberry clearwing moth (*Hemaris diffinis*), a bumble bee mimic that also uses *D. lonicera* as a larval host plant.

USDA Range Map - *Diervilla lonicera*

Few other native shrubs are as ornamental, stress tolerant, and ecologically functional as diervilla. Native to much of eastern North America, *Diervilla lonicera* is a subtly beautiful flowering native shrub with a most unfortunate common name, Northern bush honeysuckle. It is not a honeysuckle and should not be confused with the non-native invasive shrubby honeysuckles. Ask for it by scientific name, not by common name.

A small deciduous shrub typically growing to 3 or 4 feet tall (occasionally to 6 feet), diervilla has an upright arching and spreading habit. The new light-green leaves emerge in mid-May, gradually turning to a dark green as the weather warms. If the weather stays cool and wet, the newest summer leaves display a unique pattern of light green and auburn. In autumn, the leaves turn first to yellow, then orange, and finally red. Diervilla is one of our garden's loveliest fall shrubs.

Diervilla's flowers, funnel-shaped bells about a half-inch in length and clustered in the leaf axils, first appear in late June, and blooming continues through July. Pale yellow at first, the flowers slowly turn to orange or purplish red as they mature.

Diervilla makes a magnificent ground-cover, as shown here at the base of two fringe trees (*Chionanthus virginicus*).

A bumble bee forages for nectar and pollen in a diervilla blossom.

They provide steady forage for native pollinators, particularly bumble bees, during a time of the year when few other plants are flowering.

Thriving in either sun or shade, diervilla is extremely drought tolerant and can be used in soils ranging from coarse sands to heavy clays. It is not tolerant of flooding, however, so do not plant it in low areas where snowmelt and early spring rain create seasonal ponds.

We purchased our diervilla plants in one-gallon containers, well-established plants that had already developed rhizomes, and planted them 3 to 4 feet apart on both sides of the steps leading up to the house. After a single growing season, shoots from the underground stems had emerged to fill in the spaces between plants. By the end of the second summer we had what we had envisioned, a continuous thicket of foliage and flower that not only holds the soil together but provides ornamental beauty from May to November. The plant by the driveway that unfortunately gets whacked by the snow plow every winter is quick to recover, new shoots arising from the underground stems.

Hamamelis (Witch Hazels)
Common Witch Hazel (*H. virginiana*)

USDA Hardiness Zones: 3 to 8

Height: 15 to 20 feet

Width: 15 to 20 feet; multi-stemmed understory tree with an open branching habit; can produce suckers to form colonies

Sunlight: full sun to partial shade

Soil: prefers moist, acidic, organic soils; tolerates heavy clay soils

Flowers: stem-hugging clusters of bright yellow flowers, each bearing four crinkly, ribbon-shaped petals; fragrant; October to December, typically after leaf drop but often with fall foliage

Fruits: greenish seed capsules that turn light brown and woody with age

Autumn color: yellow

Wildlife use: Plants are larval hosts for a variety of moth species (see list below). Flowers are pollinated by fungus gnats, small parasitoid wasps, hoverflies, and tachinid flies.

USDA Range Map -
Hamamelis virginiana

In October, while most of our garden approaches dormancy, the common witch hazel is in full bloom. Where a few bright yellow leaves still hold fast to zigzag twigs, the flowers are hidden, but on naked twigs you can easily find the pale greenish gold and slightly fragrant blossoms clustered in threes along the stem where leaves were once attached, each flower bearing four twisted and crinkled ribbon-shaped petals. When temperatures approach freezing, the petals roll into tight curled balls, extending the life of the flower to ensure pollination when the temperature rises.

Common witch hazel can be thought of as a small, multi-trunked tree or a large understory shrub, in either case growing to no more than 20 feet in height. Inconspicuous in the summer garden, it steals the show on blue-sky October mornings as its golden leaves reflect the angled sunlight.

When the temperature approaches freezing, these flowers of common witch hazel will curl into tight balls, protecting the flower against freeze damage.

Common witch hazel's golden autumn foliage steals the show in our October garden.

The flower display begins as the leaves start to turn and continues after they fall; in some years the flowers last until December.

The fruits of witch hazels, fuzzy two-beaked woody capsules, take a full year to ripen before exploding violently, each ejecting two shiny, hard, black seeds more than 30 feet from the parent plant. After expelling their seed, the open capsules remain on the plant for yet another year.

In the wild, not far from our garden, common witch hazel grows beneath the shade of beech and birch trees, keeping company with beaked filbert (*Corylus cornuta*) and an occasional native honeysuckle (*Lonicera canadensis*), and surrounded by colonies of maple-leaf viburnum (*Viburnum acerifolium*). It frequents the drier sites, being intolerant of flooding. In the garden, use it along the edge of the dry woods or at the back of the garden border, placed where the October flowers will invite you to linger in the garden at a time of year when few other flowers beckon.

It is always a treat to come across a previously unknown cultivated variety of a favorite garden plant. Such was the case on an October afternoon at Coastal Maine Botanical

Garden in Boothbay Harbor, Maine, when we ventured for the first time into a small nook off one of the main trails and discovered several well-established common witch hazels with brick-red flowers, each petal with a yellow tip. The label identified the 6-foot-tall shrubs as *Hamamelis virginiana* 'Mohonk Red'. This cultivar was discovered at Mohonk Nature Preserve in New Paltz, New York, and introduced to the garden trade by the Arnold Arboretum. It typically grows to 9 feet tall and wide during the first 10 years, eventually reaching 15 to 20 feet in height.

The brick-red flowers of *Hamamelis virginiana* 'Mohonk Red'

H. virginiana is a larval host for numerous moth species, including many of the tussock moths that frequent our garden and the seldom seen paddled dagger moth (*Acronicta funeralis*) discussed in Chapter 2. And what insect, you might ask, goes about the business of pollination in October? Observed pollinators include fungus gnats, small parasitoid wasps, hoverflies, and tachinid flies.

Ilex (Hollies)
Winterberry (*Ilex verticillata*)

USDA Hardiness Zones: 3 to 9

Height: 6 to 8 feet

Width: 6 to 8 feet; suckers to form thickets

Sunlight: full sun to partial shade

Soil: prefers acidic, moist, organic soils; tolerates poorly drained soils of bogs and swamps

Flowers: inconspicuous, greenish-white

Fruits: bright red berries (quarter-inch diameter); late summer to fall, persistent through winter

Autumn color: insignificant in most years, occasionally turning to a mixture of green and yellow for a brief time

Wildlife use: Bumble bees and solitary bees are the primary pollinators. The berries are eaten by a wide variety of wildlife, including songbirds and small mammals (see list below). Plants serve as larval host for the Henry's elfin butterfly (*Callophrys henrici*).

In late fall, most of the plants in our garden have run their course, leaving seeds lying dormant in the soil, but not all; a few march to a different drummer. The witch hazels amaze us with their flowers in late October, and we look forward to the fruits of winterberry hollies in

USDA Range Map -
Ilex verticillata

the depths of winter. If it has been a good year for fruit set, the red winterberries clustered around leafless gray stems will brighten our garden and local roadsides into early March before the birds and mice finally eat them.

Winterberry fruits generally start to ripen in autumn as the foliage begins to yellow, although in some years the berries will turn red while the leaves are still green, and for a short time the plants resemble evergreen hollies. As winter approaches, the leaves turn brown and drop, leaving behind a feast for birds, including robins, catbirds, mockingbirds, bluebirds, cedar waxwings, woodpeckers, thrashers, thrushes, chickadees, titmice, gamebirds, and crows.

Fortunately for gardeners, birds tend to leave the berries for our visual enjoyment until a midwinter thaw, sometimes even longer. One year the berries remained on the plants in our garden until late March before they were eaten by a flock of cedar waxwings.

Found growing in the wet soils of red maple swamps and on the bare shoulders of granitic outcrops, winterberry holly is at home in most gardens throughout its native range, the entire eastern halves of the U.S and Canada. It copes well with compacted soils and withstands drought. Alkaline soils, however, cause yellowing of the foliage and stunted growth. For best fruiting, winterberry should be planted in full sun.

As with all hollies, winterberry's male and female flowers are borne on separate plants, so in order to have bright red holly berries your garden must have a ratio of one male plant for up to nine female plants. And not just any male cultivar will do, as clones selected

In some years, winterberries turn red while plants are still in leaf, taking on the appearance of evergreen hollies for a brief period in late autumn.

After the leaves drop, the bright red fruits of winterberry holly persist through winter before they are taken by birds and mice.

from different regions of the country have different flowering times. Fortunately, horticulturists have selected cultivar pairs to ensure proper timing of pollination, and an informed nurseryman can advise you on the best male partner for your chosen female cultivar.

Winterberry serves as a larval host for the Henry's elfin butterfly, and its flowers are very popular with native bees and other insects (see sidebar below). Red squirrels, chipmunks, raccoons, and white-footed mice eat winterberry fruits and seeds, as do the foxes that visit our garden, usually at night. Thoreau observed the mice, writing that they "run up the twigs at night and gather this shining fruit, take out the small seeds, and eat their kernels at the entrance to their burrows."

A few years ago the winterberries in our garden were taken early, before the first hard freeze, a mystery that remains unsolved. Crow, squirrel, chipmunk, fox, who knows? We like to believe white-footed mice took them for their seeds, scampering up the branches at night to gather the fruits, storing them near their burrows, perhaps under old tree stumps, for when the snow lies deep over the garden.

Small Holly Flowers Attract a Host of Insect Species

Growing native shrubs such as winterberry holly means being intimately involved with the garden, for much of their beauty is subtle. They are endowed with elusive qualities that we miss unless we look closely, sticking our noses or focusing our eyes in the right place, in the right season. You must look closely to appreciate the tiny flowers of winterberry in spring, watch attentively as small native bees and flies forage for a nectar shared with migrating butterflies, including the painted lady, red admiral, and question mark.

An adult thick-legged hoverfly (*Syritta pipiens*) seeks nourishment from a winterberry flower. The larvae of this species feed on rotting organic matter.

A bald-faced hornet (*Dolichovespula maculata*) sips nectar from a winterberry flower.

An adult flesh fly (*Sarcophaga* sp.), so named because its larvae eat rotting meat, nectars at a winterberry flower.

The white flowers of winterberry holly may be small, less than a quarter inch in diameter, but the pollen and nectar contained in these tiny blossoms are sought after by many species of insects. The photographs here were all taken in the summer of 2015.

A native solitary bee foraging for nectar on winterberry.

Northern crescent butterflies (*Phyciodes cocyta*) forage on winterberry flowers for nectar.

An adult tachinid fly rests on a winterberry leaf after feeding on pollen or nectar.

A thread-waisted wasp, *Ammophila procera*, feeding on winterberry flowers.

Mountain Holly *(I. mucronata)*

Note: *A recent change in the taxonomy of mountain holly from* Nemopanthus mucronatus *to* Ilex mucronata *created a new member of the genus.*

USDA Hardiness Zones: 4 to 8

Height: multi-stemmed shrub growing to at least 12 feet high

Width: broad-spreading to 12 feet or more

Sunlight: full sun to partial shade; does well as an understory shrub

Soil: neutral to acidic soils; often found growing in seasonally flooded areas

Flowers: yellow-green, late spring to early summer

Fruits: bright red berries, each attached to the stem with a long stalk

Autumn color: yellow

Wildlife use: Unlike winterberry holly, mountain holly loses its berries early in the fall when the first wave of migrating songbirds stops over for a night of rest and feasting. By morning, both berries and birds are gone. Frequent songbird consumers include Eastern bluebirds, hermit and wood thrushes, American robins, catbirds, Northern mockingbirds, brown thrashers, cedar waxwings, and white-tailed sparrows. Raccoons and white-footed mice enjoy the fruits and seeds. *I. mucronata* is a larval host plant for the Columbia silkmoth (*Hyalophora columbia*) and the Henry's elfin butterfly (*Callophrys henrici*).

USDA Range Map -
Ilex mucronata

Mountain holly forms large colonies in woodland swamps and in the swales of granite outcrops, keeping company with winterberry holly, yellow birch (*Betula alleghaniensis*), and thickets of alder (*Incana* ssp. *rugosa*). You can see the kinship to winterberry in its greenish-gray bark marked with patches of white and its colonizing habit, but its foliage is strikingly different, the leaves blue-green with purple petioles. The fruit is a distinctive long-stalked velvety red berry.

In cultivation, mountain holly can be naturalized in wet woodland landscapes, where it will form dense colonies. It can also be sited in smaller groupings or even as a single specimen in shady garden spots that offer a cool, moist root zone.

The blue-green foliage of mountain holly is the perfect foil for its bright red, velvet-textured berries. Unlike winterberry holly, the berries of *Ilex mucronata* do not persist into winter but are eaten by migrating songbirds in autumn. Thus mountain holly is an important native food source, ensuring that these birds have sufficient energy to complete their long flights.

Bright red, long-stemmed berries and blue-green leaves with purple petioles are the distinguishing characteristics of mountain holly.

Because *I. mucronata* is a dioecious species, only female plants will bear the ornamental berries. However, you should plant at least one male plant in the landscape to ensure adequate pollination for abundant fruit.

Morella (Bayberry)

Note: *While deemed necessary by systematic botanists, the frequent changes in scientific names of plants are vexing to gardeners. We have always thought of Northern bayberry as* Myrica pensylvanica, *but now must relearn it as a species in the genus* Morella. *It's getting difficult to keep it all straight! There seem to be more such changes than ever before, no doubt a result of new DNA analysis techniques that can reveal close relationships between plants. It is a trend likely to continue for the foreseeable future.*

Northern Bayberry (*M. pensylvanica*)

USDA Hardiness Zones: 3 to 7

Height: 6 to 12 feet

Width: 6 to 12 feet, commonly broader than tall

Sunlight: full sun to part shade

Soil: prefers moist soils, peaty or sandy, pH 5.0 to 6.5; tolerates a wide range of soil moisture and soil types

Flowers: small catkins; not showy

Fruits: small rounded waxy-coated berries on female plants only, gray, in clusters on old wood; particularly showy after leaves drop

Autumn color: insignificant

Wildlife use: The berries are eaten by a wide variety of birds (see list below). Bayberry thickets also provide nesting sites for songbirds, offering excellent protection from raccoons and other nest predators.

USDA Range Map -
Morella pensylvanica

Across its native range, Northern bayberry forms immense colonies in the wild, including coastal regions within the reach of salt spray. In gardens it flourishes in poor sandy soils where few other plants will grow. For sure, it is the native shrub of choice for stressful sites.

In our garden, on a warm July afternoon, we cannot pass by the bayberries without crushing a leaf to savor the spicy scent. This is why we planted them, and for their bold texture and dark green foli-

The dark green foliage of bayberry provided the perfect background for waxy grey berries.

age, and for the waxy, scented berries that cluster along the stems of female plants.

The fruits are an important food for a variety of birds, including yellow-rumpled warblers, chickadees, red-bellied woodpeckers, tree swallows, catbirds, and bluebirds. *M. pensylvanica* is a larval host plant for several moth species, including the Clemen's sphinx moth (*Sphinx luscitiosa*), a species listed as threatened throughout its range, and the beautiful Io moth (*Automeris io*).

In addition to their wildlife value, the berries of bayberry are used to scent candle wax.

Use Bayberry to Harbor Functional Perennials and Shrubs

The following photographs were taken along a winding bayberry-lined drive leading up to the Cape Cod home of Patricia Crow and James Hadley. The bayberry served as a foil for colorful herbaceous perennials and shrubs, all selected for their ability to nourish wildlife.

An informal bayberry hedge forms the perfect foil for butterfly bush (*Buddleia davidii*), shasta daisies (*Leucanthemum x superbum* 'Becky'), and the bold-textured flower clusters of oakleaf hydrangeas (*Hydrangea quercifolia*).

Shasta daisy 'Becky' flowers surrounded by bayberry foliage. The seedheads, left for the birds, enhance the textural beauty of this planting.

A swamp milkweed (*Asclepias incarnata*) cultivar, 'Ice Palace', adds a touch of color to the bayberry hedge while attracting a host of pollinators.

The fruits of American cranberrybush viburnum (*Viburnum opulus* var. *americanum*) add a splash of color to the bayberry hedge.

Rhododendron (Rhododendrons)

Rhodora *(R. canadense)*

USDA Hardiness Zones: 3 to 6

Height: 2 to 4 feet

Width: 2 to 4 feet, commonly broader than tall

Sunlight: sun to part shade

Soil: prefers moist, acidic (pH of 4.5 to 5.5), organic soils; intolerant of soil compaction, deicing salts, and drought

Flowers: terminal clusters of rose-purple flowers that appear before the leaves; April to May

Fruits: dry seed capsules that split open when ripe

Autumn color: insignificant

Wildlife value: Rhodora plays an important part in the life cycle of the bog elfin butterfly (*Callophrys lanoraieensis*), a species that is rare throughout its range and listed as an endangered species in Massachusetts, where it has the status of "Threatened." Bog elfin caterpillars feed exclusively on the needles of black spruce, a conifer that often grows in the same vicinity as rhodora. When the adult butterflies appear, rhodora flowers provide an essential nearby nectar source. Rhodora is the larval host plant for the Columbia silkmoth (*Hyalophora columbia*). The flowers also attract bees, and the seeds are occasionally eaten by songbirds and small mammals.

USDA Range Map -
Rhododendron canadense

Rhodora (*Rhododendron canadense*), a deciduous rhododendron, flowers in late May or early June on leafless stems, the purple flowers often sharing space with last year's orange-brown woody seed pods. After the flowers fade, we enjoy the blue-green summer foliage, particularly as the new rosy-tipped seed pods develop among the leaves. In winter, we look for the persistent seed pods at the branch tips, wanting to find them dusted with new snow.

In the wild, rhodora forms dense colonies of 4-foot-tall shrubs in lowland woods, often in seasonally flooded soils. In the swales between granite outcrops, where moisture is more limited, it grows to only half that height. It belongs in the wild garden, along a woodland path, or pond-side. Or, if you are fortunate enough to garden among granite outcrops, plant it in the swales, the pockets of deeper soil.

Rhodora flowers appear in early spring on leafless stems.

Rhus (Sumacs)
Staghorn Sumac (*R. typhina*)

USDA Hardiness Zones: 3 to 8
Height: 35 to 50 feet
Width: 35 to 50 feet; multi-trunked, spreading into extensive colonies
Sunlight: full sun
Soil: tolerant of any well-drained soil, from coarse sand and gravelly loams to heavy clays
Flowers: upright pyramidal spikes, 6 to 12 inches tall; yellowish-green; summer
Fruits: on female plants, bright red berries in dense terminal spikes
Autumn color: golden yellows, orange, bright red
Wildlife use: Staghorn sumac provides nectar for several butterfly species, including banded (*Satyrium calanus*) and striped (*S. liparops*) hairstreaks. It is also a larval host of the spring azure butterfly (*Celastrina ladon*). The colorful fruits persist into late winter and serve as emergency food for many species, including turkeys, bluebirds, robins, catbirds, and others. The tree colonies also provide nesting and shelter sites for many bird species.

"In summer, Staghorn Sumac lifts its immense panicles of vivid flowers among the great frond-like pinnate leaves, and in autumn the brilliant fruits and most variously brilliant foliage shout out their color to the dying year. Flaunting orange, war-paint vermilion, buttery yellow, or sometimes angry purple may be seen all together on a single tree. More, it commonly happens that half of a compound leaf, or even half of a leaflet, may retain its rich, deep, shining green, in calm contrast to the flaming autumnal hues. And at all times the lower surface of the foliage keeps its pallid, glaucus cast that, when early frost has brushed it, turns silver. Probably no tree in the country, perhaps in the world, may exhibit so many and such contrasting shades and tints, such frosty coolness with its fire."

—Donald Culross Peattie, *A Natural History of Trees of Eastern and Central North America*, 1948

USDA Range Map -
Rhus typhina

If you live and garden east of the Mississippi River, you know staghorn sumac, its common name derived from the fine felt-like hairs on young stems, giving them the texture of a deer's antlers. You know it if only from the window of your car, those roadside colonies of tropical appearance with wine-red pyramidal fruit clusters encircled by long, dark-green, pinnately compound leaves. If you are really observant, you've noticed that some colonies sport these showy fruit clusters while others lack them. Some colonies are female, some are male.

Actually, each colony can be considered a single multi-trunked shrub, each trunk derived from a suckering shoot that likely originated from a single bird-dispersed seed. The shoot that started it all may have long since died, leaving behind a group of suckers that are all the same sex and that, in time, will produce more suckering shoots. And so the colony grows, old stems dying, a multitude of young suckering shoots taking their place.

Throughout its native range, old colonies of staghorn sumac can cover an extensive area. We recall a two-acre hayfield divided in half by a colony of 20-foot-tall fruiting branches, a beautiful sight in August when the colony was fruiting, in October when the leaves were turning, and in winter when the persistent fruits were dusted with snow.

The berries of staghorn sumac, borne in cone-shaped clusters, are covered with fine red hairs.

Staghorn sumac's vegetative growth habit makes it a difficult plant to bring into some gardens. When we recommend its use as both a lovely ornamental and a valuable wildlife plant, we are likely to hear the term "invasive" tossed into the discussion. But no, a native plant, by definition, cannot be considered invasive. Aggressive it is, for sure. In the right place, in the right garden, we call it exuberant.

It comes down to a matter of placement. The suckering habit of staghorn sumac can be controlled by mowing, paving, and water. For example, a colony of fruiting plants growing between a body of water and a paved road, their spread controlled by water on one side, asphalt on the other, is naturally contained within those bounds. Reeser once lived next door to a colony of sumac in a neighbor's backyard, its spread limited by the lawn mower.

All of the plants in this colony of staghorn sumacs are female.

Staghorn sumac's shallow, wide-spreading roots make it ideal for soil stabilization along slopes, streams, or pond-side, wherever its suckering habit can be tolerated or controlled and drainage is good. Because of its tolerance of salt, it is also an excellent plant for seashore and roadside plantings.

The berries of staghorn sumac, small fleshy drupes covered with fine red hairs and borne in cone-shaped clusters, are eaten by ruffed grouse, Eastern phoebe, common crow, Northern mockingbird, gray catbird, American robin, wood thrush, hermit thrush, Eastern bluebird, and over 30 other bird species. Because the fruit persists through the winter, it is an excellent emergency source of food for these creatures.

Staghorn sumac's spring flowers, greenish-yellow and borne in conical clusters, provide nectar for bees and several butterfly species, including banded hairstreak (*Satyrium calanus*) and striped hairstreak (*S. liparops*). It is also a larval host for the luna moth (*Actias luna*) and the spring azure butterfly (*Celastrina ladon*). In late August, its leaves are riddled with the chewing of these caterpillars.

For those who can manage its exuberance, staghorn sumac belongs in the wildlife garden to nourish a host of birds and insects. And it belongs in the ornamental garden, where the gardener can watch it change in texture and color through the seasons.

Rosa (Roses)
Carolina Rose (*R. carolina*), Virginia Rose (*R. virginiana*), Swamp Rose (*R. palustris*)

USDA Hardiness Zones: 4 to 9
Height: 3 to 6 feet
Width: 6 to 12 feet; forms broad colonies
Sunlight: full sun

Soil: mesic, well-drained; tolerant of drought; pH 6.1-8.5

Flowers: deep pink with bright yellow stamens; fragrant; summer

Fruits: bright red hips; ripen in summer, persistent through winter

Autumn color: yellowish to orange and red

Wildlife use: Native rose flowers provide pollen and nectar for flower beetles, solitary bees, and other insects, such as aphids, suck the sap from the leaves and stems, while carpenter bees, sawflies, and some beetle species bore into rose stems.

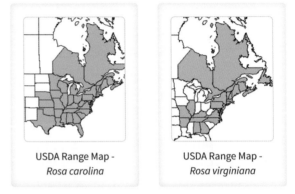

USDA Range Map -
Rosa carolina

USDA Range Map -
Rosa virginiana

In autumn, the hips are eaten by robins, mockingbirds, wild turkeys, bobwhite, cedar waxwings,

USDA Range Map -
Rosa palustris

bluebirds, goldfinches, cardinals, brown thrashers, song sparrows, skunks, and white-footed mice. Plants serve as larval hosts for mourning cloak (*Nymphalis antiopa*) and red-spotted purple (*Limenitis arthemis*) butterflies. Rose thickets provide safe nesting sites for mockingbirds, catbirds, cardinals, thrashers, and yellow warblers, while voles, shrews, squirrels, and foxes use the thickets for cover.

Replace Invasive Rugosa Rose with Native Roses

You will not find rugosa rose (*Rosa rugosa*), often called beach rose, on a list of plants native to North America. Many people believe it to be native and are astonished when they learn that it is an invasive species. And we've heard otherwise sane folks say that the invasion of beach rose is over, that it now occupies every possible coastal site where it can grow, therefore we need not worry over it anymore.

Not true! Over our 20 years in Maine, visits to the island village of Vinal-haven have revealed continuing encroachment of beach rose into the surrounding native landscape. In the open fields bordering the rocky coastline, we see

The foliage and flowers of *Rosa rugosa* distinguish it from native roses.

colonies of the invader expanding, swallowing up space previously occupied by native plants such as Northern bayberry, meadowsweet, sweet fern, and native rose. No doubt this invasion began when seeds from garden plants in the village were dispersed by birds.

Despite its beauty, beach rose should be viewed as a serious threat to the integrity of all coastal plant communities. There are still areas of New England that can be protected from the invader and other areas that can be reclaimed, but only if we stop growing beach rose in our gardens.

Encroachment of *R. rugosa* along the tideline is an all-too-common site along the New England coast.

There are beautiful alternatives to *Rosa rugosa*. Chief among them are three very similar native rose species, *R. carolina, R. virginiana,* and *R. palustris.* The differences among these species have always been obscure to us, a matter of straight versus curved spines and the abundance of hairs on the leaflets. We leave all of this to the taxonomists and lump them together as far as the garden in concerned. All three are native to the eastern U.S.

No, these three native roses are not as fragrant as beach rose, nor as long-flowering, and they have simpler flowers—a single row of deep pink petals surrounding bright yellow stamens—but their autumn displays of burgundy-red foliage and deep red hips are equal to those of *R. rugosa.* And they are far more functional than beach rose, particularly as larval host plants.

The flowers of *R. carolina, R. virginiana,* and *R. palustris* are very similar.

The hips of native roses are eaten by a variety of birds as well as white-footed mice.

Insects such as this hoverfly are attracted to the pollen and nectar of native roses.

Sambucus (Elderberries)

Common Elderberry (*S. nigra* ssp. *canadensis*)

USDA Hardiness Zones: 3 to 9
Height: 6 to 12 feet
Width: 6 to 12 feet
Sunlight: full sun to partial shade
Soil: grows in almost any soil, including coarse sands and gravels, loams, and mucks; prefers medium to wet soils and will do well in rain gardens
Flowers: small white flowers in large flat-topped clusters; summer; fragrant
Fruits: deep purple to black berries on red stems; late summer through early autumn;
Autumn color: not significant
Wildlife use: Flowers of American elder produce little nectar but are visited by pollen-collecting insects. American elder is host to the cecropia or robin moth, North America's largest moth. The fruits are eaten by over 40 bird species including catbirds, yellow-breasted chats, rose-breasted grosbeaks, and all thrushes. Fox squirrels, red squirrels, woodchucks, and white-footed mice also eat the fruits.

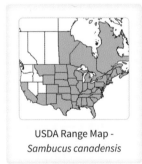

USDA Range Map - *Sambucus canadensis*

The flowers of common elderberry (*Sambucus nigra* ssp. *canadensis*), called "elderblow" by those who turn the flower clusters into fritters, appear in June. Their purple-black berries ripen in the second half of August. White-throated sparrows pluck the berries one at a time, but we cut entire fruiting clusters from the shrubs, take them inside to do the plucking, then fast-freeze them on cookie sheets before packing them in freezer boxes.

All winter we have elderberries for muffins, simply substituting them for blueberries in a favorite recipe. They offer a unique crunchy texture, and they are not as sweet as blueberries. High in antioxidants, elderberries can also be used to make jams, jellies, pies, syrups, and, of course, wine.

Common elderberry is one of the best native shrubs for sustaining a garden's birds. In addition to white-throated sparrow, over 48 other bird species, including chipping and song

Known as "elderblow," the flowers of common elderberry appear in June.

The purple-black elderberries are ready for plucking by birds and gardeners in August.

sparrows, indigo buntings, Northern cardinals, bluebirds, waxwings, thrushes, catbirds, yellow-breasted chats, and rose-breasted grosbeaks, are known to eat the berries as they ripen through the summer. Flycatchers, woodpeckers, wrens, and vireos visit elderberries in bloom to capture insects.

Elderberry flowers are a nectar source for adult butterflies, while the hollow stems provide nesting sites for solitary bee species, including mason bees (*Osmia* spp.) and small carpenter bees (*Ceratina* spp.).

We grow most of our elderberries in a bed that borders the east side of our house. From the overhanging porch we look down into the canopy of large, pinnately compound leaves raising flat-topped clusters of creamy white flowers to the June sky. And in late August we watch the sparrows feast on the fruits. They perch on the slender, pithy canes that bend toward Earth, jumping up to pluck the ripe berries.

Red Elder (*S. racemosa* var. *pubens*)

USDA Hardiness Zones: 3 to 9
Height: 6 to 12 feet
Width: 6 to 12 feet
Sunlight: full sun to light shade
Soil: prefers moist loamy soil, pH 6.1 to 8.5
Flowers: small white flowers in upright conical spikes; early spring
Fruits: clusters of bright red pea-size berries; summer
Autumn color: insignificant
Wildlife use: The fruits are eaten by ruffed grouse and several songbirds, including brown thrashers, catbirds, red-eyed vireos, warbling vireos, thrushes, and white-throated sparrows. Small mammals that eat the fruits include chipmunks, squirrels, white-footed mice, and woodland deer mice. Only pollen is offered as a reward to flower visitors such as flies, beetles, and solitary bees.

What is the true harbinger of spring in your garden, the one plant that defies the cold dampness of early April to open its buds ahead of all the others? In our garden it is a red elder rooted

USDA Range Map - *Sambucus racemosa* var. *pubens*

beneath the back steps leading up to the porch deck. When the seedling first appeared, we discussed transplanting it to a more open spot, but then forgot about it. Over time it has leaned more and more outward until now it grows on thick crooked stems into the light.

By mid-April, this red elder, protected against the damp cold by the nearby warm wall, has unpacked its leaves and flowers, the latter beginning as rounded clusters of tight green buds, a reddish-purple blush over each cluster's upper surface. They look like small heads of broccoli nested within unfolding leaves that are tiny replicates of the large, pinnately compound structures they will soon become.

In mid-May the branches of red elders are weighed down by the cluster of off-white flowers.

Fruits of red elder ripen in summer to the delight of birds, chipmunks, and squirrels.

Several other red elders, planted years ago by mice or birds, encircle the stout trunks of old yellow birches in a moist and sunny site near the house. Marjorie has pruned them into small multi-trunk trees bearing gnarly branches that grow at all angles with the trunks. All winter we enjoy their picturesque architecture.

The red elders will be in full flower by the middle of May, their branches bending nearly to breaking with the heavy clusters of off-white flowers. Insect pollinators of all descriptions are attracted to these flowers, ensuring an abundance of bright red berries in June. (Berries of red elder are toxic to humans—leave them for the birds!)

In our garden, the emerging flower buds of red elder are a welcome signal that the garden season is upon us, time to begin in earnest the gardener's work.

Spiraea (Spireas)
Meadowsweet (*S. alba* var. *latifolia*)

USDA Hardiness Zones: 3 to 7
Height: 3 to 4 feet
Width: 3 to 4 feet
Sunlight: full sun to partial shade

Soil: mesic, well-drained

Flowers: terminal cone-shaped cluster of tiny white to pink flowers; summer

Fruits: dry seed pods

Autumn color: often insignificant; sometimes yellow to bronze

Wildlife use: Plants are hosts for the spring azure butterfly (*Celastrina ladon*). The flowers are foraged by bumble bees and solitary bees. Several types of beneficial predator insects and spiders are also attracted to the plants.

USDA Range Map - *Spiraea alba* var. *latifolia*

A denizen of meadows, pastures, and roadsides through much of the eastern United States, meadowsweet begins to bloom in May and continues flowering through August. Its small soft white or pink flowers, borne in terminal branched clusters, are pollinator magnets throughout the summer. In autumn, the leaves turn to tarnished gold, and in winter the pale brown to red-brown seed heads float shadows on the garden's blanket of snow.

In a comprehensive study of native plants conducted by Michigan State University, meadowsweet was the third most attractive plant to beneficial predator insects and spiders, over four times as effective in attracting predators as a grass control. Beneficials attracted by meadowsweet included both crab and jumping spiders; soldier beetles that eat aphids and other insects; plant bugs that prey on leaf beetles; damselflies that prey on aphids, leafhoppers, mites, and caterpillars; ladybird beetles important in controlling aphid populations; and ichneumonid wasps, parasitic wasps that prey on beetles and caterpillars.

In the same study, meadowsweet attracted moderate numbers of bees, including bumble bees, sweat bees, and andrenid bees.

Meadowsweet's flowers, often pink but occasionally soft white, are pollinator magnets from May to August.

Adult Wood-boring Beetles Forage on Meadowsweet Flowers

Some beetle species in the Family Cerambycidae are commonly known as longhorn beetles for their long antennae (at least half as long as the body). Among this group are several species that are considered beneficial for the work their larvae do in recycling dead and dying trees, particularly conifers such as larch, spruce, pine, and hemlock. These larvae also serve as food for woodpeckers. The adults nourish themselves on the pollen, stamens, and nectar of conspicuous flowers, including those of meadowsweet (*Spiraea alba* var. *latifolia*).

One of the longhorn beetle species found in and around our garden is *Strangalepta abbreviata*. The larvae of this species feed on decaying conifers and hardwoods, while the adults forage on the blossoms of meadowsweet.

Adults of *Evodinus monticola*, another longhorn beetle species that we often see on the meadowsweet in our garden, prefer to lay their eggs on larch, fir, spruce, and pine.

Stictoleptura canadensis, also known as the red-shouldered pine borer, is a longhorn beetle with antennae as long as its body. It feeds as an adult on meadowsweet, laying its eggs in the decaying wood of fir, hemlock and pine.

Steeplebush (*S. tomentosa*)

USDA Hardiness Zones: 3 to 8

Height: 3 to 6 feet

Width: 3 to 6 feet

Sunlight: full sun

Soil: tolerates a wide array of soil types, including loams, fine sands, wet clays, peats, and mucks; pH 5.1 to 6.0

Flowers: erect, steeple-shaped spikes of bright pink flowers (sometimes deep rose or purple); mid-summer through early autumn

Fruits: dry dark-brown capsules; autumn through winter

Autumn color: yellow

Wildlife use: Seeds are eaten by songbirds, gamebirds, waterbirds, and small mammals. The pollen attracts bees, flies, and beetles. Plants are larval hosts for several moth species, including the Columbia silkmoth (*Hyalophora columbia*).

USDA Range Map - *Spiraea tomentosa*

Steeplebush, also known as hardhack by haymakers for its hard, brittle stems, belongs to summer, its terminal spire-like clusters of rosy-pink flowers popping up in roadside ditches and other sites where soils are sterile, acidic, and rocky, wet or dry. Like meadowsweet, the flowers attract a host of pollinators. As the flowers on the central spire are pollinated, flowering side-shoots develop that extend the blooming season into August.

Steeplebush flowers produce an abundance of pollen that attracts bees, flies, and beetles. While nectar production is minimal, butterflies have been observed nectaring on steeplebush; among them is the rare Karner blue (*Lycaeides melissa samuelis*). The caterpillars of several moth species are known to feed on the foliage, including the Columbia silkmoth (*Hyalophora columbia*).

Steeplebush gets its name from the steeple-like spikes of flowers.

Charles Newhall, in his 1893 book *The Shrubs of Northeastern America*, describes steeplebush as "often cultivated for its pretty, steeple-like clusters of late-blooming rosy flowers." It was pushed aside by the twentieth-century infatuation with exotic ornamentals, but perhaps

American gardeners are on the cusp of a reawakening, a renewal of interest in steeplebush and other native shrubs with both ornamental and ecological value.

Symphoricarpos (Snowberry)

Common snowberry (*S. albus*)

USDA Hardiness Zones: 3 to 7

Height: 3 to 6 feet

Width: 3 to 6 feet; plants spread by root suckers to form colonies

Sunlight: full sun to partial shade; best fruit production in full sun

Soil: best in mesic, well-drained soils, but can adapt to a wide range, including poor soils

Flowers: small, bell-shaped, pink, in clusters; summer

Fruits: berries (half inch diameter), pale green ripening to pure white by late summer; remain attractive through winter on naked branches

Autumn color: insignificant

Wildlife use: *S. albus* is a larval host for the Vashti sphinx moth (*Sphinx vashti*), the snowberry clearwing moth (*Hemaris diffinis*), and the beautiful cecropia moth (*Hyalophora cecropia*). Plants are used for food, cover, and nesting by songbirds, gamebirds, and small mammals. Birds that will eat the berries include grouse, pheasants, quails, towhees, thrushes, robins, grosbeaks and waxwings. Bumble bees and hummingbirds feed on the nectar.

USDA Range Map -
Symphoricarpos albus

Snowberry is not common in gardens, perhaps because the pink, bell-shaped flowers are too tiny to be noticed. The blue-green foliage color is attractive, and the white globose berries, each about a half-inch in diameter and packed into tight clusters at the stem tips, remain on the plant until well after the leaves have dropped. Borne at the stem tips, the berries cause their branches to bend toward earth, giving the entire plant a lovely arching habit from late summer into winter. The stems are hollow, providing nesting sites for native bees that build their nests in twigs with excavated piths.

Snowberries remain on the plant until winter before being taken by the birds. (Note the leaf miner trail on the left leaf.)

Vaccinium (Blueberries)

Highbush Blueberry (*V. corymbosum*)

USDA Hardiness Zones: 5 to 8

Height: 6 to 12 feet

Width: 8 to 12 feet

Sunlight: full sun

Soil: well drained, sandy loam, rich in organic matter, with a relatively acid pH range of 4.5 to 5.2

Flowers: pendulous, white, bell-shaped

Fruits: dark blue berries

Autumn color: a mix of reds, oranges, and yellows

Wildlife use: Bumble bees are major pollinators. Songbirds that eat the berries include tufted titmice, red-eyed vireos, robins, bluebirds, scarlet tanagers, towhees, catbirds, mockingbirds, brown thrashers, cardinals, and orioles. Grouse, both ruffed and spruce, also enjoy the fruits, as do small mammals, including white-footed mice, chipmunks, and striped skunks. *V. corymbosum* is also a larval host plant for several butterfly species, including the brown elfin (*Callophrys augustinus*), striped hairstreak (*Satyrium liparops*), spring azure (*Celastrina ladon*), and hummingbird clearwing (*Hemaris thysbe*), as well as at least two moths, the major datana (*Datana major*) and saddleback (*Acharia stimulea*).

USDA Range Map -
Vaccinium corymbosum

In June and July, we go to the garden to watch native bumble bees pollinate highbush blueberry blossoms as they forage for nectar. They are a joy to watch as they forage from first light to last, stopping to rest only in a cold rain, when they seek refuge under a leaf or flower cluster.

On dewy mornings in August, when the branches of the shrubs are bending under the weight of ripe fruit, we walk through wet grass to the garden, each grasping a mug of steaming coffee in one hand, a bowl for berries in the other. Holding a cupped hand beneath a cluster of berries—some further along toward full ripeness than others—and moving our fingers

A bumble bee pollinating a blueberry flower.

over the berries as if tickling the bottom of a child's foot, we coax the ripest berries to break the fragile connections with their slender stalks and fall into our hands, dark purple-black fruits bursting with sweetness.

As if the spring flowers and summer fruits were not enough, highbush blueberry shrubs delight us again in October with their scarlet red and golden-yellow leaves. On close inspection, not every leaf is the same shade of red, and some are barely red at all. Some of the blueberry leaves hang on long enough to be kissed by a late October freeze, their leaves covered with needles of ice.

We've learned to harvest the blueberries as soon as they are fully ripe; otherwise they belong to the garden's wildlife.

In addition to enriching our lives, both nutritionally and aesthetically, and the lives of native bumble bees, highbush blueberries are connected to many other members of the garden food web. In spite of the popularity of highbush blueberries among these other creatures, we manage to harvest enough ripe berries to satisfy our cravings for fresh summer berries while putting up jars of dehydrated berries for winter. We've learned to pick them just as they fully ripen. Leave them longer and they belong to the garden's wildlife.

Highbush blueberry shrubs grace the October garden with their scarlet red and golden-yellow leaves.

Viburnum (Viburnums)
Mapleleaf Viburnum (*V. acerifolium*)

USDA Hardiness Zones: 3 to 8

Height: 3 to 6 feet

Width: 2 to 4 feet

Sunlight: full sun to part shade

Soil: average, medium moisture, well-drained; prefers moist loams, but established shrubs are drought tolerant

Flowers: tiny white blossoms with extruding stamens; spring

Fruits: clusters of oblong blue-black berries; autumn

Autumn color: French rose-pink with purple blotches between the veins

Wildlife use: The flowers attract native bees, hoverflies, wasps, butterflies, skippers, and tiny beetles that crawl from flower to flower, munching pollen. The berries are taken by a variety of songbirds, including white-throated sparrows, cedar waxwings, cardinals, thrushes, flycatchers, grosbeaks, bluebirds, thrashers, robins, and vireos. Wild turkeys, ruffed grouse, and ring-necked pheasants are also fond of the fruits, as are rabbits, mice, skunks, chipmunks, and squirrels. Mapleleaf viburnums are larval host plants for a variety of lepidoptera. The list includes the holly blue butterfly (*Celastrina argiolus*), Henry's elfin butterfly (*Callophrys henrici*), Baltimore checkerspot butterfly (*Euphydryas phaeton*), and 10 moth species.

USDA Range Map -
Viburnum acerifolium

In late August through September, as butterflies sip goldenrod nectar, white-throated sparrows eat the ripened fruits of mapleleaf viburnums growing just off the porch. We consider ourselves lucky to be able to enjoy this native viburnum's spring flowers and unique fall foliage in our garden. Few nurseries grow it, few garden centers sell it. Our plants were salvaged years ago from an experiment conducted by one of Reeser's graduate students at University of Maine. She dug them, with permission, from the wild, replanted them to pots, and kept them in the research nursery until her project was done. We were not about to see them thrown away.

Fifteen years later the maple-leaf viburnums in our garden are thriving, the largest over 5 feet tall. They grow in the shade of a tall pine, nearby birches, and several common elderberries, yet they bloom profusely every year. The species is known for its tolerance of dry soils, enabling it to compete successfully with surrounding plants in the understory.

In May, tight bundles of mapleleaf viburnum's pink buds slowly open into rounded clusters of tiny white flowers.

In May these shrubs grace our garden with tight bundles of pink flower buds that slowly transform into rounded clusters of tiny white blossoms with extruding stamens. These flowers, often not fully open until early June, attract swarms of pollinating insects.

In some years the viburnum berries in our garden seem to be the exclusive property of white-throated sparrows. It is a joy to see these ground-scratching little birds hopping from branch to branch, stretching their necks to reach berries hanging just out of reach. A flock of ten or so sparrows arrives on an appointed day known only to them, and a few days later the viburnum branches are bare. We count it as a good trade, berries for their sweet whistle, *Old-Sam-Peabody-Peabody*, heard even in winter.

Mapleleaf viburnum's autumn leaves are painted with the colors of an October sunrise, French rose-pink with purple blotches between the veins, leaf colors not found in any other plant. At the same time, the slightly flattened oblong berries mature to a glossy blue-black. For a short time in early October, before the fruits are

Mapleleaf viburnum's fruits mature when the leaves are at their peak of fall color.

taken by the birds, this combination of colors is one of the highlights of our autumn garden.

The tall foliage of *Viburnum acerifolium* is unique among garden shrubs.

Two Exceptionally Functional Non-native Trees

When you decide to add a new understory tree to your garden—a functional tree that serves as a larval host plant for moths and butterflies, provides pollen and nectar for beneficial insects, or produces fruits for birds and other wildlife—most of the trees you might choose would be regionally native species, trees that have evolved relationships with wildlife species in your region of the country. But there are exceptions. For example, other than *Malus angustifolia* (Southern crabapple), a species native to the southeastern coastal plain of the U.S., any crabapple you choose to grow would be non-native yet highly functional, supporting scores of insects including pollinators and lepidopteran larvae, as

Crabapple fruits, such as these apples on the variety 'Donald Wyman', are relished by grosbeaks and other songbirds.

Metallic-green sweat bees are fond of crabapple nectar, including that of *Malus sargentii*.

This unknown species of hoverfly, a wasp mimic, is common on the flowers of the *Malus sargentii* in our garden.

well as producing fruits relished by many species of birds. Insects that we have observed foraging on the flowers of our Sargent crabapple (*Malus sargentii*), a species native to Japan, include hoverflies and metallic-green sweat bees.

Another non-native but highly functional plant you might grow is the red-vein enkianthus, *Enkianthus campanulatus*, a small multi-stemmed tree native to Japan and growing to no more than 15 feet in height. It is a member of the Ericaceae, the family to which blueberries belong, and its flowers are much like those of blueberry, bell-shaped and pendulous. Bumble bees, honeybees, and native solitary bees are the primary pollinators of these flowers, but from late May into June you may see several other insects, including butterflies and flower longhorn beetles, feeding on the nectar in enkianthus blossoms.

The bell-shaped pendulous flowers of red-vein enkianthus attract bumble bees, butterflies, and other pollinators.

Evodinus monticola, a species of flower longhorn beetle, forages on the blossoms of red-vein enkianthus.

A halictid bee, or sweat bee, forages for nectar on *Enkianthus campanulatus*.

An Eastern tiger swallowtail, *Papilio glaucus,* sips nectar from flowers high in the top of an enkianthus tree.

Choosing Functional Understory Trees and Shrubs for Your Garden

Alexander Pope, eighteenth-century poet, fervent gardener, and advisor to landscape designers, counseled his contemporaries to "consult the genius of the place in all" when creating gardens. If Pope were around today, counseling us about ecologically functional gardens, he would advise us to choose plant species that are locally native, including trees and shrubs that have co-evolved with local wildlife. He would suggest that we explore local woods, fields, stream banks, and pond edges, learning what grows where, assessing the height and width of each tree and shrub species at maturity, discerning which species favor sunny spots and which prefer dappled shade, which prefer wet areas and which like a dry root run, and observing the time of year each species flowers and fruits. Our objective in this chapter is to help you do just that.

Still, questions remain. How many plants of each species should you plant in a given area? How many species? Pope would say that the answers to these questions, too, can be found by consulting the genius of the place. Take a walk in the woods and fields, stroll along the edges of streams and ponds, note how each tree and shrub grows. Understory trees, such as mountain maple and pagoda dogwood, are typically widely spaced, while many shrub species, such as mapleleaf viburnums, form colonies. This makes sense once you know that each mapleleaf viburnum produces new shoots from underground stems, a process that leads to colony formation.

There are few native shrub species that do not spread into colonies over time. When you add a single native rose plant to your garden, know that over time it will expand several feet in all directions. The same can be said for alders (*Alnus* spp.), chokeberry (*Aronia* spp.), summersweet clethra (*Clethra alnifolia*), sweetfern (*Comptonia peregrina*), diervilla (*Diervilla lonicera*), Northern bayberry (*Morella pensylvanica*), staghorn sumac (*Rhus typhina*), and elderberry (*Sambucus canadensis*). Allow for this increase in colony size as you plan your garden.

We have planted only one pagoda dogwood in our garden, which seems right based on our observations of the species in the wild. Seedlings are widely spaced, perhaps one or two per acre, due perhaps to the dispersal of seeds over long distances by birds. There is no survival advantage in several seedlings competing with their parent tree for water and nutrients.

Rather than plant more pagoda dogwoods, we planted two other native understory tree species, serviceberry (*Amelanchier* spp.) and mountain maple (*Acer spicatum*). These two species mature their fruits much earlier in the year than pagoda dogwood, thus providing the garden's birds and small mammals with an earlier source of food.

Fifteen years ago, Marjorie decided to convert the lawn surrounding the front of her single-story office building into a native plant teaching garden, an outdoor classroom that would give Master Gardener Volunteer students and visitors an example of a landscape devoted to wildlife. The first year was devoted to eliminating the lawn, followed in the second year by construction of a small stone-paved courtyard in one half of the area, a

Once a broad expanse of lawn, this area is now a showplace for native plants, a model for the landscape of the future.

spot where classes and other groups could gather. The remaining space, approximately 900 square feet, was then planted to a wide variety of native shrubs and understory trees, leaving room for several herbaceous perennial species.

Every plant species chosen for this garden, woody and herbaceous, was chosen primarily for its ability to nurture insects, songbirds, and the humans who choose to spend time there. Many of the chosen species have something to offer in each season, including spring flowers that provide pollen and nectar, fruits that ripen in summer or fall, beautiful autumn foliage, and winter interest of branching habit or dried seed heads.

A focal point along the edge of the courtyard section is a pagoda dogwood. Other woody plants in this area include summersweet clethra, chokeberry, steeplebush, and meadowsweet. On the opposite side of a paved walk leading to the front door, a large elderberry (*Sambucus canadensis*) towers over plantings of highbush blueberry, bayberry, sweetfern, native roses, and winterberry holly.

This garden serves as an example of what can be accomplished when a homeowner decides to convert her landscape from a monoculture of turf grass to a diverse collection of functional plants, including understory trees and shrubs. Created in the middle of an urban setting, this garden is both functional and beautiful.

Gardening for wildlife has become a passion for some people. Throughout the U.S., lawns are being eliminated or reduced to a small fraction of their former expanse, replaced by landscapes of native trees, shrubs, grasses, and forbs. Nurseries and garden centers are slowly increasing their offerings of native plant species as they grudgingly give in to demands that they stop selling non-native invasive species. Still, some of the understory tree and shrub species described in this chapter are difficult to find locally.

Mapleleaf viburnum, for example, is a beautiful and highly functional native shrub that cannot be found in our local market. However, there are several online nurseries that do sell *Viburnum acerifolium;* always search for a plant by its scientific name to make sure you get what you want. Thank goodness for this surge in online plant nurseries.

To put an end to the loss of insect and other wildlife diversity caused by habitat destruction in our country, we need to pick up the pace of converting 40 million acres of lawn to functional habitat for insects, birds, and all other forms of life that can coexist with us. It is time to abandon monocultures of turf grass around our homes, businesses, schools, and churches, replacing them with functional landscapes, the bones of which must be locally native trees and shrubs.

Tachinid Fly
(*Belvosia borealis*)

Chapter 9

Functional Herbaceous Perennials

When the discussion turns to herbaceous perennials, one gardener's treasure is another's weed. Dandelions serve as an example. We delight in their early spring emergence, greeting them as essential forage for emerging bumble bee queens intent on establishing new colonies and for solitary bees that have just emerged from hibernation. Convincing other homeowners to leave the lawn mower in the garage until dandelions finish flowering can be a hard sell, but more and more gardeners are joining us every spring.

Or consider gooseneck loosestrife (*Lysimachia clethroides*), an aggressive perennial that spreads by rhizomes to form large colonies and thus is often missing from many borders and beds. In late July we make daily visits to our ever-spreading colony of gooseneck loosestrife to watch a dozen insect species crawl across small white flowers borne in slender, arching, tapered racemes. The digging and dividing necessary to keep the colony within bounds seems well worth it. (Do not confuse gooseneck loosestrife with the invasive weed called purple loosestrife, *Lythrum salicaria*.)

Among our various perennial plantings is a border that surrounds the vegetable and small fruits garden. It was created over the course of a summer, long days spent lifting boulders and rotting roots from the thin layer of soil that covered granite ledge, then digging in several inches of composted goat manure wherever possible. The width of this border varies in its 150-foot-run from two to four feet. In places the ledge erupts in boulders too heavy to move, and in other spots the thick roots and stumps of fallen pines and spruce lie exposed, slowly decomposing. Among the perennials in this border, planted to sustain pollinators through summer and into autumn, are New England asters (*Symphyotrichum* spp.), Queen Anne's lace (*Daucus carota*), swamp milkweed (*Asclepias incarnata*), goldenrods (*Solidago* spp.), and several cultivars of purple coneflower (*Echinacea* spp.).

We are partial to *functional* herbaceous perennials, growing those that attract pollinators and other insects, creating plantings that sustain garden life from the first emerging bumble bees in late April until the last hoverflies of late September. In this chapter we discuss the herbaceous perennial species that we have found to be the most functional.

The following discussion of recommended herbaceous perennials is based on hours spent observing and photographing the plants in our garden and the creatures that depend on them for food. The plant species are presented in three groups based on flowering period: early blooming, mid-season blooming, and late blooming. Many of our observations on functionality were confirmed by observations of the same plant species in other gardens, particularly a local native plant collection installed and managed by University of Maine Cooperative Extension Master Gardener Volunteers.

Functionality was documented by camera. Insects and arachnids (spiders and their kin) were photographed foraging for nectar and/or pollen or lying in wait for their prey, and in many cases it was possible to identify an arthropod to the species level. In some cases, however, after hours spent trying to identify the species of a new insect or harvestman, we had to settle for a less specific identification.

Most of the perennials we highlight below do best under standard garden culture, which includes:

- full sun to part shade, depending on species,

- well-drained soil,

- adequate moisture (one inch of water every 7 to 10 days),

- slightly acidic soil (pH 6.0 to 6.5)

- soil containing 5 to 10 percent organic matter.

We achieve the latter requirement with annual late-autumn topdressings of composted goat manure, about 2 inches deep, taking care not to cover the plant crowns.

For each of the perennials listed, we share our insights on characteristics, growth habit, and culture as well as our observations of insects seen foraging on the flowers. Thus the focus shifts from the beauty of a mass planting to the functionality of a single blossom; from nature as an aggregate entity to a natural world composed of distinct beings; from life as a random and chaotic unfolding to the extraordinary particularity of every living creature in the garden.

EARLY-SEASON FLOWERING PERENNIALS
Mountain Bluet (*Centaurea montana*)

USDA Hardiness Zones: 3 to 7
Height: 1 to 2 feet
Width: 9 to 18 inches
Sunlight: full sun
Flower Color: cornflower blue
Bloom Period: early summer
Arthropods Observed: wasps, bumble bees, hobomok skippers, solitary bees

Centaurea montana is a self-sowing perennial, its seedlings popping up here and there in the garden. We like it for its clump-forming habit and ease of division. Once the season of bloom has passed, the soft-textured foliage holds its own throughout the rest of the summer.

During the second week in June, bumble bees, including the orange-belted bumble bee, and several species of solitary bee are common visitors to our mountain bluets. Among the solitary bee species, the plasterer bee (*Colletes inaequalis*) can be recognized by the vivid white stripes on its abdomen. This species is one of the ground-nesting bees, constructing individual brood cells in underground nests and lining these cells with

The blue spidery flowers of mountain bluets open from attractive buds in late spring to midsummer.

a polyester secretion (hence the alternate common name "polyester bee").

Warmed by the early spring sun, male polyester bees emerge first from their subterranean winter nest, soon followed by the females. Mating occurs on the ground or in the air, after

Orange-belted bumble bees are frequent foragers on mountain bluets.

which the females take on the tasks of nest construction and egg laying. The males, their tasks complete, finish out their short lives foraging in the garden.

The main artery of the new nest is a foot-and-a-half-deep tunnel as wide as a pencil, dug straight down into the ground. As many as 100 such nests, each constructed by a solitary female bee, can be found in a single square meter of sandy soil. Each egg is laid in a pocket, or brood cell, dug into the side of a tunnel. The female digs out a new brood cell every night, lining the cell with polyester secreted from her abdomen, spreading it on the cell wall with her paintbrush-shaped tongue. A still unknown substance, perhaps in the bee's saliva, reacts with the polyester to form a flexible waterproof plastic that resembles cellophane.

During the day, the female forages as far as a mile from her nest, collecting pollen and nectar from a variety of flowering plants and packing it into the cell built the night before. She lays a single egg in the brood cell, suspending it on the side of the cell over the food, then seals the walls of the cell with polyester before plugging the entrance with soil, packing it down with the tip of her abdomen. The egg will hatch within the brood cell, and the resulting larva

A polyester bee, *Colletes inaequalis*, nectaring on mountain bluet blossoms.

will consume the food before pupating. Eventually the adult bee will emerge from the pupal casing only to spend much of its solitary life within the brood cell, waiting for spring.

Among solitary bee species, the life cycle of *Colletes inaequalis* is the norm. Approximately 90 percent of Earth's bee species are solitary, and 70 percent of them nest underground. And while each bee spends most of its life in solitude, hundreds may emerge from underground nests in a relatively small area.

As you might imagine, the underground nests of solitary bees are often unwittingly disturbed by gardening activities. To compensate, there are a few ways the gardener can nurture these important pollinators. Leave small undisturbed patches of well-drained, bare or sparsely vegetated ground in which solitary bees can construct their nests. Avoid overhead irrigation during daylight hours to minimize disturbance of nest entrances while female bees are foraging. Use drip irrigation to minimize damage to nest entrances. And minimize the use of weed barrier fabric, thick turf, and heavy mulch, all of which reduce the area available for underground nests.

Catmint (*Nepeta* x *faassenii*)

USDA Hardiness Zones: 3 to 8
Height: 8 to 24 inches, depending on cultivar
Width: 12 to 36 inches, depending on cultivar
Sunlight: full sun to partial shade
Flower Color: various shades of blue, or white, depending on cultivar
Bloom Period: spring through fall with some variation among cultivars
Arthropods Observed: bumble bees, butterflies, harvestmen

Nepeta is a genus of about 250 species, none native to North America and most appearing similar with respect to foliage and flower. Most species have aromatic foliage, which Marjorie describes as both minty and spicy. In addition, there are numerous cultivars for many of the species.

One of our favorite garden spots is the perennial bed in the heart of our garden. In a corner of this bed, where the deep-purple flower spikes of catmint (*Nepeta* sp.) meet and mingle with the chartreuse flowers of lady's mantle (*Alchemilla mollis*), bumble bees dance from dawn to dusk throughout July, the tall, slender catmint spikes swaying back and forth

The light blue flowers of 'Walker's Low', a cultivar of *Nepeta x faassenii*.

Bumble bees swarm over the catmint from dawn to dusk throughout July.

under the weight of these tireless pollinators. Often in early morning we find a bumble bee asleep, or so it seems, having spent the night on a catmint flower, too tired to carry its heavy load of pollen back to the nest. It awakens while we watch, warmed by a shaft of sunlight, and resumes foraging.

Nepeta thrives in lean, dry soils with little care. We fertilize ours with topdressings of compost or aged manure in late fall, taking care not to cover the plants themselves. During the growing season, as the flowers age and their stems start to fall over, lying on the ground with the fading flower spikes still pointing upward, new growth begins to emerge from the center of the plant. We cut back the aging, flopping stems to stimulate this new growth, often resulting in a second late-season bloom.

Marjorie has planted various nepetas throughout the garden, and early in the season, before the bloom, she loves to run her hands through their soft foliage, then bury her face in her hands to experience the irresistible aroma.

A red admiral butterfly nectaring on catmint.

Flowering stems can be cut and brought indoors to enjoy the foliage aroma in floral arrangements. Just be sure you don't shortchange the bees.

An Eastern tiger swallowtail nectaring on catmint.

Butterflies, including red admirals, Atlantis fritillaries, and Eastern tiger swallowtails, are also frequent visitors to the catmint patch. Adult red admirals (*Vanessa atalanta*) appear in our garden each June, having migrated north from winter hibernation in southern areas, primarily south Texas and Florida. Come October, most offspring of the spring migrants will head south, although a few start too late or fail to migrate entirely and become stranded too far north with little chance of surviving the winter.

Dandelion (*Taraxacum officinale*)

USDA Hardiness Zones: 5 to 9
Height: 1.5 to 2 feet
Width: 1 foot
Sunlight: full sun to partial shade
Flower Color: yellow
Bloom Period: early spring
Arthropods Observed: crab spiders, solitary bees, bumble bees, hoverflies, butterflies

Red admiral butterflies that arrive in our garden in early spring depend on dandelions for nectar.

In the first two weeks of May, dandelions are the only plants blooming in our garden, and they get all of our attention. We creep around the garden, camera on tripod, trying to avoid casting a shadow that will cause a bee, red admiral butterfly, or hoverfly to dart away. These pollinators depend on dandelions for the pollen and nectar they need to start egg laying, and they are the most common visitors to dandelions.

But you never know! Spend enough time going from flower to flower, and the unusual will turn up. Like a female goldenrod crab spider, *Misumena vatia*,

Many pollinators, like this bumble bee, rely on dandelions as an early source of energy for establishing a new colony.

in search of a meal. (The common name reflects this predaceous crab spider's preference for goldenrod plants as hunting ground.)

Aptly named for her short, wide, flattened body, *M. vatia* has "laterigrade leg orientation"—meaning that her legs are rotated at the base, allowing her to walk sideways like a crab. Crab spiders are common in the garden, but often missed because they spend much of their time motionless with the front pair of legs, each with two claws, spread wide apart, ready to snatch an unsuspecting fly, butterfly, grasshopper, or bee.

Hoverflies like this one (possibly *Copestylum* sp.) also depend on the early pollen and nectar of dandelions.

To further tip the odds in her favor, a *M. vatia* female, especially a young one, can change her color to yellow or white, matching the color of the flower on which she is hunting. This color change is not instantaneous, but rather can take up to 20 days, thus explaining why the *M. vatia* in the photograph is white, rather than dandelion yellow. In spite of her lack of camouflage, she was able to capture an unsuspecting honeybee.

Extremely patient, the motionless crab spider waits for its prey to pass, quickly grasping it with her front legs and immediately injecting it with venom using her small fangs. The venom immobilizes the prey and allows the spider to hold it until she has sucked out all of its bodily fluids.

Crab spiders in the garden eat pollinators, mostly bees, as well as grasshoppers, lacewings, and other insects. I've seen a crab spider take down a bumble bee twice her size, and skipper butterflies present no problem for the spider's fast-acting venom. There is little cause for concern on the part of the gardener, however, since the number of pollinators in the garden is orders of magnitude larger than that of crab spiders. What eats crab spiders? The list includes wasps, ants, other spiders, birds, lizards, and shrews.

Go in search of crab spiders in your garden. Check out all flowers that are yellow or white, as these seem to be preferred. Look closely, remembering that these spiders can change color to provide camouflage. Once

A goldenrod crab spider, *Misumena vatia*, and her captured prey, a honeybee.

you find one, go back to the same flower several times over the course of a few days. You might be surprised, as we have been, at the patience of these garden predators, at how long they will remain in the same flower, waiting for a meal.

MID-SEASON FLOWERING PERENNIALS
Yarrow (*Achillea* x 'Coronation Gold'; common yarrow hybrid)

USDA Hardiness Zones: 3 to 8
Height: 2.5 to 3 feet
Width: 1.5 to 2 feet
Sunlight: full sun
Flower Color: mustard yellow
Bloom Period: summer
Arthropods Observed: Thread-waisted wasps, butterflies, hoverflies, diurnal moths, solitary bees

In addition to its ability to attract a wide variety of insects, 'Coronation Gold' shines in our summer garden as an outstanding garden plant. Its fragrant bluish-gray foliage, different from all the other greens, adds a soft look, while its stiff flower stalks provide staying power. We grow 'Coronation Gold' together with a dark blue Siberian iris for a magical combination of

Achillea x 'Coronation Gold', along with Berry the Cat, in the perennial bed.

color and texture. 'Coronation Gold' also makes a great cut flower, but we like to leave most of the inflorescences in place for the textural interest they add to the winter garden.

Gardeners with perennial beds bordered by lawn grass tell us that dense clumps of achillea foliage inhibit easy removal of grass seedlings, another good reason to get rid of that lawn and plant more perennials!

'Coronation Gold' is host to several insect species over the course of its long summer bloom in our garden.

Ammophila procera, a sand wasp, foraging for pollen and nectar on a flower cluster of *Achillea* x 'Coronation Gold'.

A polyester bee, *Colletes inaequalis*, foraging on *Achillea* x 'Coronation Gold'.

A Northern crescent butterfly, *Phyciodes cocyta*.

The larvae of this small hoverfly (possibly *Episyrphus* sp.) prey on garden aphids.

Astilbe (*Astilbe* x *arendsii*)

USDA Hardiness Zones: 3 to 8
Height: generally 1.5 to 4 feet, but highly variable among cultivars
Width: generally 8 to 12 inches, but highly variable among cultivars
Sunlight: part shade to full shade
Flower Color: Depending on species and cultivar, flower colors include reds, violets, pinks, and white
Bloom Period: summer
Arthropods Observed: harvestmen, flower longhorn beetles, diurnal moths, wasps, butterflies

To anyone who is new to gardening and has yet to explore the virtues of astilbes, we recommend them. Part of the fun will be browsing through catalogs, deciding which of the many astilbe varieties to grow first. For example, there is the Vision series, a group of low-growing Chinese astilbes (*Astilbe chinensis*) with lacy foliage topped by dense upright plumes of lavender, red, or white flowers. They range from 12 to 18 inches in height. Many *A. chinensis* varieties flower later in the garden than other astilbe species. And there is the Gloria series (*Astilbe* x *arendsii*), red and white varieties that have exceptionally nice foliage after the flowers fade.

Astilbe 'Peaches and Cream' is an *A. x arendsii* hybrid.

Astilbes are easy to grow, will tolerate a lot of shade, and are relatively herbivore free—deer and slugs leave them alone. They will tolerate thin, acidic soils as long as you water them frequently in hot, dry weather; otherwise their foliage is likely to burn. A summer compost mulch helps retain soil water.

Divide astilbes when they grow too large, and add more compost to the beds each spring. The latter can be accomplished with annual mulching, using compost or aged manure. Some experts advise that you also rework the astilbe bed every three years, digging up the plants in early spring, adding plenty of compost, then replanting the astilbes after dividing those that need it.

Astilbes will bloom in the shade, but they need some direct sunlight to achieve full size.

Astilbes grow well in the dappled shade of tall trees.

Dappled shade that allows each plant a sufficient measure of full sun is perfect. Removing faded flower stalks will not prolong bloom but may improve plant appearance, particularly if a ground cover look is desired. On the other hand, by early September, the dried brown seed heads give the garden a beautiful autumnal look.

Of all the visitors to our garden's astilbes, a small wasp proved to be the most difficult to identify. After many hours of research, Reeser finally decided it had to be a potter wasp, in the same family as the yellow jacket and bald-faced hornet (Vespidae) but smaller and less likely to sting. Potter wasps, also known as mason wasps, are in the subfamily Eumeninae, the most diverse subfamily of vespids with over 200 genera and a vast majority of the species.

Some potter wasp species build mud nests from a mixture of soil and regurgitated water, while others prefer chewed leaves. These nests resemble a small pot turned on a potter's wheel and can be found suspended from a leaf or stem. Other species, often called mason wasps, are happy with a little of the special mud plastered on the outside wall of a building. Still others construct their nests inside hollow stems, while many species are happy to move into an old abandoned nest of any construction.

All potter wasps are predators, capturing beetle larvae and caterpillars to feed their larvae and thus reducing the populations of these herbivores in the garden. The female wasp paralyzes each victim before placing it in a cell of the nest to serve as food for a larva. She lays a single egg in the cell before provisioning it.

A potter wasp, possibly *Ancistrocerus catskill*, foraging on astilbe flowers.
Adult potter wasps feed on floral nectar and thus function as incidental pollinators.

Tickseed (*Coreopsis verticillata* 'Moonbeam'; threadleaf coreopsis)

USDA Hardiness Zones: 3 to 9
Height: 1.5 to 2.0 feet
Width: 1.5 to 2.0 feet
Sunlight: full sun
Flower Color: creamy yellow
Bloom Period: summer
Arthropods Observed: thread-waisted wasps, butterflies, hoverflies, bumble bees, solitary bees

The genus *Coreopsis* provides a good example of differences in growth habit among cultivars. In our experience, the cultivar 'Moonbeam', a sterile cultivar with soft yellow flowers, is non-aggressive and self-containing with a mounded form. It does not spread in the garden like the dark-gold-flowered 'Zagreb', which forms an impenetrable mat of viscously spreading rhizomes. The species, *Coreopsis verticillata*, is also a perennial garden bully.

A transverse hoverfly, *Eristalis transversa*, foraging on threadleaf coreopsis.

Since 'Moonbeam' is a sterile cultivar, does it attract pollinators? The marketers of this cultivar would have you believe that it is an excellent pollinator plant, yet one research study ranked it considerably lower than the species and several other cultivars. And so there may be good reason to grow 'Moonbeam' in the perennial bed or border, leaving the species and cultivars like 'Zagreb' for the wild and wooly insectary.

Insects visiting *C. verticillata* 'Zagreb' in our garden include the thread-waisted wasp, *Ammophila procera*, the transverse hoverfly (*Eristalis transversa*), Northern crescent butterfly (*Phyciodes cocyta*), cellophane bees (*Colletes* sp.) and bumble bees.

Globe Thistle (*Echinops ritro*)

USDA Hardiness Zones: 3 to 8
Height: 3 to 4 feet
Width: 2 to 2.5 feet
Sunlight: full sun
Flower Color: blue
Bloom Period: mid to late summer
Arthropods Observed: flower longhorn beetles, bumble bees

Despite its common name, *E. ritro* is not a true thistle, although it is thistle-like with a coarse-textured habit, steel-blue, globe-shaped flowers, and large, dark green, deeply cut leaves that are white tomentose beneath. The basal leaves are 6 to 8 inches long and often senesce as the season progresses. The stem leaves grow shorter. Anything but a delicate plant, its coarse foliage takes up a lot of space, and many gardeners prefer to place globe thistles at the back of a garden border.

Echinops ritro, shown here growing with purple coneflower, *Echinacea purpurea*

A flower longhorn beetle, *Evodinus monticola*, one of several species found foraging on globe thistle flowers.

The plants have a taproot that often breaks when disturbed, so do not attempt to move established plants. Globe thistles do best when planted in lean, well-drained soils.

Several species of flower longhorn beetles are ubiquitous in our garden throughout the growing season, frequent visitors to many plant species in flower, including globe thistles. The adults have a voracious appetite for pollen, nectar, and stamen tissue, and they can devastate the flowers they visit with their feeding, defecation, and copulation. They seem to go about all three of these activities with unbridled enthusiasm, often simultaneously.

Flower longhorn beetles belong to the insect family Cerambycidae. The common name refers to their love of flowers and to their long antennae, which are longer than the rest of the body in some species. They are among the most colorful of garden insects and often resemble wasps both in flight and color patterns.

Should we consider these beetles to be important pollinators of garden plants? Pollen is certainly moved around, both within a single flower and among flowers, and in the frenzy of activity there must be some transfer of pollen from stamen to pistil. While in many cases, such as native roses, the petals, stamens, and pistil are decimated by beetle feeding, the ovary wall is tough enough to avoid destruction, and thus seeds do mature. We should consider flower longhorn beetles to be "incidental pollinators" of many plants.

The larvae of many flower longhorn beetles are wood-boring, feeding on decaying wood or the fungi that grow

Orange-belted bumble bees foraging around the globe.

on decaying wood. Dead standing trees and downed logs in the garden provide habitat for these beetle larvae as well as the woodpeckers and other birds that feed on the larvae. Also, native bee species, including mason bees, carpenter bees, and leafcutter bees, nest in the abandoned wood burrows made by beetle larvae.

Bee Balm (*Monarda fistulosa;* wild bergamot)

USDA Hardiness Zones: 3 to 9
Height: 2 to 4 feet
Width: 2 to 3 feet
Sunlight: full sun to part shade
Flower Color: pink or lavender
Bloom Period: summer
Arthropods Observed: butterflies, bumble bees

Monarda fistulosa 'Claire Grace'.

A member of the mint family, wild bergamot spreads by shallow rhizomes, clumps of which are easily divided in the spring. This plant does best in gardens with good soil drainage, plenty of sun and air circulation. Its fragrant foliage is often used for tea.

The butterflies that visit wild bergamot in our garden include a still unidentified skipper, Northern crescent butterflies (*Phyciodes cocyta*), and Atlantis fritillaries (*Speyeria atlantis*). The latter is an excellent example of how maddening identification can be, of long hours spent studying photographs and reading detailed descriptions, and of permanent uncertainty. There are three very similar fritillaries found in Maine that differ in minutiae of morphology: the great spangled fritillary, the Atlantis fritillary, and the Aphrodite fritillary. We made our decision and will stand by it unless an expert sets us straight.

Adult fritillaries appear in our garden in July and August. In addition to wild bergamot, we've seen them feeding on purple coneflower (*Echinacea purpurea*), goldenrod (*Solidago* spp.), swamp milkweed (*Asclepias incarnata*), and gooseneck loosestrife (*Lysimachia clethroides*). The female lays single honey-yellow eggs on leaf litter in the vicinity of violets, the larval

An Atlantis fritillary (*Speyeria atlantis*) foraging on wild bergamot.

host plants, which are abundant in our garden. After hatching, the caterpillars feed on the violets and overwinter in the leaf litter. After emergence in spring, they continue to feed for about 50 days before pupating.

Goldenrod (*Solidago ulmifolia;* elm-leaved goldenrod)
"The sun has shown on the earth, and the goldenrod is his fruit." —Henry David Thoreau, 1853
USDA Hardiness Zones: 3 to 8
Height: 1 to 3 feet
Width: 1 to 3 feet
Sunlight: full sun to part shade
Flower Color: yellow
Bloom Period: July to October
Arthropods Observed: butterflies, bumble bees

In our experience, goldenrods planted in the garden tend to get floppy and need staking. A pair of crisscrossed bamboo stakes does the trick. Their growth habit and color combine well with robust perennials such as Joe-pye weed (*Eutrochium maculatum*) and the red or burgundy shades of sneezeweed (*Helenium autumnale*).

There are over 100 species of goldenrod, and most are native to North America, each being unique in size, leaf shape, and the form in which it displays its golden flowers in late

Queen Anne's lace (*Daucus carota*) flowering with goldenrod in the insectary.

A native aster (*Symphyotrichum* sp.) growing with goldenrod in the insectary.

summer and early autumn. In addition, a surge of interest among gardeners has resulted in cultivated forms (cultivars) of some species. Learning to identify each species in any region of the country would be an ambitious undertaking, and at the moment we are more interested in the ecological role of goldenrods in gardens.

A sand wasp, *Eremnophila aureonotata*, nectaring on goldenrod. Also called a thread-waisted wasp, this is the only species in its genus north of Mexico. When not nectaring on garden flowers, the adults hunt caterpillars of moths and skipper butterflies, dragging their prey back to an underground nest, usually constructed in sandy soils, to feed their larvae.

The ecologically functional garden is defined by which plants the gardener allows to grow and which are weeded out. Simply allowing goldenrod and its native companions to flourish in a wild corner or border, an area you could call your "insectary," will provide late-season nectar and pollen for numerous species of native pollinators. In our garden, meadowsweet (*Spiraea alba* var. *latifolia*, a shrub discussed in Chapter 8) and early goldenrods flower together along the drive in early August. The soft pink of meadowsweet's small flowers, borne in terminal branched clusters, is a pleasing contrast to goldenrod's bold bright yellow. Meanwhile, a clump of another goldenrod species is coming into bloom in the shade of a tall pine next to the porch. We planted none of these, but it is a joy to walk among them, watching pollinators and insect predators at work.

Or you can plant goldenrods in the perennial border, combining them with native asters, Queen Anne's lace, and other native perennials. There are few cultivated herbaceous perennials more ornamental or more durable than goldenrod.

Goldenrod pollen is dispersed by pollinating insects, including solitary bees, bumble bees, butterflies, diurnal moths, wasps, and flower beetles. Even spiders have been shown to move goldenrod pollen around as they prey on insects. For gardeners interested in bolstering pollinator populations in their gardens, goldenrods are hard to beat. Their late-season nectar and protein-rich pollen attract pollinators in higher numbers than any other plant species.

LATE-SEASON FLOWERING PERENNIALS
Milkweed (*Asclepias incarnata;* swamp milkweed)

USDA Hardiness Zones: 3 to 6
Height: 4 to 5 feet
Width: 2 to 3 feet
Sunlight: full sun
Flower Color: pink or mauve
Bloom Period: summer
Arthropods Observed: monarch and other butterflies, milkweed tussock moths, wasps, honeybees, bumble bees

Unlike the rhizomatous common milkweed (*A. syriaca*), swamp milkweed is a clump-forming, self-contained milkweed that stays put. It has a deep taproot and is best left undisturbed once established. Commonly found in swamps and wet meadows, it grows well both in seasonally flooded sites and average garden soils.

Be patient in spring, as swamp milkweed is slow to get started. We mark the location of each of our plants with a stake, just to make sure we don't accidentally plant something else there.

Milkweed seeds are meant to float on the wind, and it is a delight to find an occasional seedling in the garden. Marjorie transplants each of these seedlings to a place where she wants it to mature.

As a boy growing up in Georgia, Reeser learned quickly to avoid vespid wasps. The painful stings of yellow jackets rushing from their underground nest when disturbed by the lawn

Swamp milkweed (foreground), *Asclepias incarnata*, is equally at home in wet areas, such as this rain garden, and in well-drained soils.

mower, the swollen lips caused by the sting of a single yellow jacket hiding in a soda can, and the jolting repeated stings of bald-faced hornets that could knock you to the ground, all were vivid reminders to give any insect belonging to the Family Vespidae a wide berth.

These memories of past encounters with yellow jackets (*Vespula maculifrons*) and bald-faced hornets (*Dolichovespula maculata*) come rushing back every July when scores of these wasps find our garden's milkweeds in flower. We keep our distance and watch foraging butterflies, bees, and longhorn beetles join the wasps in a feeding frenzy, scrambling over the blossoms, bumping into one another as they feed. At present the record for simultaneous foraging on one cluster of flowers is five yellow jackets, two honeybees, a fritillary butterfly,

A yellow jacket, *Vespula maculifrons*, foraging on flowers of swamp milkweed, *Asclepias incarnata*.

A bald-faced hornet, *Dolichovespula maculata*, feeding on a flower of swamp milkweed.

and a pair of longhorn beetles engaged in mating while they fed. The butterfly, perched on the dome of the flower head, was the only creature nectaring in the same spot for any length of time.

Where do all these wasps come from? Where do they spend the night? What do they eat besides nectar? A yellow jacket colony containing hundreds of wasps would be underground, perhaps in an old rodent burrow or the cavity left by a rotting root—we have plenty of both around the garden. Papery in appearance and often ball-shaped, the nest is constructed from small amounts of leaf, root and dead stem fibers, and cocoon silk from pupating caterpillars. These materials are chewed into a pulp to construct multiple layers of brood cells that resemble the honeybee's comb. The nest size increases from spring through autumn. The overwintering queen starts the nest's construction, and worker females add more layers of cells as the colony grows.

Bald-faced hornets build their nests in shrubs and trees that are at least 3 feet off the ground, or sometimes on the outsides of buildings. Their nest is the familiar football-shaped, gray, papery structure. In early spring the fertile queen, having overwintered in a hollow tree, rock pile, under bark, or within the wall of a building, begins the task of nest construction by collecting cellulose from rotting wood. She chews the wood, mixing it with her saliva, then uses the resulting paste to make a papery material for nest construction. The beginning nest consists of just a few cells in which she lays the first batch of eggs. She feeds the larvae when they hatch, raising the first brood of adult wasps who take over the duties of expanding the nest, collecting food, feeding the larvae, and protecting the nest. By the middle of summer, the typical nest will have walls two inches thick, well insulated from heat and cold, and contain between 100 and 400 workers.

Vespid wasps are predators, feeding on flies, caterpillars, beetles, and other insects. Bald-faced hornets will even prey on yellow jackets. In summer yellow jackets and hornets also forage for nectar and feed on the pulp of over-ripe fruits.

Wasp nests are preyed upon by raccoons, which are regular visitors to the unfenced portions of our garden, and by fox and skunks if a nest is low enough to reach. These predators rip open the nest in fall, when the hornets are not as active, and eat the adults, pupae, and larvae. Other possible predators include birds, spiders, frogs, and mantids.

We have adopted a mutual tolerance pact with both wasp species. We've learned that they will be in the garden mainly in mid to late summer, when they need to shift their diet from animal protein to carbohydrates. We look for them rather than being caught by surprise, and are careful not to disturb their foraging for nectar. When they are around, we can approach them without disturbing their foraging, although it's certain that they know we are near. Most important, we value them for their control of many garden herbivores. It has been estimated that at least 2 pounds of insects, including caterpillars, fall webworms, aphids, and whiteflies, are captured by vespid wasps each year from a 2,000-square-foot garden.

Insect Diversity in the Milkweed Patch

During July, before monarch butterflies arrive to lay their eggs on milkweed leaves, the swamp milkweed flowers in our garden are the domain of a wide variety of insect species. Joining the yellow jackets and bald-faced hornets discussed above are the following species, each a nectar feeder, with one notable exception.

A dun skipper butterfly (*Euphyes vestris*) joins a honeybee on a cluster of swamp milkweed blossoms.

Ignoring the feeding frenzy around it, this fritillary butterfly, likely an Aphrodite fritillary (*Speyeria aphrodite*), sips nectar at a leisurely pace.

White admiral butterflies (*Limenitis arthemis*), frequent visitors to the milkweed patch, have wingspans that nearly cover a flower cluster. Notice the bee approaching from below.

Several species of bumble bee (*Bombus* spp.) are drawn to the flowers of swamp milkweed plants.

(continued on page 176)

(continued from page 175)

A ladybird beetle, *Harmonia axyridis*, joins the fray, but not for nectar. This beetle, introduced from Asia to control herbivores such as aphids and whiteflies, has become common in North American gardens.

Flower longhorn beetles, like this banded longhorn beetle (*Typocerus velutinus*), wreak havoc on the flower clusters, eating petals, stamens, and pollen.

The hummingbird clearwing moth, *Hemaris thysbe*, is seldom seen in our garden except when the swamp milkweed is in bloom.

Banded hairstreak butterflies, *Satyrium calanus*, nectar on the flowers of swamp milkweed. Larval hosts for this butterfly include oak, hickory, walnut, and butternuts. The caterpillars eat both the catkins and the foliage of these trees.

Coneflower (*Echinacea purpurea*; purple coneflower)

USDA Hardiness Zones: 3 to 8
Height: 2 to 5 feet
Width: 1.5 to 2 feet
Sunlight: full sun to part shade
Flower Color: The species has purplish-pink ray flowers. Cultivar ray flower colors within the species or hybrids include rose-purple ('Powwow Wild Berry' and 'Magnus'), orange-red ('Sombrero Salsa Red'), lemon-yellow ('Cleopatra'), and pale citron ('Sunrise')
Bloom Period: summer
Arthropods Observed: butterflies, flower longhorn beetles, bumble bees

One of the easiest perennials to grow, *E. purpurea* will grow in most well-drained garden soils and freely self-sows to produce an abundance of seedlings for transplanting throughout the garden. Growing best in full sun, it has a long blooming season. Long after the ray petals finally turn brown and shrivel, the dark brown central cone persists into winter, providing seeds for goldfinches. During the growing season, the foliage always looks great.

Purple coneflower is a magnet for pollinators, including butterflies, beetles, and bumble bees.

An interplanting of purple coneflower with the silver foliage of an artemisia makes for a striking combination.

Purple coneflower is a partner in many outstanding garden combinations. Growing it with swamp milkweed results in a sea of pink (see photograph in earlier discussion of swamp milkweed), while the delicate pink petals of coneflowers provides a striking contrast to the steel-blue flowers of globe thistle (see photograph in earlier discussion of globe thistle).

The dun skipper, *Euphyes vestris*, is a common butterfly in our area, a moth-like butterfly with a preference for nectaring on white, pink, or purple flowers. We see them in our garden when the purple coneflowers are in bloom, but it is likely they were first drawn to our garden by the presence of native sedges, their larval host plants.

In our region of the country *E. vestris* has only one brood between June and August, the female laying single eggs on the leaves of host plants. Farther south there may be two broods between May and September, and in the deep south three or more broods between March and October. Larvae from the last brood of the season overwinter encased in a leafy home made by binding together sedge leaves with silk.

The common name of "skipper" refers to their quick, darting flight habit. Indeed, it is difficult to follow one across the garden, waiting for it to come to rest on a flower. There are over 3,500 species worldwide, all with features common to the group: bodies stockier than other butterflies, large compound eyes, hooked antennae, and wings that are small in proportion to the body compared with other butterflies. Most are drab brown to gray. In general they resemble moths more than other butterflies.

A dun skipper, *Euphyes vestris,* sips nectar from flowers of purple coneflower, *Echinacea purpurea*, as a banded longhorn beetle (*Typocerus velutinus*) forages nearby.

Loosestrife (*Lysimachia clethroides;* gooseneck loosestrife)

USDA Hardiness Zones: 3 to 8
Height: 2 to 3 feet
Width: 2 to 4 feet
Sunlight: full sun to part shade
Flower Color: white
Bloom Period: summer
Arthropods Observed: wasps, bumble bees, butterflies, hoverflies, flower longhorn beetles, solitary bees

L. clethroides is often described as an "invasive" plant. Not so! An invasive plant is a non-native plant that successfully competes with native plants for resources such as water and nutrients and displaces native plants in relatively undisturbed habitats. There is no scientific evidence that gooseneck lysimachia fits this description. Quoting The New York Non-Native Invasive Species Assessment (Cornell University, 2016), "Despite anecdotal reports, there is no good evidence that the species is escaping and persisting from cultivation."

Gooseneck lysimachia is an exuberant colonizing herbaceous perennial. Give it plenty of room!

L. clethroides spreads rapidly in the garden by means of rhizomes. It should be described as aggressive, and for this reason many gardeners choose not to plant it. We love it for its unique summer flowers and the insects they attract. Why not grow it in a remote area of the border where it can be allowed to naturalize in drifts without encroaching on less vigorous perennials? Another option is to let it fill the bed along the side of the garage or shed.

One late July afternoon, we spent a half-hour in front of our small colony of *L. clethroides*, camera in hand, trying to photograph each insect as it landed

Two Atlantis fritillaries (*Speyeria atlantis*) and a flower longhorn beetle (*Strangalepta abbreviata*) forage on flowers of *Lysimachia clethroides.*

An orange-belted bumble bee, *Bombus ternarius*, sipping nectar from *Lysimachia clethroides* flowers.

on one of the gooseneck-shaped inflorescences to feed on pollen or nectar. The end result was a list of 10 insect species, including Atlantis fritillaries (*Speyeria atlantis*), two species of bumble bee (*Bombus ternarius* and an unidentified species), an unidentified hoverfly spe-

cies, three species of flower longhorn beetles (*Judolia cordifera*, *Strangalepta abbreviata*, and *Typocerus velutinus*), a metallic-green halictid bee (probably *Augochloropsis metallica*), an unidentified species of black wasp, and a tachinid fly species, probably in the genus *Tachina*.

A metallic-green halictid bee nectaring on *Lysimachia clethroides*.

With the exceptions of New England aster and swamp milkweed, no other herbaceous perennial species in our garden comes close to attracting this diversity of insect species. This begs the question, why is non-native *L. clethroides*, a plant introduced to this country from China and Japan, so effective in attracting such a large diversity of native insects, all foraging on its pollen, nectar, or both? It is doubtful that the answer lies in the composition of the nectar, as these mixtures of sugar and water are similar among most plant species, typically about 55 percent sucrose, 24 percent glucose, and 21 percent fructose. However, there are major differences in the amount of nectar per blossom of various plant species. Flower shape is another trait that is likely to influence the diversity of visiting insects. The attraction of *L. clethroides* to such a diverse group of insects may be due to the relatively large amount of nectar in each of its flow-

A tachinid fly, possibly *Tachina* sp., foraging on *Lysimachia clethroides*.

ers; a flower size and shape that accommodates long-tongued insects, such as butterflies and bumble bees, and short-tongued sweat bees; and an abundance of pollen for flower longhorn beetles and other pollen eaters.

New England Aster (*Symphyotrichum novae-angliae*)

USDA Hardiness Zones: 4 to 8
Height: 3 to 6 feet
Width: 2 to 3 feet
Sunlight: full sun
Flower Color: Ray flowers vary from light pink to bright pink ('September Ruby'), dark purple ('Purple Dome'), and mauve to soft lavender blue ('Dragon'); disk flowers yellow
Bloom Period: summer to early autumn
Arthropods Observed: bumble bees, honeybees, hoverflies, ichneumon wasps, solitary bees

New England asters demand good air circulation to minimize the impact of a fungal disease on the lower leaves. When the lower leaves do senesce, remove them to keep the disease from spreading, much like you do with tomatoes. To keep the aster stems erect, we prop up each plant with crisscrossed bamboo stakes.

In September, fall asters bloom in our garden, in a nearby wild insectary where they keep company with goldenrods, and along the lane that leads from the highway to our driveway.

'September Ruby' is one of several *Symphyotrichum novae-angliae* cultivars that we have added to the garden in recent years. They are all pollinator magnets!

Among the asters in the garden proper are cultivated forms of the New England aster as well as transplants from the lane. Late in the garden year, they are among the few plant species in full bloom, primary sources of pollen and nectar for a wide variety of insects, includ-

This monarch butterfly, just emerged from its chrysalis in late September, was eager to sip the nectar of 'September Ruby'.

ing orange-belted bumble bees (*Bombus ternarius*) and other bumble bee species, monarch butterflies (*Danaus plexippus*), honeybees (*Apis* spp.), solitary bees, transverse hoverflies (*Eristalis transversa*), winter fireflies (*Ellychnia corrusca*; a form of beetle in the firefly group that uses chemical signals rather than light to attract a mate), and the ichneumon wasp species briefly mentioned in Chapter 7.

Entering "black ichneumon wasp with orange legs and long ovipositor" in an Internet search engine led to a dozen possible genera, each with numerous species. We were prepared for a tedious search, since Ichneumonidae, the family of parasitoid wasps, is the largest family within the animal kingdom, estimated to contain 100,000 species worldwide and 3,000 species in North America. In fact, there are more ichneumon wasp species on Earth than all vertebrates combined. Identification to the level of species or even genus proved impossible. After looking at hundreds of photos, we gave up, but not before learning quite a bit about this unusual garden visitor.

The term "ichneumon" comes from the Greek word for "tracker" or "footprint," representing the female wasp's task of tracking down various insect host species to feed her larvae. Depending on the species, the host may be a beetle grub; butterfly or moth caterpillar; ant, bee or wasp larva; lacewing larva; or fly maggot. Our garden visitor was one of the ichneumon species that prey on beetle larvae burrowing beneath the bark of trees, as indicated by an ovipositor twice as long as her body. The female uses this ovipositor to drill through the bark and, once a beetle larva is located, to inject an egg into its body. When the egg hatches, the ichneumon larva becomes an internal parasite of the beetle larva, slowly eating its host and finally consuming its vital organs just prior to pupating.

What was this female ichneumon doing on a garden aster? She was likely eating pollen and/or nectar, sources of energy for drilling into wood and laying eggs.

As a group, ichneumon wasps play a large role in controlling populations of herbivores such as tomato hornworms, boll weevils, wood borers, codling moths, and asparagus beetles. Gardeners, therefore, should welcome ichneumon wasps.

This unidentified ichneumon wasp takes a break from the hunt to rest on a garden aster.

Ichneumon wasps also contributed to Charles Darwin's personal resolution of conflict between the tenants of his faith and his theory of evolution. In a letter to botanist Asa Gray, written in 1860, Darwin wrote: "*I cannot persuade myself that a beneficent & omnipotent God would have designedly created the Ichneumonidae with the express intention of their feeding within the living bodies of caterpillars.*"

Meadow Rue (*Thalictrum aquilegifolium*)
USDA Hardiness Zones: 5 to 8
Height: 2 to 3 feet
Width: 2 to 3 feet
Sunlight: full sun
Flower Color: pink, lilac-purple, white
Bloom Period: summer
Arthropods Observed: honeybees, flower longhorn beetles, tachinid flies, wasps, hoverflies, flies

The lilac-purple flowers of *Thalictrum aquilegifolium* are visited each summer by a variety of pollinators, including honeybees, flower longhorn beetles, tachinid flies, wasps, and hoverflies.

Ask Marjorie why she grows this species of *Thalictrum* and she will say for its blue-green, columbine-like foliage. Ask Reeser and he will speak about the variety of insects that forage on the flowers.

Our garden is surrounded by a forest in slow transition from mostly conifers to hardwoods. Those spruce trees that have died yet remain standing have become a hunting ground for woodpeckers that eat the insect larvae in decaying wood, including perhaps the larvae of hoverflies in the genus *Temnostoma*. It is in the forest that these hoverflies live, mate, and lay eggs in the rotting wood of trees that have been dead for at least seven to eight years. To sustain themselves, the adult syrphids visit the flowers of garden plants.

It was on the flowers of *T. aquilegifolium* that we met our first *Temnostoma*. Though still trying to determine the species, Reeser is almost certain that it is *T. balyras,* one of a group of hoverflies that are convincing wasp mimics. With markings very similar to those of a wasp, these adult hoverflies avoid predation by birds and other predators.

Insect visitors to the flowers of *T. aquilegifolium* leave covered with pollen, particularly those covered with hairs like this hoverfly (*Temnostoma* sp.).

A honeybee on the petals of meadow rue.

Choosing Functional Perennials for Your Garden

In the functional garden, the primary role of herbaceous perennial beds and borders is to nourish insects of all types, to provide pollen and nectar for bees, wasps, butterflies, hoverflies, tachinid flies, and all other insects that pollinate plants or prey on herbivores; and yes, to nourish caterpillars, aphids, and other herbivores. The garden's beds and borders should be swarming with insects. When a gardener tends her perennial garden with this objective in mind, she is also nourishing birds, rodents, amphibians, and reptiles—every member of the garden food web. She is sustained by the beauty and functionality of perennial plantings.

Marjorie plans and plants our herbaceous beds and borders, making certain that there will be functional plants in flower throughout the growing season. The perennial species included in this chapter are species that we grow and consider to be exceptionally functional; when in bloom, their flowers are constantly attended by a variety of insects. These perennials grow alongside many other species that are far less functional but irresistible as ornamental plants.

When we add a new perennial species to the garden, one that has grabbed our attention at a friend's garden or nursery, we may have no idea of how functional it might be, but its worth as a garden plant increases when we discover it is popular with the insect crowd. This is part of the joy of herbaceous perennial gardening, adding a plant for its beauty, then discovering that the insects like it too!

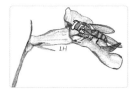

Hoverfly (*Toxomerus sp.*)

Chapter 10

Functional Annuals

"Unless someone like you cares a whole awful lot, nothing is going to get better. It's not."
—Dr. Seuss, *The Lorax*

In-ground space is always at a premium in our garden, particularly for sun-loving annuals. When all of the sunny beds are filled with plants, we turn to containers. In a typical summer there are twenty or more pots scattered about the garden. In October, as we put all the pots away for the winter, we pledge that never again will we lug the watering can about the garden on hot July afternoons. But every May the pots come out of storage and are scattered across a patch of grass to be scrubbed clean for the new season. And every year they seem to multiply, their numbers increased by Christmas gifts and such. Container gardening has become a madness without a cure.

In the winter of 2013–2014, as we made plans for the coming garden season, we decided to focus our container madness more on plants that attract and nourish garden life. We made use of porch steps, tree stumps, and rocks, all suitable perches for pots filled with annual plants that attract bees, wasps, butterflies, moths, hoverflies, harvestmen, and spiders. We also decided to make room for functional annuals in our perennial beds and vegetable garden.

Type "annual plants that attract pollinators" in a search engine and you are quickly overwhelmed with lists of dozens of species. To keep our project manageable, we narrowed the list to annuals listed among the top ten choices by university cooperative extension sources across the country.

We decided to grow twelve species, seven of which we discovered to be exceptionally functional. These seven annuals, all hardy in USDA Zones 2 through 11, are discussed below.

By no means are we suggesting that these are the only functional annuals. Rather, we want to demonstrate that annual plants, whether in containers or in beds, can be very effective in nurturing pollinators and other beneficial insects throughout the garden year, including times when little else is in flower.

When your goal is to attract beneficial insects, it is important to avoid use of annual plant species with multiple layers of petals and few, if any, pollen-bearing stamens, the "double" or "semi-double" varieties. Also, plant breeders have developed varieties of some annuals, most notably some sunflowers, that do not produce pollen. These varieties are intended for use in the florist trade, not the pollinator-friendly garden.

Pot Marigold (*Calendula officinalis*)

Height: 1 to 2 feet
Width: 1 to 2 feet
Sunlight: full sun
Flower Color: bright yellow to deep orange
Bloom Period: spring to late summer
Propagation: Start seeds indoors 6 to 8 weeks before last spring frost date or sow directly in the garden just before the last spring frost.
Arthropods Observed: solitary bees, bumble bees

Calendula 'Costa Mix' (foreground) with
Delphinium 'Dwarf Blue Butterfly'

In our garden, calendulas are the province of solitary bees. We take delight in seeing this self-sowing annual growing in drifts and patches along the edges of our vegetable garden beds, their orange and yellow flowers serving as magnets for the tiny bees. We transplant seedlings that germinate in the middle of a bed to empty spots along the bed edges. Every few years, when volunteer

A solitary bee foraging on calendula.

Self-sown calendulas growing in drifts
and patches in the vegetable garden.

seedlings seem to be sparse, we scatter a few seeds on the sides of the beds, but in most years there are more than enough volunteers popping up everywhere.

The same bees that forage on calendulas also pollinate cucumbers, squash, and melons. Calendulas keep these valuable pollinators close at hand.

Harvest Calendula Flowers for the Medicine Cabinet and Dinner Table

The small bright orange petals of calendula make a colorful addition to summer salads.

Calendula flowers can be steeped in olive oil to make a healing oil for use on minor cuts and abrasions. Harvest the flowers after the morning dew has evaporated, and place them on a tray for a day to lose their moisture. Pack them into a mason jar, cover the flowers with extra virgin olive oil, and cap the jar tightly. Place it in a sunny spot for at least two weeks, shaking it gently

(continued on page 190)

(continued from page 189)

every day. Strain the flowers out through a jelly strainer until all plant material is removed from the oil. You can use the oil directly or make it into a salve by adding melted beeswax to the oil (a quarter cup beeswax per cup of herbal oil).

The ray petals of calendula flowers make a colorful addition to summer salads. Also known as Poor Man's Saffron, the tiny petals have a subtle flavor ranging from bitter to spicy.

Bachelor's Buttons (*Centaurea cyanus;* annual bachelor's buttons)

Height: 1 to 3 feet

Width: 1 to 2 feet

Sunlight: full sun

Flower Color: blue, pink, white

Bloom Period: spring through summer

Propagation: Sow seeds indoors 6 to 8 weeks before last spring frost. Plants may self-sow in the garden

Arthropods Observed: bumble bees, thread-waisted wasp and other wasps, hoverflies, solitary bees, leafcutter bees

Note: *Annual bachelor's buttons is considered an aggressive weed in the Southeast and one state, North Carolina, has banned its use.*

Annual bachelor's buttons at the garden gate with the pink flowers of perennial sweet pea (*Lathyrus latifolius*) in the background.

Annual bachelor's buttons have been one of the most functional annuals in our garden. We grow our own transplants from seed, planting them in large patches once any chance of frost has passed. To prevent them from toppling in high winds, we either stake each stem or surround an entire bed of plants with 2-foot-high lattice. Sturdily propped and with periodic deadheading, they bloom all summer.

This annual did not perform well in containers. The plants had thin wispy stems, falling over under their own weight, and flowers were sparse compared to in-ground plants.

A leafcutter bee foraging on annual bachelor's buttons.

Most of the insects that forage on bachelor's buttons have been presented in depth elsewhere in this book, the exception being leafcutter bees in the genus *Megachile*. A foraging female resembles a bumble bee at first glance, but a closer look at the underside of her hairy abdomen will reveal that it is loaded with pollen, giving it a distinct yellow color.

Megachile is a complex genus composed of several subgenera with 242 species in North America. Many of these species are similar in appearance, and we do not attempt to identify the ones that visited our bachelor's buttons to the level of species. Within the same family, the Megachillidae, are species in the better-known genus *Osmia*, bees that readily accept the native bee nest boxes that many gardeners put out in early spring. In fact, some species of *Megachile* will also nest in these boxes, while other species prefer nesting in hollow plant stems or in the beetle tunnels of decaying wood. Still other *Megachile* bees nest in the shells of dead snails or the holes in concrete walls.

The same leafcutter bee, foraging on the flower of native sweet pea, reveals the pollen on her hairy abdomen.

Adults are the overwintering stage in the genus *Megachile*. Males and females emerge together in spring, mate, and the males soon die. The female selects a suitable nest site, typically a cavity about the diameter of a pencil that will house several egg chambers, and begins foraging for nectar and pollen. She mixes these two substances together, along with some of her saliva, which contains both antibacterial and fungicidal properties, to form a "bee loaf."

It takes many foraging trips for the female bee to form a loaf big enough to feed one grub from egg hatching to maturity. After visiting many flowers, she lays one egg on top of the loaf, then seals the small chamber with chewed-up leaves. She continues this process to fill the entire nest cavity, then builds a final thicker wall. Shortly after completion of her nest cavity, the female dies.

To seal off each nest chamber and the cap for the nest cavity, the female *Megachile* bee may rely on ornamental plants such as roses, azaleas, ash, redbud, and other smooth-leaved plants for the necessary leaf material, cutting circular pieces out of the edges of selected leaves. We have a redbud (*Cercis canadensis*) in our garden and are always pleased to discover the quarter-size holes created by this foraging, reminders of the presence of leafcutter bees in our garden.

Cosmos (*Cosmos bipinnatus*)

Height: 1 to 4 feet
Width: 2 to 3 feet
Sunlight: full sun
Flower Color: ray flowers red, shades of pink, or white; center disc flowers yellow
Bloom Period: summer to frost
Propagation: Sow seeds indoors 6 to 8 weeks before last spring frost. Sow in the garden just before last frost date.
Arthropods Observed: Northern crescent butterfly, crab spider, native bees, bumble bees

Give *Cosmos bipinnatus* plenty of space, planting the transplants 3 feet apart. Tree-like in habit, they develop thick horizontal branches and need good air circulation to grow to their full potential. The plants can be very sturdy, but benefit from staking in windy sites.

While we consider it well worth the effort, growing *C. bipinnatus* is not without its problems. For example, occasional wilting of flower stalks can occur before the flower buds open, possibly from a bacterial infection. We've also noticed that the foliage at the base may turn brown. When either of these problems arise, we remove the affected portions of the plant, placing them in the trash rather than the compost pile to prevent the problem from

A patch of *Cosmos bipinnatus* in the garden. We planted these, but *C. bipinnatus* will self-sow in the garden.

spreading. Also, pulling the plants up at the end of the season takes some muscle, as the root system is extensive. The entire plant can then be chopped up with a machete before adding it to the compost pile.

Every summer our garden is host to crescent butterflies. They come into the garden to nectar on whatever is in bloom, including the cosmos, and rely on the garden asters as host plants for their larvae. Each female butterfly lays a cluster of eggs, usually about 40, on the underside of an aster leaf. The larvae feed on aster leaves and hibernate through winter.

Are these crescent butterflies *Phyciodes cocyta*, the Northern crescent butterfly, or its look-alike, *Phyciodes tharos*, the pearl crescent butterfly? Our garden is within the overlapping ranges for both species, and we have been unable to say for sure. The more we read about these two species, the more confused we get, for the descriptions vary from one authority to the next, and the photographs for each species seem identical. We found peace with this dilemma in a quote from Robert Michael Pyle's book *The Butterflies of Cascadia*: "In naming the species after Cocytus, The River of Lamentation in the Underworld [one of the five rivers that encircle Hades], Cramer [eighteenth-century Dutch entomologist Pieter Cramer] seems to anticipate the woe in store for future students of crescentspot taxonomy." Woe indeed.

A Northern crescent butterfly (*Phyciodes cocyta*, maybe) nectaring on cosmos.

Sunflower (*Helianthus annuus;* annual sunflower)

Height: 3 to 10 feet
Width: 1.5 to 3 feet
Sunlight: full sun
Flower Color: Ray flowers are yellow, red, mahogany, or bicolor; center disc flowers are brown to purple
Bloom Period: summer
Propagation: Can be sown indoors, in pots, 2 to 3 weeks before last spring frost; best sown in the garden after the last frost
Arthropods Observed: harvestmen, bumble bees, solitary bees, maggot fly

Tall sunflowers blooming at the back of the garden.

Every summer, tall sunflowers bloom at the back of our garden, and we delight in watching bumble bees and solitary bees forage for pollen on the large discs. One mid-July afternoon, taking a break from turning the compost pile, Reeser happened to notice a colorful small fly crawling on the underside of a sunflower leaf. No more than a quarter-inch in length with a wing span of about one inch, it had a yellow body and wings with dark strips that formed an "F" shape toward the wing tip. Inspecting other leaves on the same plant, he discovered a few more of the exotic flies, creatures that we had never seen before.

Whenever a new species appears in the garden, we ask the same questions: What is it and what is it doing? This new fly turned out to be the sunflower maggot fly, *Strauzia longipennis,* a fly whose tiny larvae, called maggots, feed on the spongy tissue of the stem pith and on flower tissue. Depending on the number of larvae, injury to the pith ranges from minor to complete destruction, while the effect on seed production is minor. The maggots, tailless and only 5 mm (a fifth of an inch) long, feed for about a month before pupating through winter in the soil.

A sunflower maggot fly, *Strauzia longipennis,* on the underside of a sunflower leaf.

Sunflowers may bring the longhorn bee, named for its extremely long antennae, into your garden.

We can only guess how *S. longipennis* fits into the garden's food web. We know that it feeds on sunflower plants, but what might swoop down and grab the unsuspecting fly from the bottom of a leaf or stumble upon a pupa asleep in the soil?

We do know that we are spending more time looking under leaves.

In addition to bees, sunflowers also attract butterflies like this red admiral.

In October, when it is time to ready the vegetable garden for winter, we cut the sunflower heads from their tall stalks and hang them from the fence posts for the goldfinches.

Life in the Cilantro Bed

Allowed to flower in the sunny garden, the annual herb cilantro (*Coriandrum sativum*), also called coriander, is a magnet for several pollinators and nectar seekers. Many small insects, including tiny hoverflies, swarm over the tiny white flowers, spending more time in the air than on the plants, while larger flies, wasps, and beetles crawl among the blossoms. The following six species were among these visitors to our garden.

The American hoverfly, *Eupeodes americanus*, is one of the smallest syrphid flies (hoverflies) to visit our garden, only about a half-inch long. The small flowers of cilantro seem the perfect fit.

The common green bottle fly, *Lucilia sericata*, is one of our most familiar blow flies, best known for the larvae that feed on any form of decaying animal matter. The adult, however, is a pollinator. In our garden, we see them infrequently on several species of plants, but they are frequent visitors to cilantro flowers.

The bee fly, *Villa lateralis*, is a bumble bee imitator. It can be recognized by its stocky shape, hovering behavior, and long, stiff tongue which it uses to probe flowers as it hovers over them. This hovering behavior is an adaptation that allows the fly to avoid capture by crab spiders and other predators that might be hiding in the flower. There is a dark side to this pollinating fly. The female bee fly, having located an underground bee nest by observing the return of a solitary bee from foraging, will lay an egg at the entrance to the nest. When the egg hatches, the fly larva enters the nest and locates a larval cell, then consumes both pollen and larva. When fully grown, the fly larva remains in the nest cavity until spring.

This potter wasp, sipping nectar from a cilantro flower, seemed pleased to have its photograph taken. For a complete discussion of the potter wasp, *Ancistrocerus antilope*, see Chapter 9.

Wasps in the genus *Polistes* constitute the most common group of wasps in North America, with over 300 species and subspecies. They are disposed to construct their nests on houses and outbuildings, making them less welcome, although they will only become aggressive if disturbed. In their favor, they consume large numbers of caterpillars. They are easily identified in flight, their legs dangling below their bodies.

The ladybird beetle, *Propylea quatuordecimpunctata*, wins the prize for longest specific epithet! It roughly translates to "14-spotted ladybird beetle." Those who know her well call her P-14. There are over 100 color and pattern variations for this species, so correct identification can be a difficult task. Background colors range from cream to yellow to light orange. The "spots" are more often squares that fuse together in various patterns. Native to Africa, Asia, and Europe, P-14 was introduced to North America.

Lobelia (*Lobelia erinus*)

Height: 0.50 to 0.75 feet

Width: 0.50 to 1.00 feet

Sunlight: full sun to part shade in cool northern areas, part shade in hot summer areas

Flower Color: Cultivars are available in a variety of flower colors, including blue, violet, purple, white, red, and pink, often with white or yellow eyes

Bloom Period: Best bloom is from late spring to early summer; plants begin to decline in hot summers and should be cut back to encourage fall blooming

Propagation: Seed is as fine as dust; grow from seed in small clumps, 6 to 8 weeks before last spring frost, or obtain potted plants from garden centers and nurseries

Arthropods Observed: bumble bee moth, butterflies, skippers, hoverflies, solitary bees

Note: Lobelia erinus *is considered to be a tender perennial hardy in USDA Zones 10 and 11. Elsewhere it is an annual.*

Blue lobelia, one of the best annuals for pot culture, attracts a host of pollinators.

Growing *Lobelia erinus* in pots gave us a unique perspective on each visiting pollinator. Often we are looking up to watch bumble bee moths, bees, and butterflies, and so it felt odd to see familiar creatures nectaring just inches off the ground.

Pots of blue lobelia should be located in part shade; in hot summer sun, the leaves turn to rags and the plants die back. If plants do die back, consider cutting them back to encourage re-blooming in fall.

Growing blue lobelia and other annuals in pots requires a good bit of time, much of it dragging the hose or lugging the watering can, and yet it is well worth the effort when you encounter scenes like these.

The flowers of blue lobelia are tailor-made for the likes of this native bee, identity unknown.

It is always an exciting moment when we spot the summer's first Eastern tiger swallowtail butterfly (*Papillio glaucus*) soaring over the garden fence. Tiger swallowtails are described as having a preference for sturdy plants with red or pink flowers, yet here she was, probing the throat of a blue flower.

With its long tongue, the silver-spotted skipper, *Epargyreus clarus*, is well suited to sipping the nectar of tubular flowers such as blue lobelia. Skippers are more closely related to butterflies than to moths, although they have some moth characteristics, including hairy stout bodies and dull coloration. The name "skipper" refers to their fast, darting flight.

The silver-spotted skipper gets its common name from the metallic-silver spot on each hind wing. This bit of adornment distinguishes it as the most recognized skipper in North America. With the exception of west Texas, it is found throughout the U.S. and southern Canada.

E. clarus differs from most skippers in its choice of larval host plants. While the caterpillars of most skippers feed on grasses or sedges, *E. clarus* larvae feed on the leaves of woody legumes, including black locust (*Robinia pseudoacacia*), honey locust (*Gleditsia triacanthos*), and false indigo (*Amorpha* spp.).

Adult silver-spotted skippers seldom nectar on yellow flowers and are usually found nectaring on blue, red, pink, purple, and white blossoms. Favorite plants include milkweeds, red clover, buttonbush, blazing star, and thistles.

A metallic-green native bee, possibly the sweat bee *Augochloropsis metallica*, takes the high ground.

The silver-spotted skipper, *Epargyreus clarus*, uses its long tongue to reach the nectary of blue lobelia.

Flowering Tobacco (*Nicotiana sylvestris* 'Only the Lonely'; woodland tobacco)

USDA Hardiness Range: *Nicotiana sylvestris* is a tender perennial in USDA Zones 10 and 11.
Height: 4 to 5 feet
Width: 1 to 2 feet
Sunlight: full sun
Flower Color: The tubular white flowers are 4 inches long, nodding, trumpet-shaped, opening in the evening to release a sweet exotic scent.
Bloom Period: June to frost
Propagation: Plants can be grown from seed started 8 to 10 weeks before last frost. The extremely tiny seed size makes sowing difficult, but 'Only the Lonely' transplants are often not available locally
Arthropods Observed: hummingbird moth

We grow our woodland tobacco plants from seed because transplants of 'Only the Lonely' are not always available. The seed is as fine as dust, and no matter how thinly it is sown, you end up with a seed flat of hundreds of crowded seedlings.

Also, we have difficulty establishing the transplanted seedlings. They are slow to get established in the garden bed and plagued by slugs, snails, and earwigs. We have discovered that surrounding the transplants with wood ashes helps deter the slugs, and the earwigs can be controlled with beer traps.

Growing up to 5 feet tall, woodland tobacco is often planted at the back of a border.

Although exceedingly small as seedlings, the mature plants are huge, with large, soft but sticky leaves that can be a foot long. Place them at least 2 feet apart when planting in the garden.

A closer look at woodland tobacco's long tubular flowers. Only the hummingbird moth has a tongue long enough to reach the nectar.

A hummingbird moth (*Hemaris* sp.) resting on a tobacco leaf.

'Only the Lonely' Will Do (*Reeser*)

Woodland tobacco has increased our garden's biodiversity, as far as I know, by only two species, itself and the hummingbird moth (*Hemaris* sp., either *H. diffinis* or *H. thysbe*). And yet I could not have a garden without *Nicotiana sylvestris,* and I can have only one cultivar, 'Only the Lonely'.

This is a very personal matter. No doubt the species or any other cultivated variety of it would attract the moth, but 'Only the Lonely' brings back memories of the Roy Orbison song for which it is named, and there was a time years ago when I would lie awake on hot summer nights listening to Orbison sing this tune and feeling that it was written only for me. If you know the song—and if you know Orbison's plaintive tenor and soul-piercing falsetto—then you may know of what I speak. There are memories associated with the song that return whenever I smell the flowers of the plant for which it is named.

Woodland tobacco flowers are meant for a warm summer night, a night when you want to lie on the porch, turn off the lights, and look up at the stars. It is at this time of day that the candelabra-like sprays of tubular pure-white flowers, each 5 to 6 inches long, bring a heady jasmine-like perfume to the entire garden, and with this fragrance comes the hummingbird moth. This evening explosion of intensely fragrant flowers continues all summer into early fall.

Because the plant grows to 6 feet tall, many garden designers relegate it to the back of the border, but I suggest that you plant it as close as possible to where you sit in the garden, and let it catch the moonlight as it surrounds you with its heady perfume. Be aware that it is a prolific self-sower and that seedlings will pop up everywhere each spring. You will not be able to call these 'Only the Lonely', but that does not mean that they should all be pulled up, not if you have the space and the inclination to see what they become. Any of them should bring the moth, and that alone is sufficient reason to keep them.

The hummingbird moth, which can also be called the snowberry clearwing moth if you are sure it is *H. diffinis*, is one of the most interesting creatures to grace our garden. It flies and moves just like a hummingbird and is often mistaken for one. Like a hummingbird, it remains suspended in air in front of a flower while it unfurls its long tongue to sip nectar from the deep-throated flowers. The name "clearwing" refers to the loss of scales on the wings, making them transparent.

Larval host plants for hummingbird moths include honeysuckles (*Lonicera* sp.), dogbane (*Apocynum cannabinum*), hawthorn (*Crataegus* spp.), and cherries (*Prunus* spp.). I suspect that we owe thanks for the hummingbird moths in our garden to the bird cherries (*P. pensylvanica*) in the surrounding woods, under whose leaf litter the moth pupae hibernate through the winter.

Woodland tobacco is not the only plant that will bring hummingbird moths to your garden. During the day we see them on the annual blue lobelia, and I have read that they will also nectar on monarda and phlox. But for me they will always be associated with the gloaming and the sweet perfume of 'Only the Lonely'.

Choosing Functional Annuals for Your Garden

When it comes to attracting pollinators, not all annuals are equally functional. For example, from June through July, *Lobelia erinus* is a magnet for small solitary bees and butterflies. We've learned that no matter what other plants may be in bloom, there will be bumble bees and solitary bees foraging on bachelor's buttons through June and July. Self-sown calendulas provide pollen and nectar for solitary bees from spring until frost. Sunflowers teem with bumble bees from mid-July to the end of August. Cosmos nourish butterflies and bees from August until frost.

We feel the ability of some annuals, such as zinnias, to attract pollinators depends on the competition. Zinnias are recommended for pollinator gardens, but they have not been very functional in our garden. Bees and butterflies nectar instead on nearby lobelias and cosmos.

We have learned that annual plants seem to be preferred by the smaller bumble bees and solitary bees when the larger, more aggressive pollinators are monopolizing the perennials in bloom. For example, when the feeding frenzy of bumble bees, yellow jackets, and other wasps on swamp milkweed is at full throttle, sweat bees and other small bees are crawling into the throats of lobelia blossoms. Throughout the growing season, we seldom see vespid wasps on the garden's annuals.

The best way to discover which annuals will attract pollinators to your garden is to experiment, as we did, following the advice of experts in your area of the country. Visiting public gardens that grow a variety of annuals may also provide insight into which annual species will function best in your garden.

Grow a variety of annuals that will provide sources of pollen and nectar throughout the growing season. Grow them in empty spaces of the vegetable garden, in borders and beds, in pots perched on old stumps, and on the porch steps. Fill your garden with their vibrant colors. Know that you are doing good work.

Northern Pine Looper Moth
(*Caripeta piniata*)

Chapter 11

Sustaining Biodiversity in the Vegetable or Small Fruits Garden

"The single greatest lesson the garden teaches is that our relationship to the planet need not be zero-sum, and that as long as the sun still shines and people still can plan and plant, think and do, we can, if we bother to try, find ways to provide for ourselves without diminishing the world."
—Michael Pollan, *The Omnivore's Dilemma*

The insect life in our vegetable and small fruits garden provides a summer show filled with pollinators, herbivores, and predators, all foraging on the leaves and flowers of crop plants. Some of the herbivores—such as tortoise beetles, cucumber beetles, and flea beetles—must be controlled to avoid major crop losses. This we do with thumb and forefinger, pinching the beetle against the leaf it is eating, or by knocking a bunch of beetles into a bowl of soapy water. Hand-picking is best done at dawn, when the beetles are sluggish, and so we walk about the garden at daybreak, coffee mugs in hand, stooping to pick or pinch as needed.

This chapter describes the insects and arachnids we have found on the vegetable and small fruit plants in our garden. We routinely grow tomatoes, tomatillos (the small pineapple-flavored variety), cucumbers, summer squash, onions, leeks, garlic, spinach, highbush blueberries, blackberries, strawberries, and raspberries. Problems with herbivores are minor, due largely to a large population of predator species, including spiders, wasps, hoverfly larvae, lacewings, and predatory beetles. Several gardening practices are responsible for this abundance of predators, including interplanting crops to increase insect biodiversity, minimal tillage to avoid damaging insect nesting sites, growing self-sowing flowering annuals among the vegetables to attract both insect pollinators and insect predators, and mulching with shredded leaves to provide overwintering habitat for insect larvae and pupae, as well as conserving soil moisture. These techniques are discussed in more detail later in this chapter.

Over the course of a recent summer in our garden, we observed and photographed thirteen species of arthropods on the foliage, flowers, and fruits of one crop, raspberries. The majority of these, eleven species, were foraging on flowers, moving pollen around as they worked, while two, a nursery web spider and a harvestman, were motionless, waiting for prey to come within reach. Imagine standing in the middle of beds filled with raspberry canes in full flower, keeping company with yellow jackets, hornets, bumble bees, solitary bees, honeybees, hoverflies, and butterflies. Reeser would spend an hour there, leaving with dozens of photographs to sort through, and return the next day for more. If you are interested in boosting the insect diversity of your food garden, including the abundance of pollinators, plant raspberries.

Life Among the Raspberries

Nursery Web Spider

Marjorie reached up to pick a pair of ripe raspberries and nearly stroked the back of a nursery web spider (*Pisaurina mira*), the largest spider we encounter in our garden. The spider, its legs grasping the two fruits, remained motionless, either waiting for prey to come close or guarding a nearby nursery web. Marjorie begrudged the spider its ownership of the berries and quickly excused herself.

A nursery web spider scurries across the ground, carrying her egg sac with her fangs.

One of the most common spiders in the garden, a female *P. mira* can often be seen scurrying along the ground, carrying a white egg sac held tight with her fangs. When the eggs are ready to hatch, the mother will build a nursery web within which she hangs the egg sac. After hatching and until the first molt, the baby spiders inhabit the nursery web while the mother remains close by to defend them.

The mother does not rely on a web to trap her prey, but instead prowls in search of insects to overpower, often hanging out near outdoor lights in hopes of catching a moth or other prey that congregate there.

A nursery web spider lies motionless among the raspberries.

Hornets, Wasps, and Bees

The roster of Hymenoptera found foraging on raspberry blossoms includes bald-faced hornets, yellow jackets, ichneumon wasps, honeybees, bumble bees (including the orange-belted bumble bee), and a metallic-green halictid bee species (sweat bee). During each of our visits to the raspberry patch, we spy several of each of these species, all too busy nectaring or gathering pollen to pay us much attention.

A bald-faced hornet (*Dolichovespula maculata*) foraging on a raspberry flower.

Most of these wasps and bees have been discussed in earlier chapters, but not *Augochloropsis metallica*, a beautiful metallic-green bee belonging to the Halictidae, one of the seven bee families. Halictid bees are also called "sweat bees" because they are attracted to the salts in

Yellow jackets (*Vespula maculifrons*)
like this one are frequent foragers of
raspberry flowers.

Orange-belted bumble bees (*Bombus ternarius*)
are common visitors to the raspberry patch.

A halictid bee (sweat bee), *Augochloropsis metallica*, gatherers pollen and nectar to raise a family.

human perspiration. They are among the most colorful of bees with species of green, gold, blue, and copper.

Most halictid bees are ground-nesting bees, and many, like *A. metallica*, are solitary, each female working alone to raise her brood in an underground nest, usually on bare soil. As a generalist forager, the female will visit a wide variety of flowers to supply the pollen and nectar necessary to raise her family.

Hoverflies

Wherever there are flowers in the garden, there are hoverflies, often referred to as flower flies or syrphid flies, the latter name a reference to their family, the Syrphidae. Most are tiny and easily overlooked, while some of the larger ones are mimics of wasps or bees and thus likely to be misidentified. We gardened for decades before recognizing hoverflies or realizing the important role they play in the garden ecosystem.

This small syrphid fly was spotted resting on a raspberry leaf. It may have been temporarily displaced from a flower by a bumble bee and was waiting patiently for the bully to move on.

Adult hoverflies feed on nectar, pollen, and, when available, the sugary honeydew secreted by aphids. The adult females lay their eggs near high aphid populations, providing their larvae with plenty of food. During the seven- to ten-day larval period, a single larva will devour up to 400 aphids as well as its share of thrips, scale insects, and white-flies. Truly a gardener's friend!

Among the larger hoverflies visiting the rasp-berries is a vespid wasp mimic, *Temnostoma excentrica*. With its wings held wasp-fashion over its back and its front pair of legs extended in front of its head to mimic wasp antennae, the first one we saw was so effective in its mimicry that Reeser spent over an hour trying to identify it as a hornet before he noticed its stubby antennae, a sure indicator of a syrphid fly. With this trickery, many syrphid flies are able to avoid predation by birds and other creatures that would rather avoid a wasp's stinger.

A vespid wasp mimic, *Temnostoma excentrica*, with its front legs extended to mimic the antennae of a wasp.

The Raspberry Cane Borer: Easily Managed by the Observant Gardener with a Little Help from a Friend

If you grow raspberries or blackberries, the first sign that the raspberry cane borer (*Oberea affinis*) has found your garden may be wilting stem tips on primocanes (next year's fruiting canes), first noticeable in July. If you look closely at an infected primocane, you will notice two bands of girdled tissue about a

A wilted stem tip is a sure sign that the female raspberry cane borer has laid an egg in a primocane.

The two bands of girdled tissue are also evidence of the borer's visit.

half-inch apart that encircle the stem at the base of the wilted area. It is this girdling, the result of chewing by the female borer, that causes the stem tip to wilt.

After girdling the stem, the female lays an egg between the two girdles. The egg hatches in July, and the larva slowly burrows down the cane, eating the pith tissue as it goes, and passes its first winter inside the stem, an inch or two below the girdles. In the following growing season, the larva burrows down to the crown and spends its second winter at or below ground level. It completes its development the following spring and pupates in the soil, emerging as an adult in July.

The adult raspberry cane borer is a longhorn beetle about three-quarters of an inch long, its two antennae as long as its body. The prothorax is yellow, the head and body blue-black.

Left unchecked, larval feeding will weaken and ultimately destroy the affected canes. Damage to the primocane is easily minimized, however, by pruning off the wilting tip, making the pruning cut just above a bud below the wilted area. The removed tip, which contains the egg or larva, should be placed in the trash.

The small cobweb spider discussed in Chapter 7, *E. ovata*, is an effective predator of the adult raspberry cane borer.

The adult raspberry cane borer.

A cobweb spider finishing off its prey, a raspberry cane borer.

Highbush Blueberry Visitors
Fall Webworms and the Ichneumon Wasp

Fall webworms (*Hyphantria cunea*) make an annual appearance on our highbush blueberry shrubs, building webs at the tips of branches and feeding on the enclosed leaves until nothing is left but wood, then moving on to a nearby branch. We put up with the unsightly mess for a while, but eventually tear open the nests to expose the caterpillars, hoping that birds will have a feast.

For years we wondered at the lack of even one natural predator of the fall webworm. Cuckoos are the only birds known to break apart the silken tents and eat the caterpillars, but there are no cuckoos in Maine. And then, one August, Marjorie spotted a half-inch-long

Fall webworms encased in their web
on a highbush blueberry branch.

black wasp with a red abdomen crawling across a webworm tent. We later identified it as *Cryptus albitarsis*, an ichneumon wasp that searches for hosts primarily among foliage and fruits.

Reeser grabbed the camera from a nearby fencepost and began photographing the wasp as she moved about. Suddenly she stopped and inserted her long ovipositor into the web, apparently in an effort to deposit an egg in one of the many caterpillars. If successful, the egg would hatch, and the resulting wasp larva would feed on the caterpillar, ultimately killing it.

We cannot say how many webworms were thus dispatched by the little wasp, nor how many such wasps it would take to make a real difference in the webworm population in our August garden. But we took some comfort in realizing that the presence of webworms on our blueberry shrubs added the little wasp to our garden's biodiversity.

Other insects associated with the blueberries in our garden include pollinating bumble bees and a potter wasp in the genus *Ancistrocerus* that can beat us to some of the harvest by feeding on unripe berries.

A parasitoid wasp, *Cryptus albitarsis*, exploring a nest of fall webworms. The short ovipositor-like appendage identifies it as a male.

A potter wasp enjoying an unripe blueberry.

Herbivores Among the Vegetables
Tortoise Beetles

Tomatillos are a staple in our vegetable garden—not the salsa verde types but the small, yellow "husk cherries" that you harvest after they've been on the ground for a day or two, then eat one at a time after peeling off the husk. They have a pineapple flavor and are often offered in seed catalogs as "pineapple tomatillo." Very few ever make it to the kitchen.

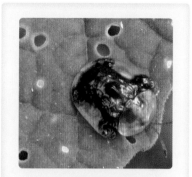

A top view of a tortoise beetle. *P. clavata* can do serious damage to young seedlings of tomatoes and their relatives.

Each year we rotate the tomatillos to a new bed all their own, their sprawling habit prohibiting interplanting with any other crop, yet the tortoise beetles (*Plagiometriona clavata*) always find them within a day or two of setting out the transplants. The first time we encountered this insect, neither of us recognized it as a beetle. Only about a quarter inch long, the adult is an oval, convex, tortoise-shaped creature with a translucent carapace (upper shell) except for the humeral areas (wing cases). In side view the body is dome-shaped with a conical peak near the middle. The color is typically a beautiful gold and brown.

P. clavata prefers to munch on the leaves of plants in the Family Solanaceae, including tomatoes and, of course, tomatillos. We find a few on the tomatoes, but they are far more abundant on tomatillos, perhaps because the sprawling habit of tomatillo plants affords them more protection from predators, including ants, spiders, and carnivorous beetle species.

Flea Beetles

Tortoise beetles keep company with another member of Order Coleoptera, the flea beetle, a general name applied to several species of jumping beetles in the leaf beetle family, Chrysomelidae.

The various species of flea beetles go by common names that reflect their dining preferences: crucifer flea beetle, eggplant flea beetle, horseradish flea beetle, spinach flea beetle, and so on. They're all tiny, typically 1 to 5 millimeters long, and they all avoid predators by jumping like a flea, a trait enabled by greatly enlarged hind legs. You have to get up very early in the morning to find them sufficiently torpid to hand pinch. This we do, or we would lose any chance at making a crop of tomatillos.

Left alone, flea beetles would make quick work of a crop of small tomatillo (or tomato) transplants, riddling the leaves with tiny round "shotgun" holes. Once the plants have increased in size, the beetles have far less overall impact, but for a couple of weeks after

Flea beetles and the "shotgun" holes they make on tomatillo leaves.
Can you spot the five tiny black beetles in this photo?

planting we visit the tomatillo bed every morning at daybreak, pinching every flea beetle we see against the surface of the leaf. Once the sun is above the horizon and the beetles have warmed up, they jump out of sight at our slightest movement.

Cucumber Beetles

As with most vegetable plant herbivores, serious eruptions of striped cucumber beetles (*Acalymma vittatum*) occur infrequently in gardens with high predator populations. Most of the time, hand-picking the beetles will prevent serious damage. When you do experience a plague, it helps to understand the creature's life cycle.

Unmated adults overwinter in wooded areas beneath the litter and under rotting logs, often as much as a mile from the garden. They leave their hibernating quarters in the spring when temperatures reach 55 degrees Fahrenheit and initially feed on the pollen, petals, and leaves of willow, apple, hawthorn, goldenrod, and asters. As soon as cucurbit plants (cucumber, squash, pumpkin) appear in your garden, the beetles fly to these plants, often in large numbers.

The beetles soon mate and continue feeding through the growing season, laying eggs 8 to 25 days after mating. Each female deposits up to 800 orange-yellow eggs in small clusters or singly in soil cracks at the base of cucurbit plants.

Eggs hatch within 8 days, and the white larvae (a third of an inch long when full-grown) spend about 15 days feeding on the roots and fruit stems in contact with the soil. The pupal period lasts about a week. The total time from egg hatching to adult for the first generation is about one month.

Cucumber beetles can quickly get out of control. It pays to carefully inspect the upper and lower surfaces of cucurbit leaves every morning, pinching the bugs while they are waking up.

In northern gardens, only one generation occurs each season, thank goodness.

Effective controls include continued hand-picking of incoming adult beetles early in the day, when they are sluggish. Growing cucurbits on trellises will reduce larval feeding on fruit stems. And row covers, supported over the cucurbit plants with wire hoops, will exclude the beetles, but only if you install the covers immediately after planting, before the beetles arrive (see sidebar). And remember to remove the row covers once female flowers appear so that the bees can pollinate them.

Be sure to look inside the flowers, as well.

Asparagus Beetles

Adults of the common asparagus beetle (*Crioceris asparagi*) appear in the asparagus bed just as the new spears are emerging from the ground in early spring, having spent the winter beneath the loose bark of nearby trees or in the hollow stems of old asparagus plants that you forgot to remove from the bed. While only about a quarter-inch long, their bright orange and black coloration with six white spots on the back gives them away.

A common asparagus beetle feeds on a newly emerged spear.

Soon after the first adults appear, numerous dark brown, oval-shaped eggs appear in rows on the spears. Later in the season these eggs can also be found on the ferns and flower buds. Eggs hatch within a week, and the slug-like larvae with visible heads and legs feed for two weeks on the asparagus plants, then pupate in the soil. The second generation of adults emerge about a week later.

Feeding by the adult beetles can cause browning and scarring of the spears and may cause the spears to bend over in a shepherd's crook. Both adults and larvae also devour the ferns, causing significant defoliation and thus weakening the plant's ability to store sufficient nutrients for the next season.

Control of asparagus beetles requires daily scouting of the plants, tossing adults and larvae into soapy water and removing egg masses. This scouting is best done in the afternoon, when the beetles are most active, and it should be done every day as new beetles fly in from surrounding areas. Be sure to remove all plant residue from the asparagus bed at the end of the season.

Floating Row Covers Foil Herbivores in the Vegetable Garden

Floating row covers are a chemical-free way to deny herbivores such as the striped cucumber beetle access to your vegetable crops. They also exclude squash bugs, Colorado potato beetles, and squash vine borers from squash, cucumbers, and pumpkins. They keep cabbageworm butterflies from finding your broccoli and other brassicas, and they will also foil bean beetles, whiteflies, grasshoppers, spinach leafminers, aphids, and leafhoppers.

Most garden row covers are a spun woven polypropylene fabric of varying weights. For insect control, we prefer a lightweight row cover (0.45 ounce per square yard) that retains very little heat in the soil while transmitting 95 percent of available light. Water from rain or irrigation easily passes through the fabric.

Available in rolls of varying length from garden stores and online, standard row covers range from 5½ to 8 feet wide, and wider is always better. Be sure to buy a width that will accommodate the upward growth of the plants.

For leaf and root crops, row covers can be kept on throughout the growing season. For crops that require pollination by insects for fruit production, row covers must be removed during flowering.

Some crops, such as tomatoes, peppers, and others with fragile growing tips, do better if the row cover is supported with hoops. Many gardeners use hoops made from 9-gauge wire cut into 6-foot-long pieces. The ends of the hoops are pushed into the ground. In raised beds framed with timbers, small holes can be drilled in the top timber to support the hoops.

Other options for hoops include inexpensive plastic pipes with their ends pushed into the soil or slipped over rebar stakes. Rebar stakes with plastic endcaps work well for supporting row covers over tall plants.

Row covers can be used for two or more seasons if properly used and stored. Small rips in the fabric can be closed with staples or clothespins, and at the end of the growing season, much of the soil can be removed by hanging the fabric on the line and rinsing it with a gentle spray from the hose. Once dry, fold the fabric for storage indoors.

Using floating row covers successfully requires knowledge of how insects overwinter. Some herbivores, like the Colorado potato beetle, spend the winter as adults in the soil near the plants on which they fed as larvae. If potatoes are planted in the same

Installed with plenty of slack between bed edges, this potato bed row cover literally floats on top of the growing plants, providing a millimeter-thick barrier to potato beetles. Because potatoes do not require pollinating insects, the row cover can remain over the potato bed throughout the summer.

bed the following spring and the bed is covered with fabric, these adults will emerge to find their favorite food handy beneath a cover that protects them from their natural enemies. Other herbivores that overwinter near last year's plant host include the onion maggot, corn rootworm, and flea beetle (which affects many vegetable seedlings). Clearly, crop rotation must be used along with row covers to foil these herbivores.

(continued on page 218)

(continued from page 217)

Some herbivores, such as slugs, cutworms, millipedes, and sowbugs, over-winter in scattered locations around the garden. These insects have the greatest potential for causing plant damage under row covers, since they could emerge anywhere in the garden. Frequent inspection is the key. If noticeable populations of these herbivores are found, the row cover should be removed to allow beneficial insects access to their prey.

Floating row covers should be used only to prevent establishment of an herbivore capable of serious damage, such as the Colorado potato beetle, but they should not be used at the expense of building strong populations of beneficial insects. Cover everything and the beneficials will disappear, a recipe for disaster.

Cutworms

Cutworms, the larval (caterpillar) stage of several species of night-flying moths, can be a major herbivore in your garden each spring, cutting down unprotected young transplants at or below the soil surface and devouring seedlings before they break through the soil. As with all garden herbivores, understanding the life cycle of the cutworm gives clues to effective controls.

Cutworms overwinter in the late-larval or pupal stage. The adults, brownish-gray moths, appear with the warm weather in spring, flying at night. They are attracted to weedy fields, particularly to mustard and quackgrass, and also lay eggs in weedy gardens during early spring.

Once gardens are planted, the young larvae feed on small roots until half-grown (about three-quarters of an inch long), at which point they become

Cutworms can be found by digging into the soil around damaged plants.

more likely to cut off plants at or just below the ground, often dragging parts of the plant into the soil where they hide during the day. Their favorite garden plants include tomatoes, peppers, beans, and corn.

Most cutworm species have only one generation per year in northern gardens, while in southern areas there can be two. Because there are several cutworm species, the larvae vary in color from gray to brown or black, striped or spotted. A mature cutworm larva can be up to 2 inches long and will curl into a tight ball when disturbed.

Cutworm collars, properly installed, will deter damage to transplanted seedlings. We use collars made by cutting out the bottoms of small paper cups, positioning them so that half of the collar will be buried beneath the soil after planting. We put these collars around every seedling transplanted to the garden.

A small paper cup with its bottom removed, positioned around a seedling so that the bottom half is buried beneath the soil, makes an excellent (and biodegradable) cutworm collar. When you dig the planting hole for a seedling, look for cutworms in the soil before you plant to avoid trapping one inside the collar.

Minimizing cutworm damage to direct-sown crops is trickier. Direct-sown beans, for example, may never make it above ground if cutworms sever the embryonic stem as it emerges from the seed. Eliminating all weeds from potential seed beds is a start, since the moth is unlikely to lay eggs in bare soil. Shallow raking and sifting of the soil before sowing is another precautionary measure, destroying any cutworms found by crushing or drowning in soapy water.

Once seedlings of crops with succulent stems, such as squash, cucumbers, and beans, have successfully emerged from the ground, we surround each seedling with a cutworm collar. These crops, the ones with juicy stems, seem to be the cutworm favorites, but only for the first week or so after emergence. The stems soon harden, and the collars can be removed.

Finally, get proactive. If you have cutworm damage, usually evidenced at the crack of dawn by a severed seedling or two lying on the ground, dig 2 or 3 inches into the soil around the damaged plant and you will likely find the culprit. And visit the garden at night with a flashlight, looking for cutworms on top of the soil.

Vegetable Garden Predators

We grow tomatoes, but I've only seen one tomato hornworm and it was dead, the victim of a parasitoid wasp. Other than the fall webworms and cutworms discussed above, the only caterpillars we encounter in large numbers are the monarch butterfly caterpillars that dine on the milkweed we planted for them and the milkweed tussock moths that finish off the foliage of these plants when the monarchs are done. Keeping in mind that both of these milkweed-eating species escape predation because their diet makes them unpalatable to predators, our vegetable garden is relatively free of lepidopteran herbivores. We give credit for this to the vegetable garden predators that abound in our garden, including many that have already been discussed as well as two that are introduced here, the green lacewing (*Chrysopa* sp.) and the six-spotted tiger beetle (*Cicindela sexguttata*).

Lacewings

Green lacewing larvae are generalist predators, feeding on a wide variety of herbivores including mealybugs, thrips, mites, white flies, aphids, small caterpillars, leaf hoppers, small beetles, scale insects, small flies, and insect eggs. The larvae have large hooked jaws, which they use to grasp the prey before sucking out the vital fluids.

Less than an inch in length with delicate transparent wings and green bodies that blend in with their surroundings, adult lacewings are seldom seen in the garden during the day, although they are there, foraging for pollen and nectar. Because they are moving pollen around, they are considered accidental pollinators. They also fly at night and can be seen when drawn to lights.

The larva of a green lacewing (*Chrysopa rufilabris*) feeding on aphids.

An adult green lacewing, possibly *C. rufilabris*.

Six-spotted Tiger Beetle

A common species of ground beetle throughout much of the U.S., the six-spotted tiger beetle is a voracious predator of small arthropods, including caterpillars, ants, and spiders. About half an inch long, it is easily recognized by the six small white dots on the metallic-green elytra (protective wing case for the hindwings, which are used for flying). Despite their ferocious appearance, they do not bite humans unless handled, and then you would feel a barely noticeable pinch. Adults can also defend themselves by secreting a foul-smelling liquid.

A six-spotted tiger beetle hunting along a garden path.

The adults live alone in wooded areas, each in its own burrow, getting together only to breed. Each adult returns to its burrow at night and also overwinters there. The female lays eggs in mid-summer, digging holes in the ground and laying one egg in each hole, then covering the hole with soil. When the eggs hatch, the larvae (grubs) burrow tunnels down into the soil. To eat, a larva pops its head out of its tunnel, like a jack-in-the-box, to grab its prey, pulling it down into the burrow. The larva stays in its burrow until the following year, changing into a pupa in July and emerging as an adult in August.

Tiger beetles are fast runners and fliers, able to catch prey in air as well as on the ground. We find them hunting along the garden's shaded paths, no doubt returning at night to their burrows in the surrounding woods.

Predators have predators, and tiger beetles are no exception. The adult beetles are preyed upon by birds, dragonflies, lizards, frogs, and salamanders, while the larvae are prey for moles, opossum, raccoons, skunks, ants, birds, and parasitoid wasps.

Increasing Biodiversity in the Food Garden
Interplanting Crops

The wise vegetable gardener eschews monoculture in favor of mixed plantings. Instead of "setting the table" for herbivores and diseases by planting entire beds or rows to a single crop, she grows a mix of compatible species within each area, thus minimizing these problems while increasing area biodiversity. The increase in biodiversity of a mixed planting includes the plants themselves and the pollinators, herbivores, and predatory insects associated with each. Taking this approach throughout the garden results in an increase in total insect biodiversity, one major indicator of a healthy, productive food garden.

Growing a blend of two or more crops in the same row or bed is called interplanting. Compared with monoculture, interplanting schemes create complex ecosystems within the garden, a rich mosaic of plantings that encourages the predators of herbivores.

Corn interplanted with squash.

An example of the benefits of interplanting in our garden makes the point. After experiencing an explosion of cucumber beetles on all of our garden's cucurbits, the following year we spread the cucumber and summer squash plants

Leeks interplanted with carrots and beans.

around the garden, interplanting them with other crops. As a result, cucumber beetles were far less numerous. At the same time, we noticed an increase in the number of harvestmen in the interplanted areas, creatures that prey on aphids, whiteflies, and small beetles.

Interplanting combinations should focus both on above-ground and below-ground compatibility. Plants that complement one another in the shapes of their top growths will fill the available garden space, leaving no room or available light for weeds to grow. Corn and beans, for example, when grown together, intercept 90 percent of the available sunlight. They are also an ideal couple for underground compatibility, since corn is a shallow-rooting crop, while beans have deeper root systems. Add winter squash in the same bed and you have the traditional Native American "Three Sisters" planting in which the corn stalks provide a scaffold for pole beans to climb, the beans fix nitrogen for all three crops, and the spiny leaves and stems of the squash deter raccoons and other corn thieves.

Interplanting schemes should also take nutrient sharing into account, mixing heavy feeders with light feeders. Fortunately, most interplanting schemes designed for sharing of aboveground and underground space, like the Three Sisters planting, also result in efficient nutrient sharing.

Imagine the mosaic of green in garden space shared by interplanted Brussels sprouts, parsley, and spinach; a bed with plants of peppers, basil, and tomato arranged in an alternating pattern; a mixture of radishes, lettuce, and peppers filling a bed from edge to edge; or a mixed bed of lettuce and cabbage bordered by trellised peas.

Chard interplanted with basil.

Another interplanting scheme to consider is alternating blocks of beans (bush or pole) and radishes. This is a very effective way to keep flea beetles away from the bean leaves, as the beetles much prefer the radish leaves. The radish foliage will be riddled with tiny holes, yet still produce a decent root crop.

Leeks can be grown along the edges of a bed of beans, carrots, or both. Lettuce partners well with carrots, onions, radishes, or any combination of these crops. Onions thrive with cabbage, peppers, and spinach. Tomatoes or peppers can be interplanted with cole crops such as broccoli, cauliflower, and cabbage. And try surrounding trellised spring peas with lettuce, carrots, and/or spinach.

Many gardeners are drawn to interplanting as a technique for maximizing the use of garden space, and indeed this is one of the benefits. More important is the integration of this method of food gardening into the goal of maximizing biodiversity garden-wide.

As biodiversity increases, so does the resilience of the garden ecosystem. When beneficial insects and arachnids are numerous, major crop losses to insect herbivores are rare.

Growing Self-Sowing Annuals Among the Vegetables

No life form is more important to the vegetable gardener's success than pollinating insects such as the small and solitary native bee and the tireless bumble bee. If these creatures are not there when we need them, the ovaries of winter squash wither on the vine, while only a fraction of the potential tomato harvest is realized. Providing essential pollen and nectar sources as well as nesting sites will enable bumble bees to build colony strength in early spring and will keep solitary bees close at hand in the garden.

Why not plant a little pollinator insurance, a few annual flowers among the vegetables? The idea is appealing, conjuring a vision of orange, red, and yellow calendula blooms poking through the dark green leaves of winter squash, with bees and beetles swarming over the blossoms of both. But would it really work that way? Would the same pollinators that visit the calendulas also service the squash? Would another species of annual flowering plant be a better choice?

These are not well-researched questions, and many authorities suggest that gardeners concentrate on perennials to attract native pollinators. There are a few annuals, however, that are known to attract pollinators, particularly the native bees.

In general, native bees prefer annual flowers in shades of purple, blue, and yellow. The lilac-colored flowers of verbena (*Verbena bonariensis*), for example, attract not only native bees but also butterflies, while the deep violet blooms of heliotrope (*Heliotropium arborescens*), with their strong vanilla fragrance, are always covered with bees in search of nectar.

Some bee-attracting annuals also provide leaves and/or flowers for human consumption and thus are excellent candidates for integration into the vegetable garden. The purple flowers of anise hyssop (*Agastache foeniculum*), an annual herb or tender perennial (depending on your location), provide nectar for bees from June to August, and you can harvest the aromatic leaves for their sweet, licorice-mint flavor. Fresh or dried, they add flavor to salads, teas, and garnishes. And the hundreds of small blue flowers of borage (*Borago officinalis*), a tall annual herb, do double duty, providing nectar and pollen to foraging bees while adding a mild cucumber flavor to salads and garnishes.

Nasturtiums (*Tropaeolum majus*) are excellent container plants for attracting native bees to the vegetable garden, as are blue lobelia (*Lobelia erinus*), cosmos (*Cosmos bipinnatus*), and bachelor's buttons (*Centaurea cyanus*).

Calendulas (*Calendula officinalis*) do make the cut, but only the single varieties. The gardener interested in attracting pollinators should avoid annuals with double flowers (varieties in which the pollen-bearing stamens have been replaced with petals), since the pollen production will be greatly reduced or eliminated entirely.

As calendulas are self-sowing annuals, coming back from seed each year, their location in the garden is managed by weeding out unwanted seedlings or transplanting them to bed edges and other desirable locations. This means a little more work, another reason to linger late in the garden at the end of the day, and it makes for delightful plant combinations that you would have never thought of yourself.

Finally, there is comfort in realizing that the yellow flowers of broccoli and other brassicas will bring native bees to the garden. This is great solace for those of us who experience bolting of these crops every spring. We can leave them be, along with a few radishes left in the ground to flower.

Flower Longhorn Beetle
(*Evodinus monticola*)

Chapter 12

A Call to Action

Planet Earth, our only home, is in peril. Victim of the HIPPO juggernaut and the significant planetary warming locked in by current atmospheric levels of greenhouse gases, Earth has passed the tipping point for sweeping extinctions and major disruptions of life-sustaining systems. Glaciers and ice sheets are melting. Extreme weather patterns, including droughts, flooding, and record heat waves, are increasing in number and intensity. Even if we could stop emitting greenhouse gases today, Earth's temperature will rise 1.5 degrees Celsius above pre-industrial levels, nearly twice the increase we have already seen. But we have not stopped emitting greenhouse gases, and there is little hope that we will be able to do so before much of Earth's biodiversity is lost.

Gus Speth, former dean of the Yale School of Forestry, put it this way in *State of the World 2013*, the annual report of The Worldwatch Institute: "All we have to do to destroy the planet's climate and ecosystem and leave a ruined world to our children and grandchildren is to keep doing exactly what we are doing today." Nearly all scientists agree with this assessment, yet business as usual continues throughout the industrialized world. While oil company CEOs and the politicians that support them continue to prosper, the rest of us feel helpless to turn the tide of climate change and, at the same time, halt the species loss associated with the unrestrained destruction of wildlife habitat.

The problem is not a lack of ideas. In his recent book *Half-Earth: Our Planet's Fight for Life* (Norton, 2016), Edward O. Wilson reasons that by setting aside fully half of the surface of the Earth—concentrating on still-existing areas of wildness such as the redwood forests of California, the longleaf pine savanna of the American South, the Amazon River basin, the Atlantic forests of South America, the Serengeti grassland ecosystem, and other relatively pristine areas—we could stave off the mass extinctions of many species, including ourselves. Such a bold step, according to Wilson, would preserve a major percentage of Earth's biodiversity if we begin now. But bold actions require rallying the will of the people, which depends on making the case fully and clearly; standing in the way of this are the bureaucrats and billionaire

corporate officers who profit from business as usual. The rest of us feel helpless.

Joni Mitchell had it right 50 years ago: It is time to get ourselves back to the garden. It is time to unleash the potential of private and public properties to nurture wildlife. In the U.S. alone, over 40 million acres of lawns, lifeless expanses of monoculture the size of Texas, could be converted to functional gardens dominated by locally native trees, shrubs, and herbaceous plants, gardens that would provide food, shelter, and habitat for countless species of plants, insects, birds, small mammals, and other wildlife. Gardens large and small, private and public, urban and rural, ground-level and rooftop should be included in this effort.

Imagine such gardens throughout your community, not only around homes, but also around (and even on top of) campus buildings, churches and businesses, all dedicated to providing wildlife habitat. Imagine these gardens linked by vegetation corridors that enable wildlife to move safely through a pesticide-free world.

Start with your own garden, then use vegetation corridors to link your functional garden with like gardens in your community. Form citizen groups working with community leaders to make entire towns and cities wildlife friendly. Such efforts are already underway in communities across the world. Use your voice and vote to elect officials that will support these efforts at all levels.

Support efforts to make knowledge of local biodiversity and its importance to our survival a major component of educational standards for all grade levels. Help build schoolyard gardens and mandate their use as classrooms, not only for science classes but also for art, history, and math. Share your knowledge of local flora and fauna with students of all ages.

Insist that colleges and universities disinvest from fossil fuel corporations and, at the same time, turn their campuses into biodiversity hotspots. Lead the charge to convert a large expanse of your church's lawn to a functional garden, then hold services in this sacred place. Patronize businesses that surround their buildings with functional landscapes.

The following actions, attitudes, and approaches, summarized from this book, will transform your own garden into a biorefuge. It's time to get back to the garden.

Make Your Garden Functional
Minimize disturbance of garden soil

- Rototillers destroy soil structure. Recycle yours, if you have one, and pull weeds by hand. Minimize weeds with mulching.

- Construct a compost pile to turn kitchen vegetable waste and non-woody garden refuse into nutrient-rich compost.

- Avoid compacting garden soil; create walkways between raised beds in the vegetable garden, and design ornamental planting areas to be worked from walkways.

- Use annual oats as a cover crop in the vegetable garden, leaving the winter-killed leaves on the bed in spring as a mulch around transplants and between rows.

- In autumn, top-dress all growing areas, including around trees and shrubs, with composted manure, leaving it on top of the soil to be incorporated by earthworms and other soil organisms.

- To conserve soil water during the growing season, mulch around plants with screened compost or shredded leaves, allowing the mulch to be slowly incorporated into the soil.

Convert all or most of your lawn to functional plantings

- Recognize that a wide expanse of lawn grass is a biodiversity wasteland.

- Begin converting your lawn into a garden with a soil test, following advice and instructions from your local university cooperative extension office.

- Plan on taking a year to convert lawn area to new garden space.

Welcome Pollinators

- Learn to recognize the pollinators in your garden, including bumble bees, solitary bees, butterflies, moths, hoverflies (syrphid flies), tachinid flies, predatory wasps, parasitic wasps, and longhorn flower beetles.

* Plant an insectary, a section of the garden devoted to nourishing pollinators and other insects. Use a combination of herbaceous plants, annual and perennial, that will ensure an abundance of nectar and pollen through the gardening year.

* Increase the abundance and diversity of butterflies in your garden by planting larval host plants as well as sources of nectar for the adults.

* Discover the diversity of moths in your garden by hanging a white sheet between two trees at night and backlighting it with a lantern. A wide variety of moths will be attracted to the light, allowing you to closely observe them. Use a field guide to identify them. Take photographs. When you have finished moth watching, turn off the lantern, and the moths will disappear safely into the night.

Build a Garden Ecosystem with Predators to Control the Herbivores

* A healthy garden ecosystem maintains a self-regulating balance between herbivores (plant eaters) and their predators. Most of the time, the gardener can stand back and let nature take its course.

* Occasionally the gardener must become a predator, hand-picking Japanese beetles, cucumber beetles, or other herbivores in order to avoid serious plant damage. No chemicals need be involved, just a keen eye and a pail of soapy water.

* Recognize that many insect species, such as hoverflies and certain wasp species, are pollinators as adults and predators as larvae.

* Keep in mind that the flowers that attract bees also attract predatory and parasitoid wasps, insects that substantially reduce populations of herbivores, including caterpillars and aphids.

* Remember that caterpillars are the primary food for garden birds, particularly nestlings. If you want a garden filled with birds, you need a garden that supports caterpillars.

* Learn to distinguish between spiders and harvestmen, recognizing both as important predators in the garden.

* Learn to identify the spiders in your garden, to distinguish a crab spider from a cobweb spider or a nursery web spider.

Favor Native Trees and Shrubs

* Native trees and shrubs are the backbone of the functional garden. Canopy trees, including oaks, maples, birches, pines, and others, are primary larval hosts for many species of moths and butterflies. Flowering and fruiting shrubs provide nectar and pollen for insects and food for birds.

* Before selecting an ecologically functional tree or shrub for your garden, make sure that it is locally native. To determine if a tree or shrub is native to your area, consult the USDA range map we provide for each woody plant, as described in Chapter 8 and Appendix 3.

* If space allows, plant a few of your favorite non-native shrubs and trees. Some of these may turn out to be functional.

Attract Pollinators and Predators with Native and Non-Native Plants

* Create herbaceous beds and borders that are both beautiful and functional. Consult Chapter 9 for some of the most functional herbaceous perennials.

* Do your own screening of herbaceous perennials to see which are most functional in your area.

* Grow a variety of herbaceous plant species that will provide nectar and pollen throughout the gardening year.

* Include functional annual flowering plants in your beds and borders.

Think of Your Garden as a Biorefuge

* Discover the life in your garden. Spend time every day walking slowly through the garden, looking closely at flowers and turning over leaves.

* Keep a list of the species you find in your garden: birds, insects, small mammals, snakes, toads, everything. Use scientific names. What better way to measure your success in gardening for biodiversity?

* Avoid stepping on wayward caterpillars. Watch where you walk. Relocate wanderers from porch steps and sidewalks to safer ground.

* Cultivate dandelions.

* Leave a dead tree standing to attract wood-boring beetles and their predators, including woodpeckers.

● Create shelters in the garden for insects, amphibians, and reptiles. Use over-turned pots, rock piles, old stumps, and rotting logs.

● Let a few broccoli plants or a bed of cilantro flower for the bees.

● Provide water for birds and "mud puddling" areas for butterflies.

● Leave seed heads on sunflowers, coneflowers, and rudbeckias for the winter birds.

● Cultivate native sedges along the edges of the garden. They are larval host plants for skipper butterflies.

● Plant milkweed for monarch butterflies. Keep a record of when the first monarch shows up each year and when the last one leaves.

Enjoy the life in your garden.

Io Moth (*Automeris*)

Appendix 1

Understanding Scientific Names

Biodiversity is measured in species, and only the unique species names of plants and animals can adequately describe the biodiversity of your garden. For example, you cannot describe the bumble bee biodiversity in your garden with the term "bumble bee," since there are 46 bumble bee species in North America, each with a unique natural history and a unique connection to your garden. When you are able to identify a bumble bee to the species level, you can discover how it interacts with the plants and other animals in your garden. And there are no common names for many insects, which make up 60 percent of all life forms on Earth, so scientific names will often be all you have to work with. You can use the common names of plants and animals much of the time, but not when you want to describe the biodiversity in your garden.

Every organism, plant and animal, is assigned a unique two-word species name (i.e., a unique binomial) consisting of a genus name and a specific epithet. As an example, let's examine the scientific name for a popular street and garden tree, the red oak. Its binomial name is *Quercus rubra*. *Quercus* is the genus name for this tree, the first letter always capitalized, while *rubra*, the specific epithet, is always lower case. The species name for red oak is *Quercus rubra*, and, like all species names, it is italicized or underlined when written.

The same rules apply for the binomial names of animals, including insects. All bumble bees are placed in the genus *Bombus*. The orange-belted bumblebee's scientific name is *Bombus ternarius*.

Specific epithets often tell us something about the plant or animal. The epithet *rubra* means "red" and, in the case of *Quercus rubra*, refers to the color of the interior wood. The epithet *alatus* means "winged," *borealis* means "from the north," *gracilis* means "graceful," *trilobatus* means "three-lobed," and so on through literally thousands of possibilities. Other

THE LIFE IN YOUR GARDEN

specific epithets are Latinized forms of places, often the location where the plant or animal was first identified. For example, the specific epithet *florida*, as in *Cornus florida* (flowering dogwood), refers to the location of its initial discovery as a unique species. An extensive list of specific epithets can be found at http://www.winternet.com/~chuckg/dictionary.html.

The person who discovers a new plant or animal is given the honor of assigning the specific epithet; thus, many specific epithets are Latinized forms of the discoverer's last name. The epithet *sargentii*, for example, honors Charles Sprague Sargent, first director of the Arnold Arboretum. Several plants bearing his name, such as the Sargent crabapple (*Malus sargentii*), were discovered by Sargent while exploring Japan in 1892.

Similar species are grouped in the same genus. For example, all 128 known maple species are in the genus *Acer*; all 250 bumble bees are in the genus *Bombus*. We owe this elegant invention of plant and animal nomenclature to the Swedish botanist Carl Linnaeus, who, in 1753, published *Species Plantarum*. He made a similar contribution to animal nomenclature with the publication of *Systema Naturae* in 1758. Before Linnaeus, plant and animal names were long, often beautifully descriptive Latin phrases. For example, the common briar rose was known as "Rosa sylvestris inodora seu canina" (odorless woodland dog rose) or "Rosa sylvestris alba cum rubore, folio glabro" (pinkish white woodland rose with hairless leaves). It is easy to see how such a system would eventually become too cumbersome as more and more species were discovered.

The binomial system developed by Linnaeus, in use now for over 260 years, greatly simplified the task of naming organisms. Each new discovery is given a simple two-word name. The common briar rose is now *R. canina*. (Note that once a genus such as *Rosa* is established, it can thereafter within the same discussion be abbreviated to its first letter unless the discussion includes another genus that also starts with that letter.)

Every plant and animal in your garden can be identified by a simple two-word scientific name. Each organism, throughout its geographical range, will have the same binomial name, while its common name may vary from region to region. Thus the use of scientific nomenclature eliminates confusion. Consider the North American tree *Acer rubrum*. Throughout its range it goes by several different common names, including red maple, swamp maple, water maple, and soft maple. *A. saccharinum*, a maple that grows in many of the same regions of North America as *A. rubrum*, shares three of these common names: swamp maple, water maple, and soft maple. It is also known as silver maple.

Gardeners should also understand the use of cultivar, variety, and hybrid names. Horticulturally, the cultivar name, for those plants that have one, is the most important part of the plant's identity. As the name implies, a cultivar is a group of cultivated plants—that is, plants that do not occur in nature—and it is distinguished from the species from which it is derived by a specific character, such as size, habit, leaf color, flower color, cold tolerance, etc. The distinguishing characteristic(s) must be retained in subsequent generations through vegetative propagation (cuttings, graftings, tissue culture). As an example, there are at least 60 cultivars of *Acer rubrum*, including 'October Glory', selected for its outstanding deep red fall foliage. Note that cultivar names are always capitalized and enclosed in single quotation marks, an easy way to recognize a cultivar. (The plant catalogs that leave out these single quotation marks are not as professional as they would like you to believe.) A cultivar's name is decided by the horticulturist who develops it.

A variety name is assigned to a group of naturally occurring individuals within a species that display a significant difference from the species. The differences are inheritable and reproduce true-to-type in succeeding generations. Varieties of woody plants often have a distinct geographic distribution. For example, the Southern population of *Acer rubrum* is *A. rubrum* var. *drummondii*. Note that variety names are Latinized, always in italics, and follow the abbreviated designator "var.," which is not italicized.

Many modern garden plants are hybrids resulting from the chance or controlled crossing of two species (rarely plants from two genera). In areas where *Acer rubrum* and *A. saccharinum* (silver maple) grow together, a naturally occurring hybrid, *A.* x *freemanii,* occurs. The two species have crossed in the wild, resulting in a hybrid form with unique intermediate characteristics. Note that hybrids are written with a designator, the "x" before the hybrid specific epithet.

You can find cultivars of hybrids. In fact, there are several cultivars selected from the Freeman hybrids, such as *Acer* x *freemanii* 'Armstrong', a cultivar with a distinctly upright, narrow habit.

Yes, nomenclature can seem tedious, and nearly impossible to absorb in one reading. And even when you have a command of scientific names, it is so much easier to resort to common names. Thanks to Linnaeus, however, use of the simple two-word binomial is all that is necessary to avoid confusion.

Appendix 2

Native Perennial *Asclepias* species for the Garden Insectary

When the two of us speak to groups about planting for monarch butterflies, we are always asked two questions: "Where can I find milkweed seeds (or plants) for my garden?" and "Which type of milkweed is best for attracting monarchs?" Often an audience member will suggest using common milkweed, *Asclepias syriaca*, but we advise against the use of this native perennial species as it will quickly take over the garden with an aggressive rhizomatous growth habit. It is better reserved for roadsides, pastures, and meadow gardens, areas where it can run rampant. For relatively small gardens, we recommend a perennial called swamp milkweed (*Asclepias incarnata*), native to the eastern U.S.

The gardener has a choice of where to plant milkweeds. They may be grown in beds and borders, their showy flowers as lovely as those of other herbaceous ornamentals, or they may be added to the garden insectary, that small patch of plants grown to provide pollen and nectar sources for pollinators and other beneficial insects. We have opted to grow our milkweeds in the garden proper. True enough, once lepidopteran larvae and aphids have had their way, milkweeds are little more than naked stems topped by seed pods, but they make up for their appearance by providing terrific caterpillar watching.

Swamp Milkweed

In its tolerance of a wide range of growing conditions and its effectiveness in attracting monarchs and other pollinators, swamp milkweed is without question one of the best perennial milkweeds for home gardens throughout its native range. It has an erect clump-forming habit, growing 3 to 4 feet tall with unbranched stems, and never grows out of bounds. In summer the end of each stem bears a cluster of small, fragrant, pink to mauve flowers that are a favorite of butterflies, bees, and other pollinating insects. These flowers are followed in late summer by attractive seed pods, each about 4 inches long, which split open when ripe to release silky-haired seeds to the wind.

'Ice Ballet' is a compact, white-flowered cultivar of swamp milkweed that grows to 3 feet in height. Reeser first saw this cultivar in a Cape Cod garden, tucked amid the deep green leaves of Northern bayberry along a winding entrance drive. (See the Chapter 8 sidebar, "Use Bayberry to Harbor Functional Perennials and Shrubs," for a photo of 'Ice Ballet'.)

The common name, swamp milkweed, belies this plant's ability to grow equally well in wet or well-drained areas. Full sun is required for optimum growth. The plants have deep taproots and are best left undisturbed once established, and their new growth is slow to emerge in spring.

Recommended Native Milkweeds for Each State

If you decide to grow perennial milkweeds in your garden, it is important to plant species that are native to your state. By doing so, you prevent the escape of a potentially competitive species that could displace populations of native milkweeds, thereby reducing regional diversity. You will also need to know the growing conditions required for each possible choice. For example, choosing a species that grows only in cool, wet areas when your garden is hot and dry would be a mistake.

There are over 100 species of *Asclepias* scattered about the U.S., some native to large regions of the country, others found only in small pockets of essential habitat within a limited region of one state. Only 27 of these function as major larval host plants for monarchs. In order to identify which of this subset are suitable for small gardens in each state, we relied heavily on the recommendations of organizations devoted to monarch butterfly conservation, including government and academic programs. Our research resulted in the following list of 18 milkweed species, the state(s) in which each can be found, and a brief description of each species, its growth habit, and its required growing conditions.

Once you identify the milkweed species you want to grow, will you be able to find either seed or plants? Start your search with local garden centers. With increasing awareness of the role that private gardens can play in sustaining populations of monarch butterflies, more and more garden centers are carrying milkweed seeds and starter plants. If there are no local sources, look online for sources of the species you need.

A. angustifolia (Arizona milkweed): AZ

Native only to Arizona, this species, also called "narrow leaf milkweed" or "talayote," is characterized by thin, narrow leaves and small white flowers. It has a clump-forming habit with a taproot and several stems growing 2 to 3 feet from a common crown. In the wild it is found in riparian woods, mountains, and canyons. In the garden it should be grown in well-drained soils, full sun or partial shade. The minimum temperature range for this species is between 10° and 20° F.

A. asperula (antelope horn): AZ, CA, CO, ID, KS, NE, NM, NV, OK, TX, UT

The common name for this species is derived from seedpods that curve upward like the horns of an antelope. The leaves are long, the stem tinged with maroon. Greenish-yellow and maroon flowers are borne in broad, round clusters on stems that grow from a central crown to a height of 2 to 3 feet. Found in desert swales, sand, and rocky hillsides, this species must have full sun, soil that is well-drained, and a minimum temperature range of −10° to −20° F. Other common names include "spider milkweed" and "trailing milkweed."

A. californica (California milkweed): CA

As in many drought-tolerant plants, the stems and leaves of this species are covered with long hairs that give the plant a woolly countenance, a striking background for the violet flowers. Mature plants have multiple stems up to 42 inches in height, all growing from a single crown. Native to flats, grassy slopes, and open woods, this species must have full sun, well-drained soil, and a minimum temperature range between 10° and 20° F.

A. cordifolia (heartleaf milkweed): CA, NV, OR

The specific epithet for this species, cordifolia, refers to its heart-shaped leaves. It is primarily found in the northern part of California. The flowers are dark red to purple, borne on upright stems with an overall height range of 1 to 4 feet. Found mostly on rocky slopes, heartleaf milkweed needs full sun to partial shade, well-drained to rocky soil, and a minimum temperature range of −10° to 0° F.

A. eriocarpa (woolly pod milkweed): CA, NV

All parts of this plant except the flowers are covered with fine hairs, those on the pods the longest, hence the common name. Stems grow erect from a central tap-rooted crown to a height of 3 to 4 feet, with pink, white, or cream-colored flowers borne on long stalks from leaf axils at the top of the plant. Native to dry flats, rocky hillsides, woods, and deserts, this is a low-maintenance garden plant that is happy in clay soils with full sun and minimum temperatures between 10° and 20° F.

A. exaltata (poke milkweed): AL, CT, DE, GA, IA, IL, IN, KY, MA, MD, ME, MI, MN, MS, NC, NH, NJ, NY, OH, PA, RI, SC, TN, VA, VT, WI, WV

Where the range of poke milkweed overlaps that of common milkweed (*A. syriaca*), the two species have been known to hybridize, making identification difficult. The flowers of poke milkweed, however, are distinctive, each blossom weeping downward from its cluster on a long stalk, the individual white flowers tinged with lavender or green. Native to shores and woodland edges, the stems emerge from a central crown to grow from 2 to 6 feet tall. In the garden, provide this species with full sun, a moist soil rich in organic matter, and a minimum temperature range of –40° to –30° F.

A. fascicularis (Mexican whorled milkweed): CA, ID, NV, OR, UT, WA

Also called "narrowleaf milkweed," this is a graceful plant with thin stems and narrow, pale-green, lanceolate leaves. Erect flower clusters branch from the tops of the stems, the small flowers ranging from pale pink to purple, white, or greenish. Overall plant height ranges from 2 to 3 feet. Native to dry climates, plains, hills, valleys, and roadsides, *A. fascicularis* thrives in full-sun locations with dry to moist soils, including clay soils, and can tolerate a minimum temperature range of –10° to 0° F.

A. humistrata (sandhill milkweed): AL, FL, GA, LA, MS, NC, SC

Sandhill milkweed is an odd fellow with purplish stems that grow nearly flat to the ground (*humistrata* means sprawling), only the clasping leaves, dull green with purplish veins, reaching for the sun. The flower color is pink to white. In the wild, this species grows in sandy soils that abut relatively open forests; similar conditions of full sun and sandy dry soil should be provided in the garden. Plants can tolerate a minimum temperature range of 10° to 20° F.

A. incarnata (swamp milkweed): AL, AR, CO, CT, DC, DE, FL, GA, IA, ID, IL, IN, KS, KY, LA, MA, MD, ME, MI, MN, MO, MT, NC, ND, NE, NH, NJ, NM, NV, NY, OH, OK, PA, RI, SC, SD, TN, TX, UT, VA, VT, WI, WV, WY

Swamp milkweed grows wild in swamps and wet meadows throughout most of the continental U.S. and eastern Canada, but it is surprisingly tolerant of average, well-drained garden soil. Blooming in July and August, it has an erect, clump-forming habit, reaching 3 to

5 feet tall with a deep taproot. Tight clusters of cinnamon-scented hourglass flowers, wide at the bottom and top but constricted in the middle, range in color from pink to mauve, almost red in some locations. These are followed by 4-inch-long seed pods, which split open at maturity to release silky-haired seeds to the wind. The cultivar 'Ice Palace' was selected from white variants found in the wild. Native habitats include the edges of lakes, ponds, marshes, swamps, and other wet areas. In the garden, grow swamp milkweed in full sun and keep plants regularly watered. Established plants can tolerate a minimum temperature range of –38º F.

A. oenotheroides (side-cluster milkweed): CO, LA, NM, OK, TX

Also called zizotes milkweed from the Spanish name for this species ("hierba de zizotes"), side-cluster milkweed is much reduced in size compared with most *Asclepias* species, only 12 to 18 inches in height. Native to prairies, ditches, and fields, all areas of sandy, rocky ground, it is one of the least conspicuous milkweeds. The flower is green with purple tinges, the leaves erect with wavy edges. In the garden, provide full sun and well-drained moist soil. Side-cluster milkweed can tolerate a minimum temperature range between –10º and 0º F.

A. perennis (aquatic milkweed): AL, AR, FL, GA, IL, IN, KY, LA, MO, MS, SC, TN, TX

Aquatic milkweed, also known as "white swamp milkweed," loves wet feet and thus is ideal for any garden spot that is continuously wet. In appearance it is much like *A. incarnata*, but smaller, its height typically between 18 and 24 inches. The flowers are typically white or light pink, the stems dark purplish-green. Native habitats include floodplains, marshes, swamps, and drainage ditches. Garden conditions include full sunlight and, of course, moist soil. *A. perennis* can tolerate minimum temperatures from –10º to 0º F.

A. speciosa (showy milkweed): AZ, CA, CO, IA, ID, IL, KS, MO, MN, MT, ND, NE, NM, NV, OK, OR, SD, TX, UT, WA, WI, WY

Similar in appearance to common milkweed (*A. syriaca*), with which it hybridizes where the two species coexist, showy milkweed differs in having a layer of fine white hairs on the leaves and flowers that look like small crowns. Most importantly, unlike *A. syriaca*, this species does not produce rhizomes and thus does not form large clones. Flower color varies from pink to red and purple. Foliage is blue-green and hairy. Height is typically to 3 feet, but plants can grow to 6 feet when conditions are favorable. Native habitats include savannas, prairies, roadsides, *Euchaetes egle* old fields, and meadows. In the garden, showy milkweed can tolerate a spectrum of soil textures, including coarse, medium, and fine, but it must have full sun. It tolerates a minimum temperature range of −40° to −30 °F.

A. subulata (rush milkweed): AZ, CA, NV

A mature plant of *A. subulata* more resembles a clump of horsetails (*Equisetum* sp.) than a milkweed. Small leaves are produced only after periods of rainfall; otherwise plants consist of leafless stems bearing either a few clusters of cream, white, or yellow flowers or a handful of pendulous, narrow seed pods. Greenish-white stems, ranging in height from 2 to 4 feet, grow from a common root crown and are the major photosynthetic organs. As you might expect, the dry slopes and plains of desert areas constitute the major native habitat of this unusual species. Xeric gardens with sandy or rocky soil and minimum temperatures ranging between 10° and 20° F are ideal for this species.

A. tuberosa (butterfly weed): AL, AR, AZ, CA, CO, CT, DC, DE, FL, GA, IA, IL, IN, KS, KY, LA, MA, MD, ME, MI, MN, MO, MS, NC, NE, NH, NJ, NM, NY, OH, OK, PA, RI, SC, SD, TN, TX, UT, VA, VT, WI, WV

This species, easily identified when not in flower by its alternate leaves, is often seen at the front of perennial borders, grown both as an ornamental for its bright orange, red, or yellow flowers and to attract butterflies. The foliage is coarse and covered with small hairs, the stems emerging from a deep, woody taproot to reach 2 feet in height. Native habitats include the sandy or loamy soils of prairies, roadsides, and open woodlands. Garden plants require full sun, well-drained soils, and winter temperatures no lower than −40° F.

A. variegata (white milkweed): AL, AR, CT, DC, DE, FL GA, IL IN, KY, LA MD, MO, MS, NC, NJ, NY, OH, OK, PA, SC, TN, TX, VA, WV

White milkweed in bloom is sure to catch every gardener's eye with clusters of flowers that form a spherical white ball, a snowball that contrasts sharply with the green foliage. Looking closely, you notice a tinge of purple at the base of the petals. The flowers are borne among the topmost leaves of a single, narrow stem that varies in color from green to a brown-red. The native habitats for white milkweed are the sandy to rocky soils of open woodlands and woodland edges. Some shade is thus required to grow this species in the garden. Minimum temperatures in the garden should not dip below −10° F.

A. verticillata (whorled milkweed): AL, AR, AZ, CT, DC, DE, FL, GA, IA, IL, IN, KS, KY, LA, MA, MD, MI, MN, MO, MS, MT, NC, ND, NE, NJ, NM, NY, OH, OK, PA, RI, SC, SD, TN, TX, VA, VT, WI, WV, WY

One of the most widely distributed milkweed species, whorled milkweed is an important late-season host plant for monarch caterpillars. Its aggressive colonizing habit should limit its use to meadow gardens, roadsides, and other large areas where it will become the dominant plant. Plants have linear leaves on thin stems that stand between 1 and 3 feet tall. The flower is greenish-white with a purple tinge. Native habitat includes the sandy, clayey, or rocky calcareous soils of prairies, flood plains, and open woods. Planting sites should offer full sunlight and medium- to fine-textured soil. This species can be grown in sites where minimum temperatures reach –40º F.

A. vestita (woolly milkweed): CA

Woolly milkweed grows only in California's dry desert slopes and plains. The common name refers to leaves that are covered with fine white hairs, giving plants a woolly grayish-green appearance. The flower is typically cream to yellow with a purple or brown tinge, borne on plants ranging between 2 and 3 feet in height. Grow woolly milkweed in full-sun gardens with winter temperatures above –10º F.

A. viridis (green antelopehorn milkweed): AL, AR, FL, GA, IL, IN, KS, KY, LA, MO, MS, NE, OH, OK, SC, TN, TX, WV

A common pasture plant through much of its range, this species can also be found along roadsides, ditches, prairies, and other open areas where competition from other plants is minimal. Mature plants are short, typically 12 inches tall, with several stems emerging from a root crown. The flowers are yellow-white with a purple tinge. *A. viridis* requires full sunlight, soils that are sandy or rocky, and winter temperatures that do not dip below –20º F.

Appendix 3

Additional Functional Understory Trees and Shrubs

The understory trees and shrubs presented in Chapter 8 are those that we grow in our garden. In this appendix, we present many other species suited to gardens across North America. A USDA Range Map shows where each species is native.

Alnus (Alders)
Brookside Alder *(A. serrulata)*
USDA Hardiness Zones: 4 to 9
Height: 12 to 20 feet; a multi-stemmed shrub with several twisted stems
Width: crown often broader than shrub height
Sunlight: full sun to shade
Soil: pH 6.8 to 7.2; moist to wet soils required; fine sandy loams, peats, and muck
Bark: shiny, gray brown; lacks conspicuous lenticels
Flowers: male catkins greenish-yellow in drooping clusters; female catkins reddish in upright clusters
Fruits: resemble small woody cones, persist through winter
Autumn color: yellow tinged with red
Wildlife use: Brookside alders and other *Alnus* species are host plants of moth caterpillars, aphids, beetles, and other insects. All told, 48 species of insects have been found on alders. Caterpillars of an unusual butterfly, the harvester (*Feniseca tarquinius*), feed on woolly aphids that are attracted to the shrubs. The seeds, buds, and catkins of alders are eaten by ruffed grouse, woodcock, swamp sparrows, goldfinches, redpolls, crossbills, and pine siskins. Alder

Alnus serrulata -
USDA hardiness zone map

shrubs also provide nesting habitat and cover for woodcock, grackles, and other birds. The woodland jumping mouse (*Napaeozapus insignis*) feeds on alder seeds.

Amelanchier (Serviceberries)
Common Serviceberry *(A. arborea)*

USDA Hardiness Zones: 4 to 9

Height: 15 to 25 feet

Width: 15 to 25 feet; suckers freely from roots

Sunlight: full sun to partial shade

Soil: average, mesic, well-drained

Flowers: white, fragrant, March to April

Fruits: purplish-black, June; resemble blueberries in size

Autumn color: yellow to bronze-red

Amelanchier arborea -
USDA hardiness zone map

Wildlife use: Fruits are relished by cardinals, waxwings, hairy woodpeckers, thrushes, catbirds, orioles, and robins, as well as squirrels and chipmunks. Butterfly caterpillars that rely on *A. arborea* as a host plant include the striped hairstreak (*Satyrium liparops*) and the red-spotted purple (*Limenitis arthemis*); moth species include the blue spring moth (*Lomigrapha semiclarata*), chokeberry underwing (*Catocala praeclara*), and several dagger moth species (*Acronicta* sp.).

Aronia (Chokeberries)
Red Chokeberry *(A. arbutifolia)*

USDA Hardiness Zones: 4 to 9

Height: 6 to 10 feet

Width: 3 to 5 feet; a suckering, spreading, colonizing shrub

Sunlight: full sun for best flowering and fruiting; will tolerate partial shade

Soil: adaptable to most soil types, wet or dry

Flowers: small, white, early May

Fruits: flat clusters of red berry-like fruits (pomes), from September into December

Aronia arbutifolia -
USDA hardiness zone map

Autumn color: Red chokeberry is one of the best shrubs for fall color, its leaves turning an intense raspberry to crimson with purplish highlights. It may also have some orange mixed in, especially in shady sites.

Wildlife use: Red chokeberry flowers are a favorite among pollinators of all types. Like *A. melanocarpa*, the fruits are taken as a last resort by a variety of overwintering birds.

Clethra (Clethras)
Cinnamonbark Clethra *(C. acuminata)*

USDA Hardiness Zones: 5 to 8

Height: 6 to 10 feet

Width: 6 to 10 feet

Sunlight: partial shade

Soil: acidic (pH less than 6.8), well-drained

Bark: exfoliating, red-brown

Flowers: white, in drooping spikes, spicy-scented; summer

Fruits: persistent, brown, peppercorn-shaped seed capsules

Autumn color: yellow-orange

Clethra acuminata -
USDA hardiness zone map

Wildlife use: Pollinators include bumble bees, solitary bees, butterflies, and hoverflies. *C. acuminata* also attracts hummingbirds.

Cornus (Dogwoods)
Silky Dogwood *(C. amomum)*

USDA Hardiness Zones: 5 to 8

Height: 6 to 12 feet

Width: 6 to 12 feet

Sunlight: full to partial

Soil: clay, loamy, or sandy; moist to wet; pH 6.1 to 7.5

Flowers: rounded clusters of white flowers, mid to late summer

Fruits: berries, porcelain blue with white blotches; late summer

Autumn color: orange, red, or purple

Cornus amomum -
USDA hardiness zone map

Wildlife use: Fruits are eaten by songbirds, waterfowl, and small mammals. Flowers serve as a nectar source for bees.

Flowering Dogwood *(C. florida)*

USDA Hardiness Zones: 5 to 9

Height: understory tree, 20 to 50 feet

Width: 20 to 50 feet

Sunlight: partial sun

Soil: loamy, dry to moist, pH 5 to 7

Flowers: white, spring

Fruits: red to orange berries

Autumn color: red to crimson-purple, best when grown in partial sun

Wildlife use: Fruits are eaten by songbirds, waterfowl, small mammals.

Cornus florida -
USDA hardiness zone map

Pacific Dogwood *(C. nuttallii)*

USDA Hardiness Zones: 7 to 8

Habit: tree or large multi-stemmed shrub, depending on growing conditions

Height: 20 to 75 feet

Width: 20 feet

Sunlight: filtered sunlight under the canopy of taller trees; one-third full sunlight is optimum

Soil: mesic to dry

Flowers: creamy-white, spring

Fruits: bright red

Autumn color: various shades of red

Wildlife use: Songbirds eat the fleshy fruits.

Cornus nuttallii -
USDA hardiness zone map

Gray Dogwood *(C. racemosa)*

USDA Hardiness Zones: 4 to 8

Height: 6 to 12 feet

Width: 6 to 12 feet

Sunlight: wide tolerance from full sun to partial shade

Soil: wide tolerance from clay to loamy

Flowers: erect cone-shaped clusters of white flowers in late spring

Fruits: white berries on red stems, late summer into fall

Autumn color: reddish to purple

Wildlife use: Songbirds, waterfowl, ruffed grouse, sharp-tailed grouse, ring-necked pheasants, white-footed mice, and small mammals eat the fruits. Bees and beetles forage the flowers for nectar. Nesting birds include willow flycatchers, gray catbirds, yellow

Cornus racemosa -
USDA hardiness zone map

warblers, and American goldfinches. Gray dogwood is a larval host plant for white-marked tussock moths (*Orgyia leucostigma*) and the cecropia moth (*Hyalophora cecropia*).

Round-leaf Dogwood (*C. rugosa*)

USDA Hardiness Zones: 3 to 7
Height: 10 feet
Width: 8 to 10 feet
Sunlight: partial shade to full shade
Soil: dry to well-drained sandy loam
Flowers: clusters of creamy-white flowers, May to June
Fruits: blue, dispersed in August
Autumn color: blends of red, purple, orange
Wildlife use: Fruits are eaten by squirrels and birds. Flowers provide nectar for bees and butterflies. Larval host: spring azure butterfly (*Celastrina ladon*).

Cornus rugosa -
USDA hardiness zone map

Red-osier Dogwood (*C. sericea, formerly C. stolonifera*)

USDA Hardiness Zones: 3 to 8
Height: 6 to 9 feet
Width: 8 to 12 feet
Sunlight: full sun to partial shade
Soil: *C. sericea* grows best in areas where the soil is saturated in spring (rain gardens, edges of ponds, streams, wetlands) and dry by late summer.
Flowers: white to cream-colored, June to August
Fruits: white, sometimes with blueish tinge
Autumn color: purple
Note: *Red-osier dogwood is often grown for the bright red color of young stems.*
Wildlife use: Thickets created by the rooting stems provide cover for wildlife. Fruits are eaten by waterbirds, marsh birds, and shorebirds. Nesting birds include willow flycatchers, gray catbirds, yellow warblers, and American goldfinches. Larval hosts: spring azure butterfly and several moth species. Pollinators include native bees, including bumble bees, syrphid flies, and longhorn beetles.

Cornus sericea -
USDA hardiness zone map

Diervilla (Bush Honeysuckles)
Southern Bush Honeysuckle (*Diervilla sessilifolia*)

USDA Hardiness Zones: 5 to 8

Height: 3 to 5 feet

Width: 3 to 5 feet

Sunlight: full sun to part shade

Soil: tolerant of most conditions; prefers acidic and dry to mesic soils

Flowers: sulfur yellow, in clusters of three to seven, summer

Fruits: brown seed pod

Autumn color: not significant

Wildlife use: Native bees, particularly bumble bees, are primary pollinators while butterflies and hummingbirds are regular nectar feeders. Plants are larval hosts for the fawn sphinx moth (*Sphinx kalmiae*).

Diervilla sessilifolia -
USDA hardiness zone map

Ilex (Hollies)
Possum Haw (*I. decidua*)

USDA Hardiness Zones: 5 to 9

Height: 7 to 15 feet with spreading, rounded crown

Width: 5 to 12 feet

Sunlight: full sun to partial shade

Soil: prefers moist, acidic, organic soils; tolerates clay soils; suitable for rain gardens

Flowers: dull white; May

Fruits: orange-red berries ripening in early autumn

Autumn color: purplish-green to yellow

Wildlife use: Deciduous holly fruits are consumed by small mammals, songbirds, and gamebirds, including wild turkeys and quail. Larvae of the pawpaw sphinx moth (*Dolba hyloeus*) feed on the leaves of *I. decidua*.

Ilex decidua -
USDA hardiness zone map

Inkberry (*I. glabra*)

USDA Hardiness Zones: 4 to 9

Height: 9 feet

Width: 9 feet, dense in youth, more open at maturity

Sunlight: full sun preferred, tolerates partial shade

Soil: rich, consistently moist, acidic soil; resistant to soil compaction and salt

Flowers: greenish-white, May to June

Fruits: The species has black berries, the cultivar 'Ivory Queen' white-fruited.

Autumn color: evergreen, but more yellow-green in winter

Wildlife use: Bobwhite, turkeys, bluebirds, brown thrashers, hermit thrushes, and other birds frequently eat inkberry fruits while raccoons, coyotes, and opossums feed on them when other food is scarce. Inkberry is also an important nectar plant for bees.

Ilex glabra -
USDA hardiness zone map

Morella (Bayberry, Sweet Fern)
California Wax Myrtle (*M. californica*)

USDA Hardiness Zones: 7 to 10

Height: 10 to 30 feet; easily kept smaller with pruning

Width: 10 to 12 feet; a fast-growing, multi-trunked shrub

Sunlight: full sun or partial shade

Soil: adaptable to sandy, clay, or loamy soils; very drought tolerant, yet performs well in wetter areas, including rain gardens

Foliage: spicy-scented

Flowers: reddish-yellow catkins, tiny and inconspicuous; late spring and summer

Fruits: brownish-purple berries that ripen in fall

Autumn color: foliage evergreen

Morella californica -
USDA hardiness zone map

Wildlife use: The berries are eaten by quail, waxwings, Eastern kingbirds, Northern mockingbirds, Northern flickers, red-bellied woodpeckers, and wood thrush. Plants are larval hosts for the red-banded hairstreak butterfly (*Calycopis cecrops*).

Rhus (Sumacs)
Fragrant Sumac (*R. aromatica*)

USDA Hardiness Zones: 3 to 9

Height: 2 to 6 feet

Width: 6 to 10 feet

Sunlight: full sun to partial shade

Soil: dry to mesic soils; tolerant of clay, dry, and shallow rocky soils

Flowers: Tiny yellow female flowers form at stem tips in early spring before the leaves appear. Male catkins form in late summer and persist through the winter before releasing pollen in early spring.

Foliage: fragrant, disagreeably so to some

Fruits: small clusters of hairy red berries

Autumn color: shades of orange, red, and purple

Wildlife use: Thickets provide excellent cover for wildlife. The berries provide winter food for small animals and over 20 species of gamebirds and songbirds, including Townsend's solitaires. Shrubs are larval hosts for red-banded hairstreak butterflies (*Calycopis cecrops*), banded hairstreak butterflies (*Satyrium calanus*), and several other lepidopterans. The flowers

Rhus aromatica -
USDA hardiness zone map

attract pollinators, including solitary bees and hoverflies, while small carpenter bees create tunnel-nests in the stem pith.

Flameleaf Sumac (*R. copallinum*)

USDA Hardiness Zones: 4 to 9

Height: 7 to 15 feet

Width: 10 to 20 feet; spreads by suckering to form large colonies

Sunlight: full sun to partial shade

Soil: dry to mesic well-drained soils

Flowers: tiny greenish-yellow flowers in pyramidal clusters, July to August; male and female flowers on separate plants

Fruits: hairy berry-like fruits in clusters; ripen in autumn, gradually turning maroon-brown; persist through winter

Autumn color: flame red

Wildlife use: Flowers are foraged for nectar and pollen by many different insects, particularly wasps, flies, and bees. The

Rhus copallinum -
USDA hardiness zone map

foliage is eaten by caterpillars of moths (at least 10 species) and butterflies (two species). Gamebirds and songbirds eat the berries during fall and winter.

Smooth Sumac (*R. glabra*)

Note: *This species is very similar to* R. typhina *except for lack of pubescence on the stems, hence the common name, and a range that extends west to the Pacific coast.*

USDA Hardiness Zones: 3 to 9

Height: 9 to 15 feet

Width: 9 to 15 feet; spreads by root suckers to form large colonies

Sunlight: full sun to partial shade

Soil: dry to mesic well-drained soil; clay, loamy, or sandy; pH 5.3 to 7.5

Flowers: yellowish-green flowers in June; male and female flowers on separate plants

Fruits: hairy berry-like fruits in clusters; ripen in autumn, gradually turning maroon-brown; persist through winter

Autumn color: bright orange to red

Wildlife use: Flower-visiting insects include numerous species of solitary bee, hoverflies, bee flies, tachinid flies, and occasional butterflies and beetles. Plants serve as larval hosts to the red-banded hairstreak butterfly (*Calycopis cecrops*) and at least 15 moth species. Bird species that eat the fruits include the ruffed grouse, bobwhite, ring-necked pheasant, red-headed woodpecker, downy woodpecker, cardinal, Northern flicker, American crow, fish crow, starling, brown thrasher, Swainson's thrush, Eastern phoebe, veery, vireos, catbird, mockingbird, robin, junco, white-throated sparrow, and pine warbler.

Rhus glabra -
USDA hardiness zone map

Rosa (Roses)

Smooth Rose (*R. blanda*)

USDA Hardiness Zones: 3 to 7

Height: 3 to 4 feet

Width: 3 feet to 4 feet; variable, depending on growing conditions

Sunlight: full sun

Soil: dry to moderate in moisture; prefers sandy, loamy soils

Flowers: pink to deep-rose petals surrounding yellow stamens; June to July

Fruits: bright red mid-summer hips

Autumn color: not significant

Wildlife use: The hips are eaten by a variety of animals including robins, mockingbirds, wild turkeys, bobwhite, cedar waxwings, bluebirds, goldfinches, cardinals, brown thrashers, song sparrows, skunks, and white-footed mice.

Rosa blanda -
USDA hardiness zone map

Swamp Rose (*R. palustris*)

USDA Hardiness Zones: 3 to 9

Height: 6 to 8 feet

Width: 6 to 7 feet

Sunlight: full sun; tolerant of shade

Soil: moist to wet; organically rich, acidic

Flowers: dark rose-pink, fragrant, showy but short-lived; May to June

Fruits: red or orange hips

Autumn color: not significant

Wildlife use: Primary pollinators are bumble bees and other long-tongued bees. Less effective pollinators include native solitary bees, hoverflies, and beetles. Only pollen is offered as a floral reward. Insects that feed on the foliage include caterpillars of moths and butterflies, larvae of sawflies, leafhoppers, aphids, beetles, rose curculio, rose chafer, and the larvae of the raspberry cane borer. The hips are eaten by gamebirds, songbirds, small rodents and other mammals. Birds that construct their nests in the shrubs include catbirds, mockingbirds, brown thrashers, yellow warblers, and cardinals.

Rosa palustris - USDA hardiness zone map

Prairie Rose (*R. setigera*)

USDA Hardiness Zones: 5 to 8

Height: vining with branches growing 6 to 15 feet tall

Width: spreading to 6 feet or more

Sunlight: full sun to partial shade

Soil: fertile loamy soil preferred, but adaptable to clay and sand; moist soil, dislikes standing water or droughty conditions

Flowers: light pink to rosy-pink fading to white, yellow stamens; typical rosy fragrance; May

Fruits: red hips

Autumn color: not significant

Wildlife use: Honeybees and solitary bees are the primary pollinators. Beetles and hoverflies move some pollen around as they forage for pollen. Plants serve as larval host for at least 12 moth species. The hips are eaten by prairie chickens and other birds.

Rosa setigera - USDA hardiness zone map

Nootka Rose (*R. nutkana*)

USDA Hardiness Zones: 4 to 8

Height: typically 3 to 6 feet

Width: 6 feet; new plants arise from the mother plant through underground runners.

Sunlight: full to partial sun

Soil: tolerant of moist soils and periodic flooding; pH 4 to 7; withstands long summer drought

Flowers: cinnamon-like fragrance, pink, May to July

Fruits: orange-red hips that persist through winter

Autumn color: deep pink to orange-red

Rosa nutkana -
USDA hardiness zone map

Wildlife use: In summer, hummingbirds and bees forage among the flowers for nectar and pollen while birds seek shelter and build their nests in nootka rose thickets. In winter, towhees, thrashers, Stellar's jays, and other songbirds feed on the hips. This rose species also serves as a larval host for the mourning cloak butterfly (*Nymphalis antiopa*) and grey hairstreak butterfly (*Strymon melinus*).

Arkansas Rose (*R. arkansana*)

USDA Hardiness Zones: 4 to 8

Height: a small shrub, 0.5 to 2 feet tall

Width: 3 to 4 feet

Sunlight: full sun to partial shade

Soil: mesic to dry conditions; prefers poor soils that contain some clay, rocky material, or sand

Flowers: petals nearly pure white to deep rose-pink, often bicolored, yellow stamens; fragrant; late spring to mid-summer

Fruits: round bright red hips; ripen in summer

Autumn color: not significant

Rosa arkansana -
USDA hardiness zone map

Wildlife use: Flowers offer only pollen as a reward to foraging insects, including bumble bees, solitary bees, beetles, and hoverflies. Insects that feed on the foliage, stems, and other parts of the plant include grasshoppers, thrips, plant bugs, aphids, leafhoppers, gall wasp larvae, flea beetles, and moth caterpillars. Prairie chickens and bobwhite quail feed on the hips.

Spiraea (Spireas)
Rose spirea *(S. douglasii)*

USDA Hardiness Zones: 5 to 8

Height: 4 to 6 feet

Width: 3 to 6 feet

Sunlight: full sun to partial shade

Soil: well-drained acidic soils,

Flowers: rose-pink in terminal spike-like clusters

Autumn color: not significant

Wildlife use: The flowers attract bees, butterflies, and beetles.

Spiraea douglasii -
USDA hardiness zone map

Symphoricarpos (Snowberries)
Coralberry *(S. orbiculatus)*

USDA Hardiness Zones: 2 to 7

Height: 2 to 5 feet with arching stems

Width: 4 to 8 feet; spreads by runners to form thickets

Sunlight: full sun to partial shade

Soil: tolerates a wide range of soils, performing best in mesic well-drained soils

Flowers: white, bell-shaped, pink-tinged; summer, along the stems in axillary clusters and at stem ends in spikes

Fruits: round coral-red berries that mature in autumn

Autumn color: insignificant

Wildlife use: Wasps, flies, and bees suck nectar from the flow-ers, but bees are the primary pollinators. Plants serve as larval

Symphoricarpos orbiculatus -
USDA hardiness zone map

hosts for the snowberry clearwing moth (*Hemaris diffinis*), hummingbird clearwing moth (*H. thysbe*), and the sulfur moth (*Hesperumia sulphuraria*). Berries are eaten primarily by robins, also bobwhite quail.

Vaccinium (Blueberries)
Lowbush Blueberry *(V. angustifolium)*

USDA Hardiness Zones: 3 to 6

Height: 1 to 3 feet

Width: spreading groundcover

Sunlight: full sun to partial shade

Soil: acidic (pH 6.8 or lower); dry to mesic

Flowers: white, May and June

Fruits: blue berries

Autumn color: brilliant red

Wildlife use: In addition to bumble bees, which use high frequency vibration of their thoracic muscles to pollinate blueberry flowers (a process called "buzz pollination"), lowbush blueberries are also visited by solitary bees in search of both pollen and nectar rewards. Caterpillars of two butterflies, the brown elfin (*Callophyrus augustinus*) and Henry's elfin (*C. henrici*), feed on the flowers and developing berries, while over 40 moth species feed on the foliage. The berries are an important food source for many animals, including terrestrial turtles, gamebirds, over 25 species of songbirds, foxes, raccoons, skunks, opossums, squirrels, chipmunks, and mice.

Vaccinium angustifolium -
USDA hardiness zone map

California Huckleberry *(V. ovatum)*

USDA Hardiness Zones: 3 to 7

Height: 4 to 8 feet in full sun, taller in shade

Width: 3 to- 6 feet

Sunlight: prefers full to partial shade, but will tolerate sun in coastal areas

Soil: dry to mesic, well-drained; pH 4 to 6

Flowers: pinkish-white, bell-shaped; spring and summer

Fruits: blue-black

Autumn color: evergreen

Wildlife use: The flowers attract butterflies while the fruits are eaten by grouse, chipmunks, mice, scarlet tanagers, bluebirds, thrushes, and other songbirds.

Vaccinium ovatum -
USDA hardiness zone map

Viburnum (Viburnums)

Arrowwood Viburnum *(V. dentatum)*

USDA Hardiness Zones: 2 to 8

Height: an upright, mounded, multi-branched shrub from 6 to 10 feet

Width: 6 to 10 feet

Sunlight: full sun to partial shade

Soil: dry to wet, pH 6.6 to 7.5

Flowers: white with yellow stamens, May to June

Fruits: blue-black, berry-like

Autumn color: yellow to orange and red

Wildlife use: Fruits eaten by over 35 species of birds, including Eastern bluebirds, Northern flickers, gray catbirds, grosbeaks, thrushes, waxwings, thrashers, towhees, bobwhite quail, cardinals, bluebirds, flycatchers, redpolls, and American robins. Plants are larval hosts of the spring azure butterfly (*Celastrina ladon*), Baltimore checkerspot butterfly, saddleback caterpillar moth (*Acharia stimulea*), and hummingbird moths, as well as a nectar source for red admiral butterflies.

Viburnum dentatum -
USDA hardiness zone map

Possumhaw *(V. nudum)*

USDA Hardiness Zones: 5 to 9

Habit: rounded, multi-stemmed, upright spreading

Height: 5 to 12 feet

Width: 5 to 12 feet

Sunlight: full sun to partial shade

Soil: prefers wet, mucky, acidic (pH less than 6.8) soils

Flowers: white, fragrant, flat-topped clusters, May to June

Fruits: Ovoid berry-like fruits change color as they mature from light pink to dark pink to blue to purplish-black at maturity.

Autumn color: maroon to dark red-purple

Wildlife use: The berries are eaten by songbirds, including robins, cardinals, and woodpeckers, as well as waterbirds, shorebirds, and small mammals. Possumhaws serve as larval host plants for the Baltimore checkerspot butterfly (*Euphydryas phaeton*) and 45 other lepidopteran species.

Viburnum nudum -
USDA hardiness zone map

Blackhaw *(V. prunifolium)*

USDA Hardiness Zones: 3 to 9

Height: 15 feet

Width: 6 to 12 feet

Sunlight: light shade to partial sun

Soil: mesic to dry; loamy, clayish-loamy, sandy-loamy, or somewhat rocky

Flowers: clusters of small white flowers with extruding stamens; strong, pleasant fragrance; mid to late spring

Fruits: fruits berry-like, blue-black at maturity, often with whitish bloom

Autumn color: purplish to brilliant red, highly variable

Wildlife use: The flowers provide pollen and nectar for butterflies, skippers, hummingbird moths, cuckoo bees (*Nomada* spp.), native solitary bees, hoverflies, bee flies, and tachinid flies. Plants serve as larval hosts for the holly blue butterfly, Baltimore checkerspot butterfly, and several moth species. The berries are eaten by songbirds, including robins, cardinals, and woodpeckers, as well as waterbirds, shorebirds, and small mammals.

Viburnum prunifolium -
USDA hardiness zone map

Nannyberry *(V. lentago)*

USDA Hardiness Zones: 2 to 8

Height: 14 to 16 feet

Width: 6 to 12 feet

Sunlight: full sun to part shade

Soil: average moisture, loamy, well-drained

Flowers: non-fragrant, white, in flat-topped clusters

Fruits: blue-black, berry-like

Autumn color: variable, greenish-yellow to reddish-purple

Wildlife use: The foliage of nannyberry viburnum is host to several moth caterpillars, including two owlet moths: the unsated sallow (*Metaxaglaea inulta*) and the horrid zale (*Zale horrida*). Chief feeders of the fruits include ruffed grouse, brown thrashers, cedar waxwings, robins, cardinals, woodpeckers, Eastern chipmunks, and red squirrels.

Viburnum lentago -
USDA hardiness zone map

Suggested Reading

The following is a list of works that have been pivotal in framing our view of the gardener's role in a changing world.

Buchmann, S. L. and G. P. Nabham. 1996. *The Forgotten Pollinators* (Washington, D.C.: Shearwater Books).

Darke, R. and D. Tallamy. 2014. *The Living Landscape: Designing for beauty and biodiversity in the home garden* (Portland, OR: Timber Press).

Evans, A. V. 2014. *Beetles of Eastern North America* (Princeton and Oxford: Princeton University Press).

Grissell, E. 2001. *Insects and Gardens* (Portland, OR: Timber Press).

Himmelman, J. 2002. *Discovering Moths: Nighttime jewels in your own backyard* (Camden, ME: Down East Books).

Lowenfels, J. and W. Lewis. 2010. *Teaming with Microbes: The organic gardener's guide to the soil food web* (Portland, OR: Timber Press).

Manley, R. and M. Peronto. 2013. *The New England Gardener's Year: A month-by-month guide for Maine, New Hampshire, Vermont, Massachusetts, Rhode Island, Connecticut, and Upstate New York* (Thomaston, ME: Cadent Publishing).

Moore, K.D. 2016. *Great Tide Rising: Toward Clarity and Moral Courage in a Time of Planetary Change* (Berkeley, CA: Counterpoint).

Moore, K. D. and M. P. Nelson, Editors. 2010. *Moral Ground: Ethical action for a planet in peril* (San Antonio: Trinity University Press).

Pollan, M 1991. *Second Nature: A gardener's education* (New York: Bantam Doubleday Dell Publishing Group, Inc.).

Tallamy, D. W. and R. Darke. 2009. *Bringing Nature Home: How you can sustain wildlife with native plants* (Portland, OR: Timber Press, Inc.).

The Xerces Society. 2011. *Attracting Native Pollinators: Protecting North America's Bees and Butterflies* (North Adams, MA: Storey Publishing).

Dean, B. P., editor. 2000. *Wild Fruits: Thoreau's rediscovered last manuscript* (New York: W. W. Norton).

Williams, P., Thorp, R., Richardson, L., and Colla, S. 2014. *Bumble Bees of North America* (Princeton and Oxford: Princeton University Press).

Wilson, E. O. 2006. *The Creation: An appeal to save life on Earth* (New York: W. W. Norton).

Wilson, E. O. 2016. *Half-Earth: Our Planet's Fight for Life* (New York: Liveright Publishing/W. W. Norton).

Index

Page numbers in bold refer to photographs.

J
Japanese beetles, control of, 67–68, **67**, 96
Japanese knotweed. *see Fallopia japonica*

K
Karner blue butterfly *(Lycaeides melissa samuelis). see* butterflies

L
ladybird beetle, 14-spotted *(Propylea quatuordecimpunctata). see* beetles
ladybird beetle *(Harmonia axyridis). see* beetles
ladybird beetles, as garden predators, 89
landscape industry, limited native plant selections in, 152
larval host plants
   and importance in butterfly gardens, 55
   and importance in gardens for songbirds, 76–77
   importance of native trees and shrubs as, 78
lawns
   acreage of in U.S., 43
   biodiversity benefits in elimination of, 228–229
   and conversion to gardens, 42–43, 230
leafcutter bees *(Megachile spp.). see* bees
leaves, use of, 36–37
Lepidoptera. *see* butterflies; moths
lobelia. *see Lobelia erinus*
Lobelia erinus, 197–199
locally native plants, 98
longhorn bees. *see* bees
longhorn beetle, banded *(Typocerus velutinus). see* beetles
longhorn beetle *(Evodinus monticola). see* beetles
longhorn beetles, flower *(Cerambycidae)*, 69–70; see also beetles
looper moth, Northern pine *(Caripeta piniata). see* moths
luna moths *(Actias luna). see* moths

Lysimachia clethroides, 153, 179–181
Lythrum salicaria, 153

M
major datana *(Datana major). see* moths
mapleleaf viburnums. *see Viburnum acerifolium*
mason bees *(Osmia spp.). see* bees
mass extinctions, rates of, 1–3
Master Gardener Volunteers, 154
Master Gardener Volunteers, University of Maine, 151, 154
meadow rue. *see Thalictrum aquilegifolium*
meadowsweet. *see Spiraea alba* var. *latifolia*
medicinal flowers, 189–190
migration, 57–58
milkweed, common. *see Asclepias syriaca*
milkweed, swamp. *see Asclepias incarnata*
milkweed, tropical. *see Asclepias curassavica*
milkweed tussock moth *(Euchaetes egle). see* caterpillars; moths
mimicry, 59, 65–66, 209
monarch butterfly *(Danaus plexippus). see also* butterflies
   biology of, 19–22
   and decline in population of, 18
   monitoring of, 21
Monarch Watch, 21
Monarda fistulosa, 168–169
Morella pensylvanica, 127–129
moth diversity, technique for determining, 61
moths
   ailanthus webworm *(Atteva aurea)*, 64, **64**
   arched hooktip *(Drepana arcuata)*, **61**
   banded tussock *(Halysidota tessellaris)*, 75, **75**
   blinded sphinx *(Paonias excaecata)*, **62**
   brown-hooded owlet *(Cucullia convexipennis)*, 72–73, **73**
   bumble bee *(Hemaris spp.)*, **63**
   cecropia *(Hyalophora cecropia)*, 143
   Clemen's sphinx *(Sphinx luscitiosa)*, 128
   Columbia silkmoth *(Hyalophora columbia)*,

see butterflies
pistils, 45, 48
pollen tube, 48
pollination
    diversity of insects involved in, 45–47
    and efficiency of bumble bees in, 49–50
    process of, 48
pollinators, 8
polyester bees (*Colletes inaequalis*). *see* bees
polyphemus moth (*Antheraea polyphemus*). *see* moths
pot marigold. *see* Calendula officinalis
potter wasps (*Ancistrocerus antilope*). *see* wasps/ hornets
predators, gardeners as, 8–9
predatory beetles, 89–91
predatory insects, as part of garden ecosystems, 8–10, 183, 231–232
predatory wasps, 86–88
primrose moth (*Schinia florida*), 60; see also moths
puddle club, 56, **56**
purple coneflowers. *see* Echinacea purpurea
purple loosestrife. *see* Lythrum salicana
Pyle, Robert Michael, 193

Q
question mark butterfly (*Polygonia interrogationis*). *see* butterflies

R
raspberries, common insects found on, 206–211
raspberry cane borer (*Oberea affinis*). *see* beetles
red admiral butterfly (*Vanessa atalanta*), 57–58; see also butterflies
red elders. *see* Sambucus racemosa var. *pubens*
redbud. *see* Cercis canadensis
red-shouldered pine borer (*Stictoleptura canadensis*). *see* beetles
redvein enkianthus. *see* Enkianthus campanulatus

resiliency, 3–4
rhizosphere, 26–27
Rhododendron canadense, 130
rhodora. *see* Rhododendron canadense
Rhus typhina, 131–133
Rosa carolina, 133–134
Rosa palustris, 133–134
Rosa rugosa, 134–136
Rosa virginiana, 133–134
row covers, as method to exclude insect herbivores, 215, 216–218
rugosa rose. *see* Rosa rugosa

S
saddleback (*Acharia stimulea*). *see* moths
Sambucus canadensis, 137–138
Sambucus racemosa var. *pubens*, 138–139
saprotrophs, 28, 66
seeds, 48
self-fertilization, 49
self-sowing perennials, 155
serviceberry, shadblow. *see* Amelanchier canadensis
silkmoth, Columbia (*Hyalophora columbia*). *see* moths
silver-spotted skipper butterfly (*Epargyreus clarus*). *see* butterflies
skipper butterfly, dun (*Euphyes vestris*). *see* butterflies
skipper butterfly, silver-spotted (*Epargyreus clarus*). *see* butterflies
snail-eating beetle (*Scaphimotus andrewsii*). *see* beetles
snowberries, common. *see* Symphoricarpos albus
snowberry clearwing moth (*Hemaris diffinis*). *see* moths
soil ecosystems
    benefits of minimum tillage to, 33
    biodiversity in, 27–29, **28**
    nutrient cycling in, 25–27, **26**
    use of organic mulches to support, 34–37

Acknowledgments

We thank Jonathan Friedman of Frame25 Productions for the book's design, including the cover, text design, and page layout. We also extend sincere thanks to our friend and fellow horticulturist, Barbara Murphy, for her excellent work in indexing the book.

We wish to acknowledge the USDA for permission to use range maps from its website (The Plants Database, *http://plants.usda.gov*) in Chapter 8 and Appendix 3 of this book. Each map was modified to show only the states and provinces in which the species is considered native.

Lynne Hundhammer, Marjorie's daughter, spent many hours creating twelve drawings of garden insects for *The Life in Your Garden*, one for the last page of each chapter. We are very grateful for her contribution to the book.

Once again, Jon Eaton, our editor and publisher, turned an idea into the reality of a book. Watching *The Life in Your Garden* grow from the seed of an idea to fruition was an extraordinary experience that would not have happened without his insight and guidance.

About the Authors

REESER MANLEY has gardened in South Carolina, Washington state (while earning a Ph.D. in Horticultural Science), Massachusetts, and, for the last 15 years, in Maine. From 2007 through 2015, he wrote about the garden in a weekly column for the *Bangor Daily News*. He taught courses in horticulture at the University of Massachusetts, Amherst, and the University of Maine, Orono. In 2013 he retired from teaching chemistry and physics at a small high school on the coast of Maine to devote his time to gardening and garden writing.

MARJORIE PERONTO, a professor for the University of Maine Cooperative Extension, has been teaching courses in fruit and vegetable gardening, ecological landscaping, and pruning for 26 years. She is a resource among her colleagues on native and invasive plants of the Northeast. Marjorie oversees Downeast Maine's Master Gardener Volunteers program, training individuals to conduct community outreach projects that promote sustainable gardening and food security. She has developed nationally recognized school gardening courses for teachers.

Marjorie and Reeser live and garden in Ellsworth, Maine, along with Berry the cat, their black lab Sophie, and a worm bin in a corner of the living room. Their first book, *The New England Gardener's Year*, was published by Tilbury House in 2013.